WATERFALLS USA

A HIKING GUIDE AND TRAVEL PLANNER

First Edition

THE ULTIMATE WATERFALL GUIDE TO OVER 600 UNIQUE WATERFALLS THROUGHOUT THE 48 CONTIGUOUS UNITED STATES

James Grass and Carla Bowers

Waterfalls USA
A Division of JRG Inc.

Published by Waterfalls USA
A Division of JRG Inc., Bloomingdale, IL
E-mail address: info@waterfallsusa.com
www.waterfallsusa.com

Manufactured in the United States of America
Cover photograph: Lower Calf Creek Falls, Utah   © 1996 Grass/Bowers
All photographs and text by authors except where noted
Color copies of any falls pictured in this book are available for purchase

ISBN 0-9672871-0-3

The authors and publisher have presented this book to promote fun, adventure, self-discovery and an awareness of the beauty and workings of nature. With all these activities, the ingredients the reader must supply are common sense, responsibility for safety, caution, and a prior awareness of weather conditions. The authors and publisher of this book assume no responsibility for any loss of property, injuries, accidents or death occurring to visitors while exploring any of the waterfall locations described in this guide. Danger and hazards exist around waterfalls as in other situations in life, and by keeping safety a priority, enjoyment can be experienced by all.

CONTENTS

PREFACE

The birth of *WATERFALLS USA* came about through a dream one night back in 1993 about waterfalls. Both of us were between jobs and looking for a new endeavor to sink our teeth into. The dream was our lead-in. We both had always loved nature and waterfalls, so we thought it would be fun to find the five tallest waterfalls in each state and visit them for a "kind of" vacation and photo book project. Plus, we had a previous goal of seeing every state in the United States, so the falls idea fit the bill.

Our initial correspondence was to the USGS, Library of Congress, Forest Service Headquarters, State Geology Offices, Chambers of Commerce and Visitors Bureaus of each state inquiring about waterfalls. The USGS had loads of information on over 2500 waterfalls, useful but incomplete, with no height designations. The other contacts had bits and pieces of information, mostly on falls that were tourist destinations, again with very few height designations. So, with incomplete data except for the falls name, county, state, and topo map references, and a few books found on separate states, our initial plan of visiting the five tallest falls in each state was nullified. No one knew what they were!

This surprising discovery fueled our desire to know more about what was unknown about as many waterfalls as possible throughout each state in the contiguous U.S. We unfortunately could not visit all of them, as it would take a lifetime or more, but we assembled a fine representation of what each state had to offer. We had to choose the falls randomly, only to discover their height once we found them. We still do not know the five tallest falls in every state, but we have come much closer to knowing these facts than ever before.

After months of trip planning, preparing, responsibility juggling, lifestyle changing and purchasing 'Sunny Boy', our trusty 18' RV, off we went on our search for waterfalls across the U.S. over a 4-year time period (with some time off in between trips to accumulate more travel cash and research data). Once on the road, we collected directions and tips firsthand about waterfalls from libraries, stores, restaurants, government offices, newspaper companies, historical societies, radio stations, local citizens, police, construction workers, etc. Searching out the falls like detectives was as much fun and excitement as finally seeing and photographing them in person. We probably doubled our mileage by all the backtracking and going in circles that was necessary to find some of these cataracts, both on the road and on the trail (something we trust this book will help you avoid).

Years of research, travel, sleuthing and cataloging have created a stack over eight feet tall of maps, computer printouts, state literature, letters of correspondence, directions, slide and photographic film records, daily experience journals (which in themselves warrant another whole book on *THE MAKING OF WATERFALLS USA*), and more—all the foundation of *WATERFALLS USA*. We have preserved on film over 550 wonderous waterfalls, accumulating 6,000 slides and 300 photographic negatives, and have traveled 80,000 miles through this majestic United States of America, an experience of a lifetime, to say the least.

This volume is a tribute to all the waterfalls of the United States, huge and tiny, and to the joy and wonder they bring mankind. Our wish is to increase public awareness and encourage the continued preservation and care of these special natural areas for current and future generations.

ACKNOWLEDGMENTS

We would like to thank the numerous organizations and individuals that offered information and assistance during the making of *WATERFALLS USA*, namely, the U.S. Geological Survey for their thorough series of topographic maps and falls listings, Stanford and UCLA University Libraries, Library of Congress, U.S. Forest Service, State Park Headquarters, State Geological Survey Offices, Chambers of Commerce, Tourist Bureaus, County Libraries, Historical Societies, town Mayors, Police Chiefs, newspaper staffs, shop owners, and local citizens from all around the country. You were our angels throughout our journeys. Your kindness and willingness to share your time and information is gratefully appreciated.

We would like to acknowledge, as well, the handful of waterfall books that have been published on individual states for the reader's reference, namely, *A Waterfall Lover's Guide to the Pacific Northwest* by Gregory Plumb; *Waterfalls of Colorado* by Marc Conly; *Wisconsin Waterfalls* by Patrick Lisi and *Waterfalls of the Southern Appalachians* by Brian Boyd.

Also, we would like to thank our family and friends for their enthusiasm and unwavering support throughout this entire mammoth project.

INTRODUCTION

Waterfalls are one of Mother Nature's creations that move the soul. They have a hypnotic drawing power that is irresistible to most people, due in part to the negative ions they produce which, according to scientific studies, are soothing to humans. And, each falls is as distinct and different from one another as are people. Whether it is a powerful, voluminous, thundering falls or a tranquil, romantic, trickling one, each has its own 'fingerprint' that touches the senses and creates a myriad of deep impressions upon the mind.

As to what qualifies a waterfall to be called a waterfall, opinions vary. Some believe if a boat cannot safely navigate the drop, it is a waterfall. Others claim if the cataract can be seen as a defining, specific landmark from land or sky, it is a waterfall. In many eyes, the definition is relative and quite subjective. To honor the tiniest drop, as well as the monster whitewater sensation, is the intention of *WATERFALLS USA*.

In this guide, each state in the 48 contiguous United States is represented by its own waterfall uniqueness (except for Delaware and North Dakota where no falls were found). A few states have over a hundred falls, namely, California, Colorado, Maine, Michigan, Montana, New York, North Carolina, Oregon, Washington and Wyoming. (As noted in the Preface, we could not visit all of them.) However, most states have just a small number of cataracts. The unsuspecting reader will be surprised to discover that falling waters exist in many states not known for waterfalls at all, for example, Oklahoma, Kansas, Nebraska, and Mississippi.

In the following pages, the U.S. is divided into six regions, each region comprising a chapter. These chapters/regions are arranged geographically from the West to the East, with the states within each chapter ordered alphabetically. Exact locations and directions are given and, for the interested or technical traveler, individual falls facts are included as an added feature to the waterfall destinations.

The authors have made every effort to provide accurate directions, however, these may alter with the passage of time as road and trail systems change or are improved. The authors would appreciate being notified of any changes or alterations in any directions that may be discovered by new visiting explorers. Send the information to the e-mail address shown at the beginning of this book. Also, most State and National Parks charge a small entry fee. Other fees are noted in the text.

Additionally, visitors to these scenic wonders are advised to exercise safety precautions—potential hazard and danger co-exist with a waterfall's beauty and splendor. Several falls noted in these pages are in remote, undeveloped areas with no guardrails or viewing platforms to ensure the public's safety. Many have precarious cliffs, straight-down dropoffs, slippery or rocky surfaces and other hazards which require your personal awareness and responsibility to safeguard yourself and your children. Beware also of poison ivy and poison oak; they thrive near the trail and water environment.

The following parameters were utilized in the falls selection process for this guide:

    1)   to photograph lesser-known, yet still awe-inspiring falls, eliminating those in most National Parks and most of those already acclaimed,

2)   to enable the visitor to access the falls from the trailhead and return in 6 hours or less via auto, hike, combination of both, or other means (with a few noted worthwhile exceptions), and

3)   to represent different regions of each state if possible.

The state maps provided at the beginning of each state's waterfall collection are merely an overview to give an approximation of waterfall locations. They are not to scale. The town or landmark that begins the written directions is represented by the symbol:

Headings in the falls facts listings bear brief explanations. Regarding the 'Type' of waterfall pictured, the definitions below are used [adapted from Gregory A. Plumbs' *A Waterfall Lover's Guide to the Pacific Northwest* (Seattle: The Mountaineers Books)]. Note that the type of falls identified can change with the season as the water flow increases or decreases.

1)   Block - a very wide square or rectangular-shaped drop

2)   Cascade - many small stair-like drops flowing down into the next

3)   Fan - drop touches rock wall surface on descent, width expanding noticeably at bottom

4)   Horsetail - drop touches rock wall surface on descent, width remaining fairly constant top to bottom

5)   Plunge - drop does not touch rock wall surface on descent

6)   Punch Bowl - drop usually descends from a constricted upper stream or pool directly into a lower pool

7)   Segmented - 2 or more drops descending from the same origination point (also termed double or triple)

8)   Tiered - a series of separate, distinct drops that descend in stairstep fashion down to the next

9)   Slide - drop slides down an angular smooth rock face

In addition, the 'Variant Name' is a nickname or alias for the same falls. Some falls were unnamed, so the authors refer to them by the creek or stream name. The references to 'Height in feet' are either estimates or figures obtained from source material. The 'Topo Map' refers to the 7.5 minute maps published by the U.S. Geological Survey. The maps are available at most outdoor adventure stores, commercial map dealers, large libraries or through the USGS, Department of the Interior (in the government pages of the phone book). For those not familiar with Topo maps, the 'Geo Coord' indicates the falls location on the map by using horizontal and vertical coordinates to locate the point of intersection. The 'Map Ref Code' will help when ordering maps from the USGS or other sources.

The 'Elevation' is the approximate altitude above sea level. Elevations above 3000 feet may have limited access in the winter months. Check with local road and park officials for accessibility in the off season. The 'Season of Flow' is abbreviated Sp for Spring, Sm for Summer, F for Fall, and W for Winter. In other words, this is the best time of the year to see the falls and to have the highest probability of water flowing. The 'Section of State' consists of NW for the Northwest quadrant, NE for the Northeast quadrant, SW for the Southwest quadrant, and SE for the Southeast quadrant of each state. The 'Directions' start from a town, city or significant landmark that can be located on most state maps and atlases.

The authors have a reverence for all falls, large and small, and therefore have purposefully not included any form of rating system. The 'not knowing' exactly what one will find at the end of the trail is part of the joy of personal discovery that each adventurer deserves to experience on his own.

Whether you are an armchair traveler or planning your next adventure, sit back and let your imagination go as you turn these pages and journey through *WATERFALLS USA*. Feast your eyes on the shimmering spectacle; inhale the pure, cool freshness into every cell; feel the moist, delicate mist on your cheeks; touch the icy rivulets with wiggling toes; listen to the babbling bubbles or thunderous roar; marvel at the whole experience—

Drown your senses and fill your soul

with all the magic that is a waterfall.

A final thought—please do not litter. Follow the nature lover's slogan:

Take only pictures; leave only footprints.

CHAPTER 1

The Western States

Arizona
California
Idaho
Nevada
Oregon
Utah
Washington

Fall Creek Falls
IDAHO

Waterfall Name	Fifty Foot Falls
State	Arizona
Type	Fan
Variant Name	Supai Falls
Height in feet	50
County	Coconino
Topo Map	Supai
Geo Coord	361442N1124157W
Map Ref Code	36112-B6
Elevation ft	3800
Water Source	Havasu Creek
Seasonal Flow	Year
Section of State	NW

Directions   See directions for Havasu Falls. Hike from Supai Village to falls is approx. 1 mile.

Waterfall Name	Grand Falls
State	Arizona
Type	Block
Variant Name	
Height in feet	185
County	Coconino
Topo Map	Grand Falls
Geo Coord	352539N1111200W
Map Ref Code	35111-D2
Elevation ft	4650
Water Source	Little Colorado River
Seasonal Flow	Sp
Section of State	NE

Directions   From Flagstaff, take US 89 N. to Leupp Rd. and turn right. Proceed 8 miles to the Leupp turnoff (Indian Route 15). Turn left and go 13.8 miles to Rt. 70 (look for green and white sign saying "Grand Falls 10 Miles"). Turn left on 70 (dirt road can be slick, muddy, or dusty depending on season, use caution). Just before reaching the Little Colorado River (end of road), veer left onto unmarked dirt road and proceed over the knoll to the picnic area and falls viewing areas.

Waterfall Name	Havasu Falls
State	Arizona
Type	Segmented/Plunge
Variant Name	
Height in feet	170
County	Coconino
Topo Map	Havasu Falls
Geo Coord	361518N1124148W
Map Ref Code	36112-C6
Elevation ft	3500
Water Source	Havasu Creek
Seasonal Flow	Year
Section of State	NW

Directions   From Peach Springs, take Rt. 66 E. for 7 miles to the Supai Hilltop turnoff. Go north for 62 miles to the parking area. The hike is 8 miles (losing 3000 ft.) to reach Supai Village in the Havasupai Indian Reservation. The 4 waterfalls in this part of the Grand Canyon are an additional 6 miles round trip from Supai Village. Prior reservations are recommended to visit this part of the Canyon. The distance from the Hilltop to the Village is a difficult hike, especially the return. Horseback or helicopter are other modes of reaching the Village. Best to take one day to reach the Village, one day to view the falls, and one day to return to the Hilltop. The hike from Supai Village to Havasu Falls is approx. 2 miles.

Waterfall Name	Mooney Falls
State	Arizona
Type	Plunge
Variant Name	Hualapai Falls
Height in feet	220
County	Coconino
Topo Map	Havasu Falls
Geo Coord	361546N1124224W
Map Ref Code	36112-C6
Elevation ft	3400
Water Source	Havasu Creek
Seasonal Flow	Year
Section of State	NW

Directions   See directions for Havasu Falls. From the Village to Mooney Falls is about 3 miles. The last 200 yards of the trail is steep going through two tunnels and scaling vertical cliffside steps that require holding onto a chain handrail. Not for the faint of heart, but well worth the view at the bottom.

Waterfall Name	Navajo Falls
State	Arizona
Type	Segmented/Plunge/Fan
Variant Name	
Height in feet	60
County	Coconino
Topo Map	Supai
Geo Coord	361458N1124151W
Map Ref Code	36112-B6
Elevation ft	3600
Water Source	Havasu Creek
Seasonal Flow	Year
Section of State	NW

Directions   See directions for Havasu Falls. From Supai Village to Navajo Falls is about 1.5 miles.

Waterfall Name	Pine Creek Falls
State	Arizona
Type	Fan
Variant Name	
Height in feet	50
County	Gila
Topo Map	Buckhead Mesa
Geo Coord	341950N1112652W
Map Ref Code	34111-C4
Elevation ft	4600
Water Source	Pine Creek
Seasonal Flow	Sp
Section of State	SW

Directions   See directions for Tonto Natural Bridge Falls. Take the Waterfall Trail; hike down a short, steep stairway with a cable railing to the falls.

Waterfall Name   Slide Rock Falls

State   Arizona

Type   Tiered

Variant Name

Height in feet   10

County   Yavapai

Topo Map   Munds Park

Geo Coord   345805N1114440W

Map Ref Code   34111-H6

Elevation ft   5600

Water Source   Oak Creek

Seasonal Flow   Year

Section of State   NW

Directions   From Sedona, take Rt. 179 N. to Slide Rock State Park in Oak Creek Canyon. The pools, waterfalls, and slides are a 5-minute walk from the parking lot.

Waterfall Name   Tonto Natural Bridge Falls

State   Arizona

Type   Plunge

Variant Name   Arch Falls

Height in feet   180

County   Gila

Topo Map   Buckhead Mesa

Geo Coord   341940N1112730W

Map Ref Code   34111-C4

Elevation ft   4600

Water Source   Tonto Spring

Seasonal Flow   Sp

Section of State   SW

Directions   From Strawberry, take Rt. 260 S. for several miles to the Tonto Natural Bridge turnoff (very well-marked). Turn right and follow this gravel road for 3 miles to the parking area. To see the falls and natural bridge, take either the "Gowan Trail" or the trail to Viewpoints 3 and 4. Hike will take about 15 minutes.

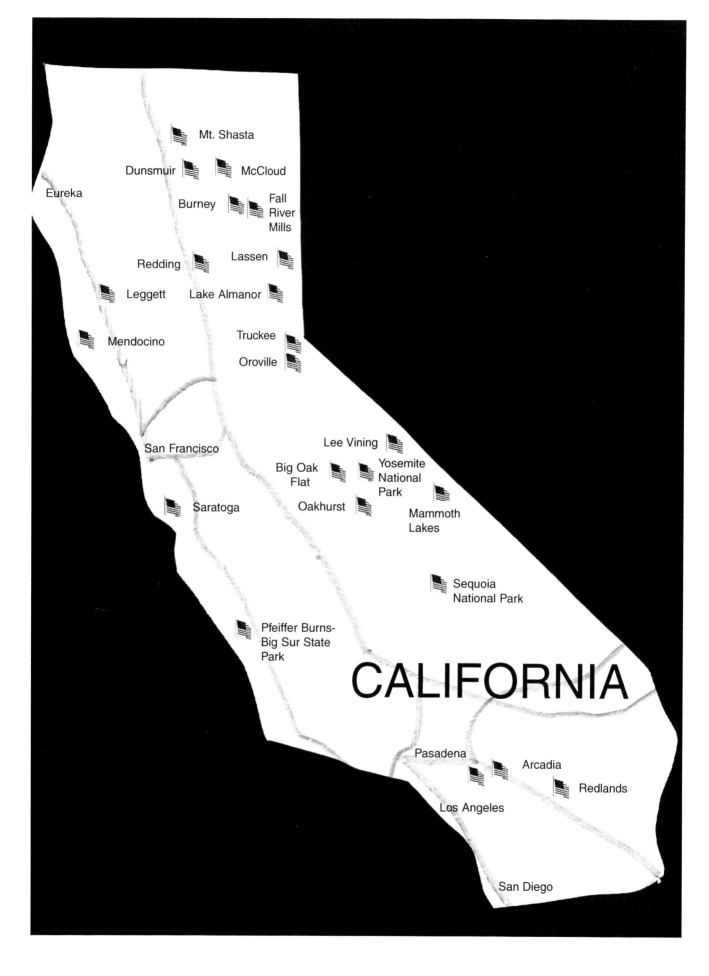

Mt. Shasta

Dunsmuir   McCloud

Eureka

Burney   Fall River Mills

Redding   Lassen

Leggett   Lake Almanor

Mendocino   Truckee

Oroville

Lee Vining

San Francisco

Big Oak Flat   Yosemite National Park

Saratoga   Oakhurst   Mammoth Lakes

Sequoia National Park

Pfeiffer Burns-Big Sur State Park

CALIFORNIA

Pasadena   Arcadia

Redlands

Los Angeles

San Diego

Waterfall Name	Angel Falls
State	California
Type	Slide/Fan
Variant Name	
Height in feet	100
County	Madera
Topo Map	Bass Lake
Geo Coord	372018N1193411W
Map Ref Code	37119-C5
Elevation ft	3000
Water Source	North Fork Willow Creek
Seasonal Flow	W,Sp,Sm
Section of State	NE

Directions   From Oakhurst, take Rt. 41 N. approx. 3 miles to Bass Lake Road 222. Turn right, then veer left at first Y intersection onto Road 274, cross bridge over Willow Creek (unmarked) and park in the first turnout on the right past the bridge. (Total mileage is about 4.5 miles from 222/41 intersection to bridge.) Walk back to the bridge, cross over the road and take the dirt road (on the right of the creek) upstream to the trailhead sign. Sign is to the left of the Water Filtration Building. Hike up the McCloud Trail about 1/2 mile to the falls.

Waterfall Name	Big Falls
State	California
Type	Tiered/Horsetail
Variant Name	
Height in feet	120
County	San Bernadino
Topo Map	Forest Falls
Geo Coord	340509N1165342W
Map Ref Code	34116-A8
Elevation ft	6200
Water Source	Falls Creek
Seasonal Flow	Sp
Section of State	SE

Directions   From Redlands, take Rt. 38 toward Big Bear (north). Turn right (east) onto Valley of the Falls Drive; pass Forest Falls Community. Go to Big Falls Trailhead on left and park. Cross the creek and hike up Falls Creek approx. 1 mile to falls.

Waterfall Name	Burney Falls
State	California
Type	Segmented/Plunge/Block
Variant Name	McArthur-Burney Falls
Height in feet	130
County	Shasta
Topo Map	Burney Falls
Geo Coord	410039N1213906W
Map Ref Code	41121-A6
Elevation ft	3000
Water Source	Burney Creek
Seasonal Flow	Year
Section of State	NE

Directions   From the junction of Routes 89 and 299 (just north of Burney), take Rt. 89 N. 6 miles to Burney Falls State Park. The falls is a short distance from parking lot.

Waterfall Name	Castle Rock Falls
State	California
Type	Horsetail
Variant Name	
Height in feet	70
County	Santa Cruz
Topo Map	Castle Rock Ridge
Geo Coord	371335N1220617W
Map Ref Code	37122-B1
Elevation ft	2600
Water Source	Kings Creek
Seasonal Flow	W, Sp
Section of State	NW

Directions   From the intersection of Routes 35 and 9 in Santa Cruz County above Saratoga, take Rt. 35 S. (Skyline Blvd.) to Castle Rock State Park on right. From parking lot to falls is about 1.5 miles.

Waterfall Name	Corlieu Falls
State	California
Type	Segmented/Horsetail
Variant Name	
Height in feet	80
County	Madera
Topo Map	White Chief Mountain
Geo Coord	372458N1193725W
Map Ref Code	37119-D5
Elevation ft	4000
Water Source	Lewis Creek
Seasonal Flow	Sp
Section of State	NE

Directions From Oakhurst, take Rt. 41 N. Go 4 miles past Bass Lake Road and park in large turnout on the right. The turnout is just after the green 4000 ft. elevation sign and just past the Litter Removal sign. A large dirt trail at the north end of the turnout leads down to the trailhead sign. Follow the Lewis Creek Trail to the right for 0.1 mile to reach upper Corlieu Falls. Middle and lower drops are further on the trail; follow the switchbacks.

Waterfall Name	Crystal Creek Cascade
State	California
Type	Cascade
Variant Name	Lower Crystal Creek Cascade
Height in feet	150
County	Shasta
Topo Map	French Gulch
Geo Coord	403702N1224117W
Map Ref Code	40122-F6
Elevation ft	2000
Water Source	Crystal Creek
Seasonal Flow	W,Sp,Sm
Section of State	NE

Directions From Redding, take Rt. 299 W. for 15 miles to Crystal Creek Road. Turn left and follow for 3 miles to unmarked gravel road on left; park here (this is past the gravel pit on the left and before the end of the road). The unmarked gravel road leads to a primitive campground. An undeveloped trail leads off to the right from the gravel road and follows the river downstream to the falls, about a 20-minute hike to the Upper Falls and another 10 minutes to the Cascade (just past the powerhouse).

Waterfall Name	Crystal Creek Upper Falls
State	California
Type	Cascade
Variant Name	Upper Crystal Creek Falls
Height in feet	150
County	Shasta
Topo Map	Shasta Bally
Geo Coord	403630N1224120W
Map Ref Code	40122-E6
Elevation ft	2200
Water Source	Crystal Creek
Seasonal Flow	W,Sp,Sm
Section of State	NE

Directions   See directions to Crystal Creek Cascade.

Waterfall Name	Deer Creek Falls
State	California
Type	Punchbowl
Variant Name	
Height in feet	15
County	Tehama
Topo Map	Onion Butte
Geo Coord	401209N1213044W
Map Ref Code	40121-B5
Elevation ft	3720
Water Source	Deer Creek
Seasonal Flow	Year
Section of State	NE

Directions   From the junction of Routes 36W/89N/32 near Lake Almanor, take Rt. 32 S. for 8.6 miles to the turnout on the left (east) side of the road (1.3 miles south of FS Alder Campground). A trail (unmarked) leads down to the falls. A very short, easy hike.

Waterfall Name	Feather Falls
State	California
Type	Horsetail
Variant Name	
Height in feet	640
County	Butte
Topo Map	Brush Creek
Geo Coord	393835N1211624W
Map Ref Code	39121-F3
Elevation ft	3000
Water Source	Fall River
Seasonal Flow	Year
Section of State	NE

Directions   From Oroville, take Rt. 162 W. Turn right onto Forrestown Road (look for sign to Feather Falls). Turn left onto Lumpkin Road (sign for Feather Falls) and go 18 miles. Turn left at sign "National Forest Feather Falls Recreation Area". Follow this road for 1.5 miles to the parking lot and trailhead. The trail is 3.8 miles to the falls. The falls is the 5th tallest in the U.S.

Waterfall Name	Fern Canyon Falls
State	California
Type	Plunge
Variant Name	
Height in feet	30
County	Mendocino
Topo Map	Mendocino
Geo Coord	391702N1233620W
Map Ref Code	39123-C7
Elevation ft	400
Water Source	Fern Canyon Creek
Seasonal Flow	Year
Section of State	NW

Directions   From Mendocino, take Hwy 1 N. Go approx. 2 miles and turn left into Russian Gulch State Park (follow signs). Turn left onto the main park road and follow the signs down to the campground. Go to the very end of the campground and park. Hike along the Fern Canyon Trail for 2.3 miles to the falls. The first 1.5 miles of the trail is paved and level. The remaining 0.8 mile is an up and down, narrow dirt trail.

Waterfall Name	Frazier Falls
State	California
Type	Horsetail/Cascade
Variant Name	
Height in feet	250
County	Plumas
Topo Map	Gold Lake
Geo Coord	394225N1203829W
Map Ref Code	39120-F6
Elevation ft	6000
Water Source	Frazier Creek
Seasonal Flow	Year
Section of State	NE

Directions   From Truckee, take Rt. 89 N. for approx. 30 miles, then take Rt. 49 W. for 10 miles to Gold Lake Road (near town of Bassett). Go right on Gold Lake Road for 7 miles and turn right on the gravel road marked "Gold Lake/Frazier Falls". Go 1.5 miles to the trailhead and parking area on the right. A well-developed trail for 1/2 mile leads to the overlook of the falls.

Waterfall Name	Hedge Creek Falls
State	California
Type	Plunge
Variant Name	
Height in feet	30
County	Siskiyou
Topo Map	Dunsmuir
Geo Coord	414022N1222508W
Map Ref Code	41122-B3
Elevation ft	1200
Water Source	Hedge Creek
Seasonal Flow	W,Sp
Section of State	NE

Directions   From Interstate 5, take the north Dunsmuir exit. Go to the parking area (follow sign) that is about 100 feet from the exit ramp on the west side of the Interstate. There is a well-maintained trail that leads down about 200 yards to the falls.

Waterfall Name	King Creek Cascade
State	California
Type	Cascade
Variant Name	
Height in feet	200
County	Shasta
Topo Map	Reading Peak
Geo Coord	402735N1212620W
Map Ref Code	40121-D4
Elevation ft	7600
Water Source	King Creek
Seasonal Flow	Year
Section of State	NE

Directions   See directions to King Creek Falls.

Waterfall Name	King Creek Falls
State	California
Type	Cascade
Variant Name	
Height in feet	50
County	Shasta
Topo Map	Reading Peak
Geo Coord	402734N1212619W
Map Ref Code	40121-D4
Elevation ft	7400
Water Source	King Creek
Seasonal Flow	Year
Section of State	NE

Directions   Take Rt. 89 N. through Lassen National Park. The trailhead to the falls is on the right just past the Kings Creek Picnic Area. It is unmarked but there are large turnouts on both sides of the road. Hike is 0.9 mile to the cascades and another 0.2 mile to the falls. The trail is not marked at the road but is well-marked along the way.

Waterfall Name   Lake Ellery Falls

State   California

Type   Plunge/Cascade

Variant Name

Height in feet   100

County   Mariposa

Topo Map   Mt. Dana

Geo Coord   375540N1191303W

Map Ref Code   37119-H2

Elevation ft   9000

Water Source   Lee Vining Creek

Seasonal Flow   Year

Section of State   NE

Directions   Near Lee Vining and the intersection of Routes 395/120, take Rt. 120 W. up Tioga Pass towards Yosemite. The falls will be on the left a short distance before reaching the summit. There will be several parking turnouts to view the falls.

Waterfall Name   Lewis Creek Lower Cascade

State   California

Type   Cascade

Variant Name   Lower Cascade of Lewis Creek

Height in feet   30

County   Madera

Topo Map   Fish Camp

Geo Coord   372440N1193715W

Map Ref Code   37119-D6

Elevation ft   4000

Water Source   Lewis Creek

Seasonal Flow   W,Sp,Sm

Section of State   NE

Directions   See directions for Corlieu Falls. Lower Cascade is about 1/4 mile further along the trail from Middle Cascade.

Waterfall Name	Lewis Creek Middle Cascade
State	California
Type	Cascade
Variant Name	Middle Cascade of Lewis Creek
Height in feet	30
County	Madera
Topo Map	Fish Camp
Geo Coord	372510N1193740W
Map Ref Code	37119-D6
Elevation ft	4000
Water Source	Lewis Creek
Seasonal Flow	W,Sp,Sm
Section of State	NE

Directions See directions for Corlieu Falls. Middle Cascade is about 1/2 mile further along the trail.

Waterfall Name	McCloud River Middle Falls
State	California
Type	Block
Variant Name	Middle Falls McCloud River
Height in feet	80
County	Siskiyou
Topo Map	Lake McCloud
Geo Coord	411438N1220031W
Map Ref Code	41122-B1
Elevation ft	3000
Water Source	McCloud River
Seasonal Flow	Year
Section of State	NE

Directions See directions to McCloud River Upper Falls. Instead of going 1 mile on Road 40N44, go only 0.6 mile to a large turnout on the left. There will be a large pine tree in the middle of the turnout; park here. Cross over the road to a well-worn trail that leads to the cliff's edge and view of the falls. A steep, undeveloped path leads off to the right to the river and falls base.

Waterfall Name	McCloud River Upper Falls
State	California
Type	Tiered/Punchbowl
Variant Name	Upper Falls McCloud River
Height in feet	60
County	Siskiyou
Topo Map	Lake McCloud
Geo Coord	411427N1220025W
Map Ref Code	41122-B1
Elevation ft	3200
Water Source	McCloud River
Seasonal Flow	Year
Section of State	NE

Directions
From McCloud, take Rt. 89 S. about 5 miles to Road 39N28 (sign reads NFS Upper and Lower Falls Campground). Turn right and go 0.7 mile to the second dirt road on the left (Road 40N44). Look for sign for Upper Falls. Go 1 mile on 40N44 and turn right onto dirt Road M9 (marked with a yellow sign). Follow this road a short distance to the parking lot.

Waterfall Name	McWay Falls
State	California
Type	Plunge
Variant Name	
Height in feet	70
County	Monterey
Topo Map	Partington Ridge
Geo Coord	361040N1213912W
Map Ref Code	36121-B6
Elevation ft	70
Water Source	McWay Creek
Seasonal Flow	Year
Section of State	NW

Directions
From Pfeiffer-Big Sur State Park on Hwy. 1, go south for approx.12 miles to McWay Falls parking area. The parking area is just past Mile Mark 36 on the left (east) side of the road. Follow the well-maintained trail for about 1/4 mile to the falls viewpoint.

Waterfall Name	Mill Creek Falls
State	California
Type	Horsetail
Variant Name	
Height in feet	35
County	Mendocino
Topo Map	Noble Butte
Geo Coord	395253N1234440W
Map Ref Code	39123-H6
Elevation ft	600
Water Source	Mill Creek
Seasonal Flow	Year
Section of State	NW

Directions   From Leggett, go north on Hwy. 101. Go 4 miles and turn left into the parking lot for Smithe Redwoods State Reserve. Walk about 20 yards to the north end of the parking lot to the culvert under Hwy. 101 with Mill Creek flowing through it. Cross the highway (use CAUTION) and follow the creekside trail upstream for about 100 yards to the falls.

Waterfall Name	Millard Falls
State	California
Type	Segmented/Horsetail
Variant Name	
Height in feet	50
County	Los Angeles
Topo Map	Pasadena
Geo Coord	340805N1180820W
Map Ref Code	34118-B2
Elevation ft	3300
Water Source	Millard Creek
Seasonal Flow	W,Sp
Section of State	SE

Directions   From Interstate 210 near Pasadena, take Lake Ave. north. In the town of Altadena, Lake will turn into Loma Alta Dr. heading west. Go 1 mile and turn right onto Chaney Trail; follow this to the parking lot. The 0.7-mile trail starts on the right near the lot entrance.

Waterfall Name	Minaret Falls
State	California
Type	Cascade
Variant Name	
Height in feet	100
County	Madera
Topo Map	Mammoth Mountain
Geo Coord	373827N1190538W
Map Ref Code	37119-F1
Elevation ft	2420
Water Source	Minaret Creek
Seasonal Flow	Year
Section of State	NE

Directions   From the junction of Routes 395/203 near Mammoth Lakes, take Rt. 203 W. through town and turn right onto Minaret Road. Turn right on the road to Minaret Falls Campground. Veer left at the information board in the campground and park at the south end of the parking lot. There is an unmarked trail to the right. The 0.3-mile hike goes through a couple meadows and across two small streams.

Waterfall Name	Monkeyface Falls
State	California
Type	Horsetail
Variant Name	
Height in feet	50
County	San Bernadino
Topo Map	Forest Falls
Geo Coord	340555N1165720W
Map Ref Code	34116-A8
Elevation ft	4900
Water Source	Monkeyface Creek
Seasonal Flow	Sp
Section of State	SE

Directions   From Redlands, take Rt. 38 towards Big Bear (north). Turn right (east) onto Valley of the Falls Drive. Monkeyface Falls will be on the left at the first large pullout on the right.

Waterfall Name	Mossbrae Falls
State	California
Type	Fan
Variant Name	
Height in feet	60
County	Siskiyou
Topo Map	Dunsmuir
Geo Coord	414130N1221557W
Map Ref Code	41122-B3
Elevation ft	2600
Water Source	Shasta Springs
Seasonal Flow	Year
Section of State	NE

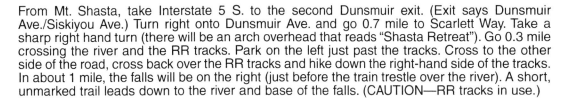

Directions From Mt. Shasta, take Interstate 5 S. to the second Dunsmuir exit. (Exit says Dunsmuir Ave./Siskiyou Ave.) Turn right onto Dunsmuir Ave. and go 0.7 mile to Scarlett Way. Take a sharp right hand turn (there will be an arch overhead that reads "Shasta Retreat"). Go 0.3 mile crossing the river and the RR tracks. Park on the left just past the tracks. Cross to the other side of the road, cross back over the RR tracks and hike down the right-hand side of the tracks. In about 1 mile, the falls will be on the right (just before the train trestle over the river). A short, unmarked trail leads down to the river and base of the falls. (CAUTION—RR tracks in use.)

Waterfall Name	Pit River Falls
State	California
Type	Block
Variant Name	
Height in feet	50
County	Shasta
Topo Map	Hogback Ridge
Geo Coord	405910N1212815W
Map Ref Code	40121-H4
Elevation ft	4000
Water Source	Pit River
Seasonal Flow	Year
Section of State	NE

Directions From Fall River Mills, go SW on Rt. 299 for 3.2 miles. Turn left (south) at Pit 1 Power House sign. Veer right and follow the road to the old tennis court on the left (about 1 mile). Turn left just past the tennis court and go about 0.3 mile to the end of the road and park. Walk around the gate and cross the footbridge over the spillway. Follow the dirt road veering left twice (stay near power plant). Take the footbridge across the Pit River. Follow a faint trail up a small hill and turn left at the base of the bluff, following the old stagecoach trail along the river. Go about 1.3 miles upstream (stepping over lots of boulders from a previous rock slide) to the old, dilapidated bridge over the river. The falls can be seen from here.

Waterfall Name   Rainbow Falls

State   California

Type   Block/Fan

Variant Name

Height in feet   100

County   Madera

Topo Map   Crystal Crag

Geo Coord   373706N1190457W

Map Ref Code   37119-E1

Elevation ft   7600

Water Source   Middle Fork San Joaquin River

Seasonal Flow   Year

Section of State   NE

Directions   From the junction of Routes 395/203 near Mammoth Lakes, take Rt. 203 through town. Turn right onto Minaret Road and go to the end (past Devil's Postpile). Follow signs to trailhead and parking lot. Trail is about 1.25 miles to the falls. At the first junction in the trail, follow the middle trail towards Fish Creek. After this point, there are well-marked signs to Rainbow Falls. There are three well-developed overlooks to view the falls.

Waterfall Name   Sturtevant Falls

State   California

Type   Plunge

Variant Name

Height in feet   50

County   Los Angeles

Topo Map   Mt. Wilson

Geo Coord   341242N1180108W

Map Ref Code   34118-B1

Elevation ft   2660

Water Source   Santa Anita Creek

Seasonal Flow   W,Sp

Section of State   SE

Directions   From Interstate 210 in Arcadia, take Santa Anita Ave. north for about 6 miles to the end at Chantry Flat. The 2-mile trail starts at the gate on the right side of the road at the lot entrance. Follow the signs and the creek to the falls.

Waterfall Name	Tokopah Falls
State	California
Type	Horsetail
Variant Name	
Height in feet	60
County	Tulare
Topo Map	Lodge Pole
Geo Coord	363610N1184002W
Map Ref Code	36118-E6
Elevation ft	8500
Water Source	Kaweah River
Seasonal Flow	Year
Section of State	NE

Directions   From the Lodgepole Visitors Center in Sequoia National Park, obtain a Park map. The hike starts a short distance from the Visitors Center at the Lodgepole Campground. Follow the Tokopah Falls Trail for approx. 3/4 mile to the falls.

Waterfall Name	Vivian Creek Falls
State	California
Type	Plunge
Variant Name	
Height in feet	70
County	San Bernadino
Topo Map	Forest Falls
Geo Coord	340515N1165235W
Map Ref Code	34116-A8
Elevation ft	7400
Water Source	Vivian Creek
Seasonal Flow	Sp
Section of State	SE

Directions   See directions for Big Falls. Follow the dirt road at the east end of the campground to the first creek on the left. Go up the creekside trail for 200 yards to the falls.

Waterfall Name	Wapama Falls
State	California
Type	Horsetail
Variant Name	
Height in feet	400
County	Tuolumne
Topo Map	Lake Eleanor
Geo Coord	375759N1194552W
Map Ref Code	37119-H7
Elevation ft	6000
Water Source	Falls River
Seasonal Flow	Year
Section of State	NE

Directions   From Big Oak Flat, take Rt. 120 E. (Big Oak Flat Road) towards upper Yosemite. Turn left onto Evergreen Road and right on Hetch Hetchy Road. Follow to the dam and parking lot. Hike over the dam and through the tunnel, then veer right at the Y. The hike is about 2.6 fairly level miles to the falls.

Waterfall Name	White Cascade
State	California
Type	Cascade
Variant Name	
Height in feet	200
County	Mariposa
Topo Map	Falls Ridge
Geo Coord	374046N1192435W
Map Ref Code	37119-H4
Elevation ft	8000
Water Source	Tuolumne River
Seasonal Flow	Year
Section of State	NE

Directions   In Yosemite National Park, the trail begins at Soda Springs in the Tuolumne Meadows Area. The trail goes toward Glen Aulin and the falls is just after the footbridge over the Tuolumne River (about 4 miles).

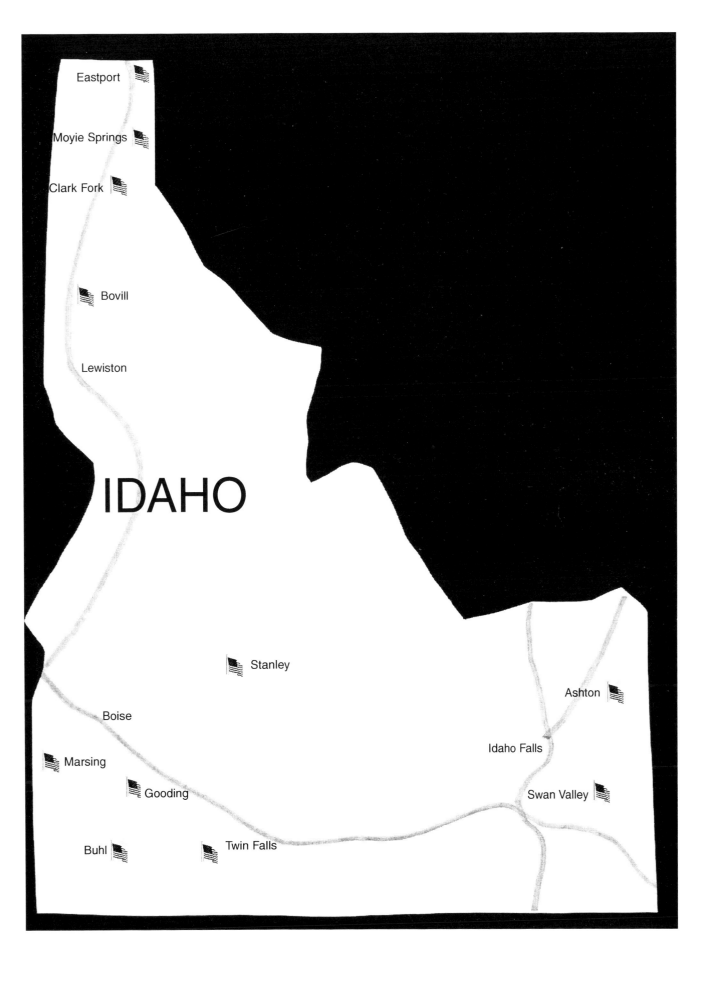

IDAHO

Eastport

Moyie Springs

Clark Fork

Bovill

Lewiston

Stanley

Ashton

Boise

Idaho Falls

Marsing

Gooding

Swan Valley

Buhl

Twin Falls

Waterfall Name	Copper Falls
State	Idaho
Type	Horsetail/Plunge
Variant Name	Copper Creek Falls
Height in feet	160
County	Boundry
Topo Map	Eastport
Geo Coord	485818N1160828W
Map Ref Code	48116-H2
Elevation ft	3400
Water Source	Copper Creek
Seasonal Flow	Year
Section of State	NW

Directions   From Eastport, take Hwy 95 S. about 3/4 mile to Road 2517. Go east on 2517 for 2 miles (gravel) to Copper Falls Trail 207. From here, go uphill 1/2 mile to the falls.

Waterfall Name	Elk Creek Lower Falls
State	Idaho
Type	Plunge
Variant Name	Lower Elk Falls
Height in feet	100
County	Clearwater
Topo Map	Elk Creek Falls
Geo Coord	464411N1161030W
Map Ref Code	46116-F2
Elevation ft	2400
Water Source	Elk Creek
Seasonal Flow	Year
Section of State	NW

Directions   From Bovill, drive south on S.R. 8 towards Elk River. In about 16 miles, turn south (right) at the unmarked road near the large gravel pile. From here, go about 2.5 miles to the parking lot and trailhead. The hike is 1 mile to Elk Falls and about 1/4 mile further to the Lower Falls.

Waterfall Name	Elk Falls
State	Idaho
Type	Horsetail
Variant Name	Elk Creek Falls
Height in feet	150
County	Clearwater
Topo Map	Elk Creek Falls
Geo Coord	464412N1161031W
Map Ref Code	46116-F2
Elevation ft	2720
Water Source	Elk Creek
Seasonal Flow	Year
Section of State	NW

Directions	Follow directions to Elk Creek Lower Falls.

Waterfall Name	Fall Creek Falls
State	Idaho
Type	Fan
Variant Name	
Height in feet	60
County	Bonneville
Topo Map	Conant Valley
Geo Coord	432629N1112235W
Map Ref Code	43111-D4
Elevation ft	5300
Water Source	Snake River
Seasonal Flow	Year
Section of State	SE

Directions	From Swan Valley, take Hwy. 26 W. for 3.25 miles to Snake River/Palisades Dam Road. Go south on this gravel road for 1.4 miles and park where the road widens. The trail is marked by a small sign and is a short walk to the falls.

Waterfall Name	Falls of a Thousand Springs
State	Idaho
Type	Various
Variant Name	Thousand Springs Falls
Height in feet	100
County	Twin Falls
Topo Map	Thousand Springs
Geo Coord	424430N1145002W
Map Ref Code	42114-F7
Elevation ft	3000
Water Source	A Thousand Springs
Seasonal Flow	Year
Section of State	SW

Directions From Buhl, take Hwy. 30 N. for about 15 miles. Looking across the Snake River from this point and also for the next mile, many falls can be observed descending from springs along the northern canyon walls. There are several pullouts to park along the way.

Waterfall Name	Goat Falls
State	Idaho
Type	Fan
Variant Name	
Height in feet	350
County	Custer
Topo Map	Stanley Lake
Geo Coord	441035N1150101W
Map Ref Code	44115-B1
Elevation ft	8160
Water Source	Goat Creek
Seasonal Flow	Year
Section of State	SW

Directions From Stanley, take S.R. 21 W. for 2.25 miles to Iron Creek Road 619. Turn left and go about 4 miles to the end of the road and park. Hike Trail 640 (Alpine Lake/Sawtooth Lake) for 1 mile, then turn left (southeast) onto Trail 528 (Alpine Trail). Continue on 2.5 miles to Goat Creek and falls.

Waterfall Name	Jump Creek Falls
State	Idaho
Type	Horsetail
Variant Name	
Height in feet	60
County	Owyhee
Topo Map	Jump Creek Canyon
Geo Coord	432837N1165528W
Map Ref Code	43116-D8
Elevation ft	2900
Water Source	Jump Creek
Seasonal Flow	Year
Section of State	SW

Directions   At the junction of Routes 95 and 55 (2 miles west of Marsing), take Rt. 95 W. for 2 miles. At this point, Rt. 95 will turn right (north), but continue straight west on Cemetery Road (cemetery on the right). Go 1 mile to Jump Creek Road (T intersection) and turn left. Proceed 3 miles, then Jump Creek Road turns into gravel; go another 1/2 mile and turn right over the cattle guard. Veer right at the Y (left is private ranch). Continue over the second cattle guard and to the parking lot at the end of road (from the cattle guard to the parking area is about 1.4 miles). From here (unmarked trailhead), follow the trail up the canyon boulder hopping for about 0.2 mile to the falls.

Waterfall Name	Lady Face Falls
State	Idaho
Type	Punchbowl
Variant Name	
Height in feet	75
County	Custer
Topo Map	Stanley Lake
Geo Coord	441354N1150542W
Map Ref Code	44115-B1
Elevation ft	6600
Water Source	Stanley Lake Creek
Seasonal Flow	Year
Section of State	SW

Directions   From Stanley, take S.R. 21 W. for 5 miles and turn left at Stanley Lake Road 455 (gravel). Go 3.5 miles to Inlet Campground and park. Hike about 2 miles on the Iron Creek/Greenback Trail to the junction with Lady Face Trail (not highly traveled; small sign nailed to tree facing opposite direction). Turn left onto Lady Face Trail and follow it about 1/4 mile to the falls.

Waterfall Name	Malad Gorge Falls
State	Idaho
Type	Block
Variant Name	Devil's Washbowl
Height in feet	60
County	Twin Falls
Topo Map	Tuttle
Geo Coord	425120N1145150W
Map Ref Code	42114-G7
Elevation ft	3050
Water Source	Malad River
Seasonal Flow	Year
Section of State	SW

Directions   Take Interstate 84 S. of Gooding and follow the signs to Malad Gorge State Park. From the parking area in the State Park, a short walk leads to the overlook of Devil's Washbowl and the falls.

Waterfall Name	Mesa Lower Falls
State	Idaho
Type	Block
Variant Name	Lower Mesa Falls, Lower Falls
Height in feet	65
County	Fremont
Topo Map	Snake River Butte
Geo Coord	441032N1111908W
Map Ref Code	44111-B3
Elevation ft	5300
Water Source	Henry's Fork of Snake River
Seasonal Flow	Year
Section of State	SE

Directions   From Ashton, take S.R. 47 N. for 15 miles to the turnout called Grandview. The falls can be seen here from a distance.

Waterfall Name	Mesa Upper Falls
State	Idaho
Type	Block
Variant Name	Big Falls, Mesa Falls, Upper Falls
Height in feet	110
County	Fremont
Topo Map	Snake River Butte
Geo Coord	441117N1111945W
Map Ref Code	44111-B3
Elevation ft	5600
Water Source	Henry's Fork of Snake River
Seasonal Flow	Year
Section of State	SE

Directions   See directions for Mesa Lower Falls. Drive about 3/4 mile further along S.R. 47 to Upper Mesa Falls Road 295 and go left (west). In about a mile, the road will end; park here. Follow the boardwalk trail to the falls (about 200 feet).

Waterfall Name	Moyie Falls
State	Idaho
Type	Tiered
Variant Name	Moyie River Falls
Height in feet	140
County	Boundary
Topo Map	Moyie Springs
Geo Coord	484359N1161028W
Map Ref Code	48116-F2
Elevation ft	2000
Water Source	Moyie River
Seasonal Flow	Year
Section of State	NW

Directions   From Moyie Springs exit off of U.S. 2 (immediately west of the Moyie River Bridge), go about 1/2 mile to the lumber yard and turn left. There will be several turnouts along this road in the next 1/2 mile that will provide viewpoints of the falls. Please note that this waterfall is very difficult to see in its entirety without doing dangerous maneuvers. Use CAUTION.

Waterfall Name	Perrine Coulee Falls
State	Idaho
Type	Plunge
Variant Name	
Height in feet	200
County	Twin Falls
Topo Map	Twin Falls
Geo Coord	423548N1142818W
Map Ref Code	42114-E4
Elevation ft	3600
Water Source	Coulee Creek
Seasonal Flow	Year
Section of State	SW

Directions   From Twin Falls, take U.S. 93 N. a short distance to Canyon Springs Road and turn west. In about 3/4 mile, there will be a turnout on the left (before the golf course); park here. The falls is a short distance away.

Waterfall Name	Wellington Falls
State	Idaho
Type	Punchbowl
Variant Name	Wellington Creek Falls
Height in feet	75
County	Bonner
Topo Map	Trestle Peak
Geo Coord	481733N1161040W
Map Ref Code	48116-C2
Elevation ft	3500
Water Source	Wellington Creek
Seasonal Flow	Year
Section of State	NW

Directions   From Clark Fork, take S.R. 200 N. for about 12 miles and turn right onto Trestle Creek Road 275. Go 13 miles to Lightening Creek Road 419. Turn right (south) and proceed 4.8 miles to Auxor Road 489 and turn right (west). Cross Lightening Creek and hike or drive (depending on conditions) down the primitive road to the left. In about 0.4 mile, veer right at the Y and continue on this bumpy road to the end. Follow a very faint trail for about 0.3 mile in a SW direction towards the river. Let the sound of the falls help guide you.

NEVADA

Reno

Las Vegas

Waterfall Name	Big Falls
State	Nevada
Type	Plunge
Variant Name	
Height in feet	120
County	Clark
Topo Map	Charleston Peak
Geo Coord	361608N1154035W
Map Ref Code	36115-C6
Elevation ft	8800
Water Source	Big Falls Spring
Seasonal Flow	Sp
Section of State	SE

Directions   From Las Vegas, take Rt. 95 N. about 15 miles and turn left (west) onto Rt. 157 (towards Mt. Charleston). Upon reaching the town of Mt. Charleston (about 18 miles from Rt. 95), turn right (north) onto Echo Road. Veer left at the Y onto a gravel road (see sign for Mary Jane Falls Trailhead) and park at the end of the road. Hike up the trail towards Mary Jane Falls. At the sign that reads "Off Trail Shortcuts Ruin Trail", go off the main trail onto a faint trail to the left. This trail will soon turn into a wider gravel trail. At the first Y, veer left; at the second Y, veer right. Continue up this gravel-like road until it becomes a narrower dirt trail. This trail will curve to the left and lead directly into the streambed of Big Falls. The trail at this point will be heading in a SW direction. From here, boulder hop and crisscross the streambed upstream to reach the falls. The total length of the hike from trailhead to falls is about 1.5 fairly strenuous miles. In Spring Mountain Recreation Area, Toiyabe National Forest.

Waterfall Name	Little Falls
State	Nevada
Type	Plunge/Horsetail
Variant Name	
Height in feet	100
County	Clark
Topo Map	Charleston Peak
Geo Coord	361530N1153805W
Map Ref Code	36115-C6
Elevation ft	8000
Water Source	Little Falls Spring
Seasonal Flow	Sp
Section of State	SE

Directions   From the picnic area in the town of Mt. Charleston, take the foot path to the SW for about 3/4 mile to the falls.

Waterfall Name	Mary Jane Falls
State	Nevada
Type	Fan
Variant Name	
Height in feet	100
County	Clark
Topo Map	Charleston Peak
Geo Coord	361646N1154013W
Map Ref Code	36115-C6
Elevation ft	8800
Water Source	Mary Jane Springs
Seasonal Flow	Sp
Section of State	SE

Directions   See directions for Big Falls. At the sign reading "Off Trail Shortcuts Ruin Trail", continue to the right on the main, rock-lined trail. Follow the switchbacks up to Mary Jane Falls. Total distance from trailhead to falls is a strenuous 1.2 miles.

Waterfall Name	Mirage Falls
State	Nevada
Type	Tiered/Fan
Variant Name	Man-Made
Height in feet	30
County	Clark
Topo Map	Las Vegas N.W.
Geo Coord	
Map Ref Code	36115-B2
Elevation ft	2100
Water Source	Man-Made
Seasonal Flow	Year
Section of State	SE

Directions   Located at the Mirage Hotel on "The Strip" in downtown Las Vegas. Becomes a volcano at night. The authors were told by a Nevada geology expert that this was the only falls in the State of Nevada!!

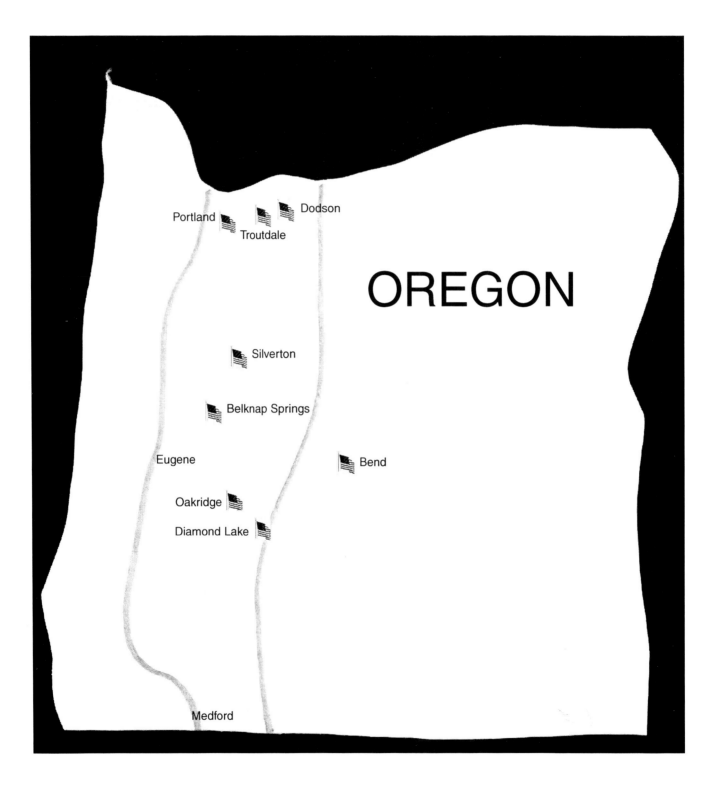

Waterfall Name	Elowah Falls
State	Oregon
Type	Plunge
Variant Name	Kelley Falls
Height in feet	290
County	Multnomah
Topo Map	Tanner Butte
Geo Coord	453641N1215935W
Map Ref Code	45121-E8
Elevation ft	500
Water Source	McCord Creek
Seasonal Flow	Year
Section of State	NW

Directions   From Dodson, take the Columbia Gorge Scenic Highway east. Turn right into John Yeon State Park just before the junction with Interstate 84. From the parking area, take Gorge Trail 400 and turn left at the first junction. Continue on Trail 400 for a total of 0.4 mile to the base of the falls.

Waterfall Name	Koosah Falls
State	Oregon
Type	Block
Variant Name	
Height in feet	120
County	Linn
Topo Map	Clear Lake
Geo Coord	442039N1215958W
Map Ref Code	44121-C8
Elevation ft	2700
Water Source	McKenzie River
Seasonal Flow	Year
Section of State	NW

Directions   From Belknap Springs, take Rt. 126 N. Go 5.5 miles and turn left into the Ice Camp Campground. From the parking area, a 0.3-mile hike leads to the falls viewpoint.

Waterfall Name	Latourell Falls
State	Oregon
Type	Plunge
Variant Name	
Height in feet	250
County	Multnomah
Topo Map	Bridal Veil
Geo Coord	453212N1221303W
Map Ref Code	45122-E2
Elevation ft	400
Water Source	Latourell Creek
Seasonal Flow	Year
Section of State	NW

Directions   From Troutdale, take Interstate 84 E. Go approx. 9 miles. At Exit 28, take the Scenic Highway to the west for 3.4 miles and turn left into Guy Talbot State Park. A 5-minute walk from the parking area leads to the falls viewpoint.

Waterfall Name	Lemolo Falls
State	Oregon
Type	Horsetail
Variant Name	
Height in feet	100
County	Douglas
Topo Map	Lemolo Lake
Geo Coord	432045N1221307W
Map Ref Code	43122-C2
Elevation ft	3800
Water Source	North Umpqua River
Seasonal Flow	Year
Section of State	SW

Directions   From Diamond Lake, take Rt. 138 N. Turn left (north) onto Lemolo Lake Road 2610 towards Lemolo Lake. In 4.3 miles, veer left (north) onto Thorn Prairie Road 3401. Go 0.4 mile and turn right onto Lemolo Falls Road 3401/800. Go 1.8 miles and park at the trailhead on the right. Hike Lemolo Falls Trail 1468 for 1 mile (steep downhill) to the base of the falls.

Waterfall Name	Multnomah Falls
State	Oregon
Type	Tiered/Plunge
Variant Name	
Height in feet	630
County	Multnomah
Topo Map	Multnomah Falls
Geo Coord	453420N1220710W
Map Ref Code	45122-E1
Elevation ft	640
Water Source	Big River
Seasonal Flow	Year
Section of State	NW

Directions   From Troutdale, take Interstate 84 E. At Exit 31, follow the signs to Multnomah Falls. The falls can be seen on a very short, well-maintained trail from the parking area.

Waterfall Name	North Falls
State	Oregon
Type	Plunge
Variant Name	
Height in feet	140
County	Marion
Topo Map	Elk Prarie
Geo Coord	445301N1223721W
Map Ref Code	44122-H5
Elevation ft	1400
Water Source	North Fork Silver Creek
Seasonal Flow	Year
Section of State	NW

Directions   From Silverton, take S.R. 214 S. Go 14 miles and turn right into Silver Falls State Park (follow signs). Go to the east end of the Park to the parking area. Take the trail at the south end of the parking area to the west for 0.3 mile to the falls. Several falls in this Park. Entry fee.

Waterfall Name	Paulina Creek Falls
State	Oregon
Type	Segmented/Plunge
Variant Name	Paulina Falls, Upper Falls
Height in feet	100
County	Deschutes
Topo Map	Paulina Peak
Geo Coord	434245N1211655W
Map Ref Code	43121-F3
Elevation ft	6200
Water Source	Paulina Creek
Seasonal Flow	Sp,Sm
Section of State	SW

Directions   From Bend, take Rt. 97 S. Go about 25 miles and turn left (east) onto Paulina Lake Rd. Go approx. 13 miles and park in the Paulina Creek Falls Picnic Grounds on the left. A short trail leads to the falls.

Waterfall Name	Proxy Falls
State	Oregon
Type	Segmented/Fan
Variant Name	
Height in feet	200
County	Lane
Topo Map	Linton Lake
Geo Coord	440943N1215536W
Map Ref Code	44121-B8
Elevation ft	3200
Water Source	Proxy Creek
Seasonal Flow	Year
Section of State	SW

Directions   From the junction of Routes 126 and 242 (near Belknap Springs), take Rt. 242 E. Go about 8.3 miles and park in the pullouts on either side of the road. There is a small sign with a picture of 2 hikers on it just before the pullouts. There is a small wooden sign at the trailhead on the south side of the road that reads Proxy Falls. Hike the right spur of Trail 3532 for about 15 minutes to the falls viewpoint.

Waterfall Name	Punchbowl Falls
State	Oregon
Type	Punchbowl
Variant Name	
Height in feet	15
County	Hood River
Topo Map	Tanner Butte
Geo Coord	453718N1215335W
Map Ref Code	45121-E8
Elevation ft	400
Water Source	Eagle Creek
Seasonal Flow	Year
Section of State	NW

Directions   From Portland, take Interstate 84 E. At Exit 41, follow the signs to Eagle Creek Park. Once in the Park, hike Eagle Creek Trail 440 gradually uphill for 2.1 miles to the falls. A great example of a true punchbowl falls.

Waterfall Name	Sahalie Falls
State	Oregon
Type	Segmented/Plunge
Variant Name	Upper Falls
Height in feet	140
County	Linn
Topo Map	Clear Lake
Geo Coord	442057N1215945W
Map Ref Code	44121-C8
Elevation ft	2940
Water Source	McKenzie River
Seasonal Flow	Year
Section of State	NW

Directions   From Belknap Springs, take S.R. 126 N. Go about 6 miles and follow the point-of-interest sign to the falls. The falls can be seen a short distance from the parking area.

Waterfall Name	Salt Creek Falls
State	Oregon
Type	Plunge
Variant Name	
Height in feet	285
County	Lane
Topo Map	Diamond Peak
Geo Coord	433643N1220738W
Map Ref Code	43122-E2
Elevation ft	4000
Water Source	Salt Creek
Seasonal Flow	Year
Section of State	SE

Directions   From Oakridge, take S.R. 58 E. Go about 21 miles and park in the Salt Creek Falls turnout on the right. The falls is a short walk from the parking area.

Waterfall Name	South Falls
State	Oregon
Type	Plunge
Variant Name	
Height in feet	175
County	Marion
Topo Map	Drake Crossing
Geo Coord	445244N1223926W
Map Ref Code	44122-H6
Elevation ft	1200
Water Source	South Silver Creek
Seasonal Flow	Year
Section of State	NW

Directions   From Silverton, take S.R. 214 S. Go approx. 14 miles to Silver Falls State Park. Park in the western portion of the park. Follow the trail to the west for about 0.4 mile to the falls viewpoints. Several falls in this Park. Entry fee.

Waterfall Name	Toketee Falls
State	Oregon
Type	Tiered/Plunge
Variant Name	Toketie Falls
Height in feet	120
County	Douglas
Topo Map	Toketee Falls
Geo Coord	431548N1222549W
Map Ref Code	43122-C4
Elevation ft	2500
Water Source	North Umpqua River
Seasonal Flow	Year
Section of State	SW

Directions   From Diamond Lake, take S.R. 138 W. In about 20 miles, turn right (north) onto Toketee Lake Road (34/268). Go 0.3 mile and turn left (west) towards Toketee Falls Trail 1495. Park and follow the trail for 0.6 mile to the falls.

Waterfall Name	Triple Falls
State	Oregon
Type	Segmented
Variant Name	
Height in feet	135
County	Multnomah
Topo Map	Multnomah Falls
Geo Coord	453450N1220415W
Map Ref Code	45122-E1
Elevation ft	1100
Water Source	Oneonta Creek
Seasonal Flow	Year
Section of State	NW

Directions   From Dodson, take the Scenic Highway west for about 3 miles to the trailhead parking area for Oneonta Trail 424. Hike up the moderately strenuous trail for a total distance of 1.7 miles to the falls. At the junction with Horsetail Trail 438, be sure to stay on the Oneonta Trail 424. From this junction, continue 0.8 mile to the falls viewpoint.

Waterfall Name	Wahkeena Falls
State	Oregon
Type	Tiered
Variant Name	Gordon Falls
Height in feet	240
County	Multnomah
Topo Map	Bridal Veil
Geo Coord	453423N1220737W
Map Ref Code	45122-E2
Elevation ft	600
Water Source	Wahkeena Creek
Seasonal Flow	Year
Section of State	NW

Directions   From Troutdale, take the Scenic Highway east. Go about 1/2 mile to the picnic area on the right. The falls can be seen from here.

Waterfall Name	Watson Falls
State	Oregon
Type	Plunge
Variant Name	
Height in feet	275
County	Douglas
Topo Map	Fish Creek Desert
Geo Coord	431430N1222320W
Map Ref Code	43122-B4
Elevation ft	3200
Water Source	Watson Creek
Seasonal Flow	Year
Section of State	SW

Directions   From Diamond Lake, take S.R. 138 W. Go about 18 miles and turn left (south) onto Fish Creek Road 37. Go 0.2 mile and park in the Watson Falls Picnic Ground. Hike Watson Falls Trail 1495 for about 0.3 mile to the falls viewpoint.

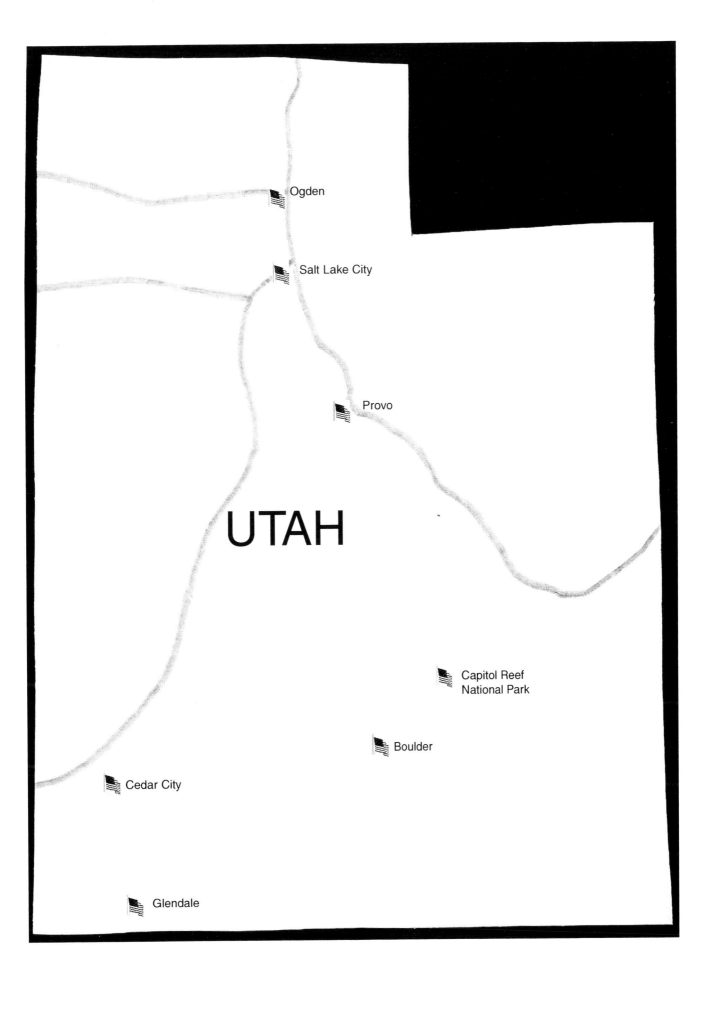

Waterfall Name	Bridal Veil Falls
State	Utah
Type	Tiered/Plunge
Variant Name	
Height in feet	100
County	Utah
Topo Map	Bridal Veil Falls
Geo Coord	402018N1113602W
Map Ref Code	40111-C5
Elevation ft	6000
Water Source	Bridal Veil Creek
Seasonal Flow	Year
Section of State	NE

Directions   From Provo, take Rt. 189 N. Go about 15 miles (follow signs) to view the falls off to the right.

Waterfall Name	Calf Creek Lower Falls
State	Utah
Type	Horsetail
Variant Name	Lower Calf Creek Falls
Height in feet	125
County	Garfield
Topo Map	Calf Creek
Geo Coord	374945N1112509W
Map Ref Code	37111-G4
Elevation ft	5600
Water Source	Calf Creek
Seasonal Flow	Year
Section of State	SE

Directions   From Boulder, take Rt. 12 S.W. Go about 12 miles and park in the Calf Creek Recreation Area on the right. From the picnic area, a 3-mile hike follows the creek through the sandstone canyon. The trail has 24 points of interest along the way. Located in the Calf Creek Recreation Area of the Grand Staircase-Escalante National Monument.

Waterfall Name	Calf Creek Upper Falls
State	Utah
Type	Horsetail
Variant Name	Upper Calf Creek Falls
Height in feet	90
County	Garfield
Topo Map	Calf Creek
Geo Coord	375119N1112704W
Map Ref Code	37111-G4
Elevation ft	6000
Water Source	Calf Creek
Seasonal Flow	Year
Section of State	SE

Directions   See directions for Calf Creek Lower Falls. From the parking area at Calf Creek Lower Falls, take Rt. 12 N.E. towards Boulder. Go about 5.5 miles and turn left onto the second unnamed bumpy gravel road. The turn is 1/2 mile past Mile Mark 81. Park in the large parking area. Hike from the well-marked trailhead down the steep rocks following the chevrons and the faint trail for about 20 minutes to the falls.

Waterfall Name	Cascade Falls
State	Utah
Type	Cascade
Variant Name	
Height in feet	100
County	Kane
Topo Map	Navajo Lake
Geo Coord	373007N1124523W
Map Ref Code	37112-B7
Elevation ft	8800
Water Source	Underground Spring
Seasonal Flow	Year
Section of State	SW

Directions   From Cedar City, take Rt.14 E. After passing Navajo Lake, turn right onto the unnamed dirt road (directly across from Duck Creek Campground). Go 3 miles (follow signs) and park at the trailhead at the end of the road. The falls are about a 1/2-mile hike from the parking area. The falls flow directly out of a cave.

Waterfall Name   Doughnut Falls

State   Utah

Type   Plunge/Cascade

Variant Name

Height in feet   20

County   Salt Lake

Topo Map   Mount Aire

Geo Coord   403747N1113915W

Map Ref Code   40111-F6

Elevation ft   8000

Water Source   Mill D South Fork

Seasonal Flow   Year

Section of State NE

Directions   From Salt Lake City, take Interstate 80 W. Then take Interstate 215 S. At Exit 6, follow Rt. 190 E. (Cottonwood Canyon Road) towards Solitude and Brighton. Go about 9 miles and turn right towards the Doughnut Falls parking area (follow sign). In about 1 mile, park in the parking area. From here, a 3/4-mile hike leads to the falls. This falls is a true doughnut with the water-formed hole going directly through the rock.

Waterfall Name   Fremont River Falls

State   Utah

Type   Cascade

Variant Name

Height in feet   20

County   Wayne

Topo Map   Fruita

Geo Coord   381723N1110937W

Map Ref Code   38111-C2

Elevation ft   5100

Water Source   Fremont River

Seasonal Flow   Year

Section of State SE

Directions   From the Visitors Center at Capitol Reef National Park, take Hwy. 24 E. Go 7.2 miles and park in the parking area on the north side of the road. The falls can be seen from here (unmarked).

Waterfall Name	Hidden Falls
State	Utah
Type	Horsetail
Variant Name	
Height in feet	40
County	Salt Lake
Topo Map	Mount Aire
Geo Coord	403807N1114321W
Map Ref Code	40111-F6
Elevation ft	6800
Water Source	Mill B North Fork
Seasonal Flow	Year
Section of State	NE

Directions   See directions for Doughnut Falls. Before reaching the turn for Doughnut Falls, turn right into the Mill B North Fork Trail picnic area (the turn is between the two hairpin turns). The picnic area is just past Mile Mark 6. From the picnic area, hike across Rt.190 to the MBNFT Trailhead. From here, follow the creek (do not follow the stairway off to the right) for about 100 yards to the falls (unmarked).

Waterfall Name	Lisa Falls
State	Utah
Type	Tiered/Horsetail
Variant Name	
Height in feet	75
County	Salt Lake
Topo Map	Dromedary Peak
Geo Coord	403422N1114337W
Map Ref Code	40111-E6
Elevation ft	7200
Water Source	Lisa Canyon Creek
Seasonal Flow	Sp
Section of State	NE

Directions   From Salt Lake City, take Interstate 80 W. to Intertstate 215 S. At Exit 6, follow the signs to Alta and Snowbird following Rt. 210 S. At the Y, veer left onto Little Cottonwood Canyon Road. Pass the 2 defunct power plants. Pass 2 pullouts on the right-hand side. Park in the next large pull-out on the left. The trail begins at the "Camping Prohibited" sign. The falls is a 1/4-mile hike (unmarked).

Waterfall Name	Scout Falls
State	Utah
Type	Cascade
Variant Name	
Height in feet	30
County	Utah
Topo Map	Timpanogos Cave
Geo Coord	402502N1113821W
Map Ref Code	40111-D6
Elevation ft	8000
Water Source	Timpanogos Spring
Seasonal Flow	Sp
Section of State	NE

Directions   From Salt Lake City, take Interstate 15 S. Go 25 miles and turn left (east) onto Rt. 92 (Alpine Scenic Loop). At the Timponeke Campground, park in parking lot for Camps 6 and 7. Hike the Mt. Timponeke Trail for 2 miles (crossing the creek twice) to the falls (unmarked).

Waterfall Name	Stewart Falls
State	Utah
Type	Tiered/Plunge
Variant Name	Stewarts Cascades
Height in feet	100
County	Utah
Topo Map	Aspen Grove
Geo Coord	402311N1113611W
Map Ref Code	40111-D5
Elevation ft	7400
Water Source	Cascade Cirque Creek
Seasonal Flow	Year
Section of State	NE

Directions   See directions for Scout Falls. Take Alpine Scenic Loop (Rt. 92) to the parking area in Timpagonos Campground. The trailhead is out of the picnic area near Theater in the Pines. Hike the Stewart Cascade Trail for about 2 miles to the falls. The other access to the falls is through the trails at the Mandan Cottages in Sundance. Permission and directions can be obtained there.

Waterfall Name	The Falls
State	Utah
Type	Plunge
Variant Name	Falls
Height in feet	20
County	Kane
Topo Map	Bald Knoll
Geo Coord	371728N1122930W
Map Ref Code	37112-C4
Elevation ft	6200
Water Source	Kanab Creek
Seasonal Flow	Sp
Section of State	SW

Directions   From Glendale, take Rt. 89 N. At the north end of town, turn east onto gravel Glendale Bench Road (across from the Smith Hotel). Go 7.3 miles to where the creek flows over the road. The falls can be seen from here off to the right.

Waterfall Name	Upper Falls
State	Utah
Type	Tiered
Variant Name	
Height in feet	30
County	Utah
Topo Map	Bridal Veil Falls
Geo Coord	402038N1113524W
Map Ref Code	40111-C5
Elevation ft	5900
Water Source	Davis Canyon Creek
Seasonal Flow	Sp
Section of State	NE

Directions   See directions to Bridal Veil Falls. Continue north on Rt. 189 for 1 more mile. Just past the Upper Falls Picnic Area, the falls can be seen off to the right.

Waterfall Name	Waterfall Canyon Falls
State	Utah
Type	Fan
Variant Name	Falls at Waterfall Canyon
Height in feet	150
County	Weber
Topo Map	Ogden
Geo Coord	411222N1115517W
Map Ref Code	41111-B8
Elevation ft	6200
Water Source	Waterfall Canyon Creek
Seasonal Flow	Sp
Section of State	NE

Directions   From Ogden, take Interstate 15 S. to the 25th St. exit. Go east on 25th St., then right onto Washington Blvd. Turn left onto 36th St. After passing the second "Mt. Ogden Exercise Trail" sign, park on the right side of the road (trailhead on left side of road). Follow the exercise trail along the golf course, pass the water tanks, cross Strong Creek, and cross another bridge to another falls trailhead sign on right. The distance from the roadside parking to the falls trailhead is about 1 mile. Follow the trail uphill, veering right at the Y intersections. This section of the trail is about 1.2 miles. The total hike from the roadside parking to the falls takes about 1 hour. Second half of hike fairly strenuous.

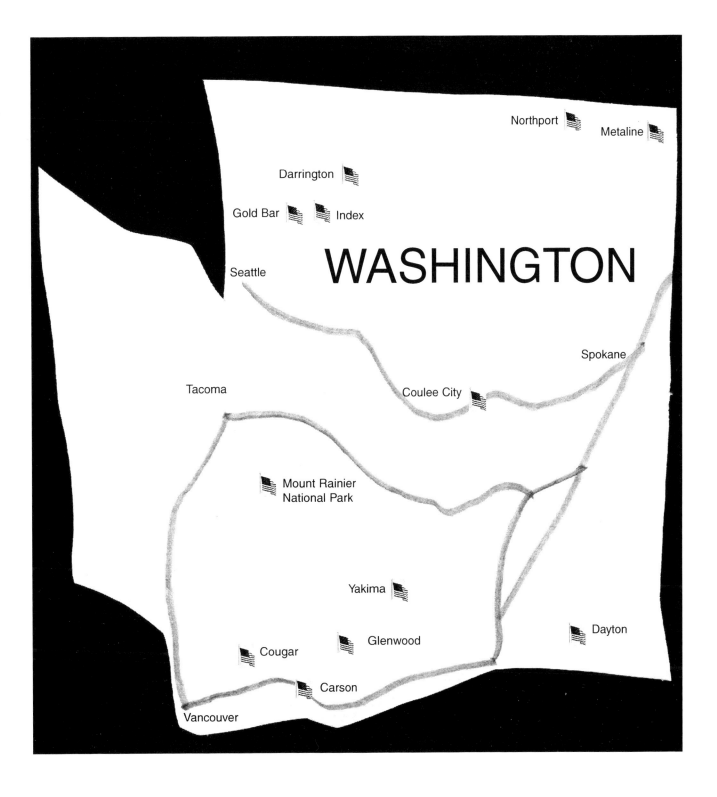

Waterfall Name	Big Creek Falls
State	Washington
Type	Plunge
Variant Name	
Height in feet	125
County	Skamania
Topo Map	Burnt Peak
Geo Coord	460607N1215444W
Map Ref Code	46121-A8
Elevation ft	1600
Water Source	Big Creek
Seasonal Flow	Year
Section of State	SW

Directions   From Cougar, drive east on Lewis River Road (90). Go about 19 miles to the bridge over Eagle Cliff. Go another 8.8 miles on Lewis River Road and park on the north side where Big Creek crosses the road. Follow the trail for a short distance along the south side of the gorge, in a downstream direction, to view the falls.

Waterfall Name	Canyon Falls
State	Washington
Type	Punchbowl
Variant Name	Eagle Falls
Height in feet	30
County	Snohomish
Topo Map	Index
Geo Coord	474816N1213205W
Map Ref Code	47121-G5
Elevation ft	600
Water Source	South Fork Skykomish River
Seasonal Flow	Year
Section of State	NW

Directions   From Index, take U.S. 2 E. Go about 1.5 miles and turn right onto the unnamed private road. Go about 0.2 mile and park where a gate blocks the road. Follow the gravel road for about 1 mile (veer left at the first Y) to the falls off to the right. Listen for the sound of the rushing water to guide the last 50 feet (unmarked).

Waterfall Name	Christine Falls
State	Washington
Type	Plunge
Variant Name	
Height in feet	60
County	Pierce
Topo Map	Mt. Rainier West
Geo Coord	464652N1214643W
Map Ref Code	46121-G7
Elevation ft	3600
Water Source	Van Trump Creek
Seasonal Flow	Year
Section of State	SW

Directions   From the west entrance of Mt. Rainier National Park, take Rt. 706 E. Go about 1/4 mile past Comet Falls Trailhead and park in the turnout on the east side of the Van Trump Creek Bridge. Follow the stairway down from the bridge to the falls.

Waterfall Name	Clear Creek Falls
State	Washington
Type	Plunge
Variant Name	
Height in feet	300
County	Yakima
Topo Map	Spiral Butte
Geo Coord	463932N1212106W
Map Ref Code	46121-F3
Elevation ft	4000
Water Source	Clear Creek
Seasonal Flow	Year
Section of State	SW

Directions   From White Pass (about 50 miles west of Yakima), take Rt.12 E. Go 2.5 miles and park in the parking area for Clear Creek Falls on the right (follow sign). Follow the short trail to the falls viewpoint.

Waterfall Name	Comet Falls
State	Washington
Type	Plunge
Variant Name	
Height in feet	320
County	Pierce
Topo Map	Mt. Rainier West
Geo Coord	464746N1214644W
Map Ref Code	46121-G7
Elevation ft	5200
Water Source	Van Trump Creek
Seasonal Flow	Year
Section of State	SW

Directions From the west entrance of Mt. Rainier National Park, take Rt. 706 E. Go about 10 miles and park in the parking area for Comet Falls on the left (follow signs). Follow the well-marked trail for 1.9 miles to the falls, fairly steep.

Waterfall Name	Cougar Falls
State	Washington
Type	Plunge
Variant Name	
Height in feet	120
County	Lewis
Topo Map	Mt. Rainier East
Geo Coord	464536N1213738W
Map Ref Code	46121-G6
Elevation ft	2600
Water Source	Nickel Creek
Seasonal Flow	Year
Section of State	SW

Directions Drive east on Rt. 706 from the west entrance of Mt. Rainier National Park. Go 0.6 mile past Box Canyon (look for sign) and park in the turnout that is NW of the Nickel Creek Bridge. Follow the path from here for 0.2 mile to the falls viewpoint.

Waterfall Name	Dry Falls
State	Washington
Type	Dry
Variant Name	
Height in feet	400
County	Grant
Topo Map	Coulee City
Geo Coord	473642N1192110W
Map Ref Code	47119-E3
Elevation ft	1680
Water Source	None
Seasonal Flow	None
Section of State	SE

Directions   From Coulee City, take Rt. 2 W., then turn left (south) onto Rt.17. Go 2 miles and park in the scenic viewpoint to observe the area that the world's largest falls once plunged over. The falls dried up long ago, but used to be 400 feet tall and 3.5 miles wide.

Waterfall Name	Falls Creek Falls
State	Washington
Type	Tiered
Variant Name	
Height in feet	250
County	Skamania
Topo Map	Termination Point
Geo Coord	455412N1215407W
Map Ref Code	45121-H8
Elevation ft	2250
Water Source	Falls Creek
Seasonal Flow	Year
Section of State	SW

Directions   From Carson, take Wind River Road 30 N. Go about 16 miles and turn right onto Road 3062-057. Go 2.3 miles and park at the Trailhead for Lower Falls Creek Trail 152A. Follow the trail for about 1.5 miles to the falls, a gradual, steep climb.

Waterfall Name	Martha Falls
State	Washington
Type	Fan
Variant Name	Martha's Falls
Height in feet	130
County	Lewis
Topo Map	Mt. Rainier East
Geo Coord	464603N1214135W
Map Ref Code	46121-G6
Elevation ft	3700
Water Source	Unicorn Creek
Seasonal Flow	Year
Section of State	SW

Directions   From the west entrance to Mt. Rainier National Park, take Rt. 706 E. Go 2 miles past "The Bench" (look for sign) and park in the Martha Falls Wayside (follow sign). The falls can be viewed from here.

Waterfall Name	Myrtle Falls
State	Washington
Type	Fan
Variant Name	
Height in feet	80
County	Pierce
Topo Map	Mt. Rainier East
Geo Coord	464724N1214352W
Map Ref Code	46121-G6
Elevation ft	5600
Water Source	Edith Creek
Seasonal Flow	Year
Section of State	SW

Directions   From the west entrance to Mt. Rainier National Park, take Rt. 706 E. Go about 15 miles and turn left onto Paradise Loop Road. Go about 1.5 miles and park at the Paradise Inn. Hike the Skyline Trail for about 1/2 mile to the falls viewpoint. Majestic Mt. Rainier makes up the backdrop.

Waterfall Name	Narada Falls
State	Washington
Type	Horsetail
Variant Name	
Height in feet	240
County	Lewis
Topo Map	Mt. Rainier East
Geo Coord	464631N1214443W
Map Ref Code	46121-G6
Elevation ft	5000
Water Source	Paradise River
Seasonal Flow	Year
Section of State	SW

Directions From the west entrance to Mt. Rainier National Park, take Rt. 706 E. Go about 14 miles and park in the parking area for Narada Falls (follow sign). The parking area is 1 mile west of the turnoff for Paradise. Follow the well-developed trail for about 0.1 mile to the falls.

Waterfall Name	North Fork Falls
State	Washington
Type	Punchbowl
Variant Name	North Fork Sauk River Falls
Height in feet	70
County	Snohomish
Topo Map	Sloan Peak
Geo Coord	480552N1212205W
Map Ref Code	48121-A3
Elevation ft	1500
Water Source	North Fork Sauk River
Seasonal Flow	Year
Section of State	NW

Directions From Darrington, take Sauk River Road 20 S. (gravel). Go 15.5 miles and turn left onto North Fork Road 49. Go 1.2 miles and park at the trailhead for Trail 660. Hike on Trail 660 for about 1/4 mile to the falls.

Waterfall Name	Outlet Falls
State	Washington
Type	Plunge
Variant Name	
Height in feet	150
County	Klickitat
Topo Map	Outlet Falls
Geo Coord	460105N1211021W
Map Ref Code	46121-A2
Elevation ft	1600
Water Source	Outlet Creek
Seasonal Flow	Year
Section of State	SW

Directions   From Glenwood, take the unnamed road east for 6 miles. Park in the parking area on the left (sign here reads "No Fires Without Permit"). The falls are a short distance from the parking area (unguarded cliffside-CAUTION).

Waterfall Name	Palouse Falls
State	Washington
Type	Plunge
Variant Name	Aputapat Falls
Height in feet	185
County	Whitman
Topo Map	Palouse Falls
Geo Coord	463949N1181321W
Map Ref Code	46118-F2
Elevation ft	650
Water Source	Palouse River
Seasonal Flow	Year
Section of State	SE

Directions   From Dayton, take Rt.12 E. Go about 15 miles and turn left (west) onto Rt. 261. Go 21 miles and turn right into Palouse Falls State Park. The falls can be viewed a short distance from the parking area.

Waterfall Name	Pewee Falls
State	Washington
Type	Horsetail
Variant Name	Periwee Falls/PeeWee Falls
Height in feet	200
County	Pend Oreille
Topo Map	Boundary Dam
Geo Coord	485815N1172114W
Map Ref Code	48117-H3
Elevation ft	2100
Water Source	Pewee Creek
Seasonal Flow	Year
Section of State	NE

Directions   From Metaline, take C.R. 2975 north towards Crawford State Park. Go about 9 miles to the Y intersection (gravel Road 340). Turn right onto Road 340 and follow to the Y and park. Hike on the road to the left of the Y for about 10 minutes to view the upper section of the falls through the trees on the left. The best view of the falls can be seen by taking a boat from the dock at Boundary Dam. The dam can be reached by taking C.R. 2975 north from Metaline. Go about 12 miles to the boat dock. Bring a boat.

Waterfall Name	Sheep Creek Falls
State	Washington
Type	Fan
Variant Name	
Height in feet	150
County	Stevens
Topo Map	Northport
Geo Coord	485653N1174738W
Map Ref Code	48117-H7
Elevation ft	1400
Water Source	Sheep Creek
Seasonal Flow	Year
Section of State	NE

Directions   From Northport, take Rt. 25 N. Go about 1 mile and turn left onto the first gravel road after the bridge (Sheep Creek Road). In a short distance, park opposite the entrance to the International Speedway at unmarked trailhead. Hike on the wide trail for about 1 mile to the hydroelectric sign (veer left at the Y). Go another 1/2 mile to view the falls off to the right.

Waterfall Name	Sluiskin Falls
State	Washington
Type	Horsetail
Variant Name	
Height in feet	300
County	Pierce
Topo Map	Mt. Rainier East
Geo Coord	464736N1214258W
Map Ref Code	46121-G6
Elevation ft	5900
Water Source	Paradise River
Seasonal Flow	Year
Section of State	SW

Directions   See directions for Mrytle Falls. Hike on the Skyline Trail for about 1.9 miles to reach the falls. From a distance, Sluiskin Falls can be seen from the trail near Mrytle Falls.

Waterfall Name	Sweet Creek Falls
State	Washington
Type	Fan/Cascade
Variant Name	
Height in feet	50
County	Pend Oreille
Topo Map	Metaline
Geo Coord	484930N1172350W
Map Ref Code	48117-G4
Elevation ft	2200
Water Source	Sweet Creek
Seasonal Flow	Year
Section of State	NE

Directions   From Metaline, take Rt. 31 S. about 2 miles to marked Roadside Park on the right (west) side of the road. (The Roadside Park is just before the crossover bridge above Sweet Creek and before Selkirk High School on the east side of the road.) Hike about 1/4 mile on the log-lined path to the falls.

Waterfall Name	Wallace Falls
State	Washington
Type	Horsetail
Variant Name	
Height in feet	250
County	Snohomish
Topo Map	Gold Bar
Geo Coord	475224N1213852W
Map Ref Code	47121-G6
Elevation ft	1400
Water Source	Wallace River
Seasonal Flow	Year
Section of State	NW

Directions   From Gold Bar, take the road towards Wallace Falls State Park. Go about 2 miles and park at the Woody Trail Trailhead (just past the camping area). Follow the trail for about 2 miles to the first viewpoint of the falls. The best viewpoint is another 1/2 mile, some gradual, steep climbs.

CHAPTER 2

The Eastern Rocky Mountain States

Colorado
Montana
New Mexico
Wyoming

North Clear Creek Falls
COLORADO

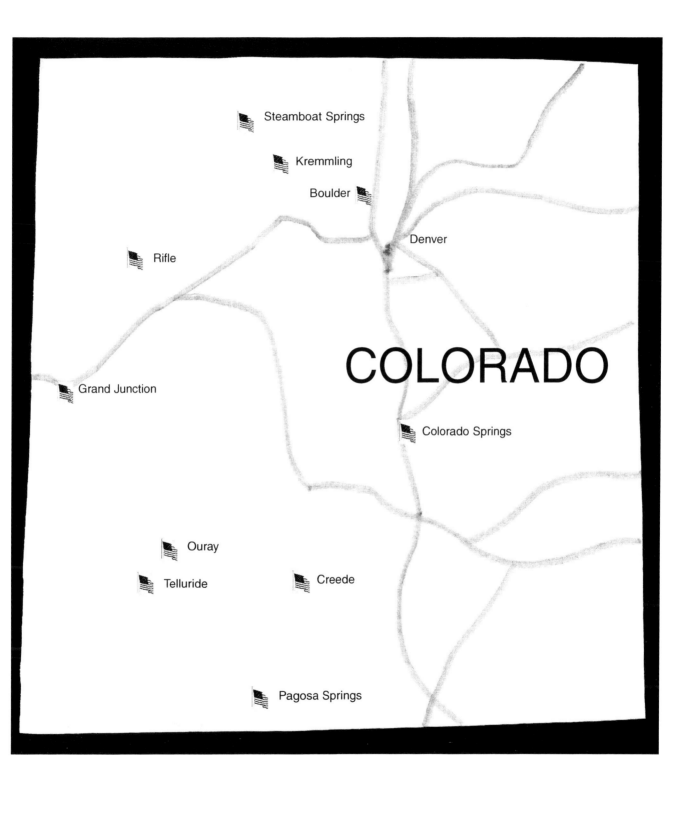

Steamboat Springs

Kremmling

Boulder

Denver

Rifle

Grand Junction

COLORADO

Colorado Springs

Ouray

Telluride

Creede

Pagosa Springs

Waterfall Name	Bear Creek Falls
State	Colorado
Type	Plunge/Horsetail
Variant Name	
Height in feet	100
County	Ouray
Topo Map	Ironton
Geo Coord	375959N1073934W
Map Ref Code	37107-H6
Elevation ft	8550
Water Source	Bear Creek
Seasonal Flow	Year
Section of State	SW

Directions   From Ouray, take Hwy. 550 S. for 2.6 miles to the turnout on the right. The falls can be viewed from the south end of the parking area.

Waterfall Name	Boulder Falls
State	Colorado
Type	Segmented/Plunge
Variant Name	
Height in feet	40
County	Boulder
Topo Map	Gold Hill
Geo Coord	400025N1052419W
Map Ref Code	40105-A4
Elevation ft	7050
Water Source	North Boulder Creek
Seasonal Flow	Year
Section of State	NE

Directions   From Boulder, take Highway 119 W. for 8 miles to the turnout on the right (look for sign to Boulder Falls). The hike is an easy 0.1 mile to the falls.

Waterfall Name	Bridal Veil Falls
State	Colorado
Type	Plunge
Variant Name	
Height in feet	360
County	San Miguel
Topo Map	Telluride
Geo Coord	375509N1074610W
Map Ref Code	37107-H7
Elevation ft	10000
Water Source	Bridal Veil Creek
Seasonal Flow	Year
Section of State	SW

Directions   Take Rt. 145 into the town of Telluride and keep going past the Pandora Mill. The road will end; park here and hike the switchback trail up the mountain about 1.2 miles to view the bottom of the falls. The top of the falls is 0.6 mile further. This is the largest drop of any falls in Colorado.

Waterfall Name	Cascade Falls
State	Colorado
Type	Tiered/Plunge
Variant Name	
Height in feet	80
County	Ouray
Topo Map	Ouray
Geo Coord	380135N1073950W
Map Ref Code	38107-A6
Elevation ft	8360
Water Source	Cascade Creek
Seasonal Flow	Year
Section of State	SW

Directions   From Main St. in the town of Ouray, drive up 8th St. about 5 blocks to the parking lot. Hike to the base of the falls on the well-marked trail (about 1/4 mile).

Waterfall Name	Cataract Falls
State	Colorado
Type	Segmented/Fan
Variant Name	Cataract Creek Falls
Height in feet	300
County	Summit
Topo Map	Mount Powell
Geo Coord	394950N1061748W
Map Ref Code	39106-G3
Elevation ft	9000
Water Source	Cataract Creek
Seasonal Flow	Year
Section of State	NW

Directions   From the junction of Interstate 40 and Hwy. 9 in the town of Kremmling, take Hwy. 9 S. for 12.8 miles to Heeney Rd. (30). Turn right (south) and go 5.2 miles to Cataract Creek Road (dirt). This is the SW side of Green Mountain Reservoir. Turn right (south) and go approx. 2.5 miles to the end of the road (past Cataract Creek Campground). The trailhead leads to a loop trail that circles the lake (about 2 miles RT). At the halfway point, there is a footbridge at the base of the falls. There are lots of trees blocking the view, so hike up the trail at the side of the falls for a closer look.

Waterfall Name	Fish Creek Falls
State	Colorado
Type	Segmented/Horsetail
Variant Name	
Height in feet	280
County	Routt
Topo Map	Steamboat Springs
Geo Coord	402854N1064614W
Map Ref Code	40106-D7
Elevation ft	7600
Water Source	Fish Creek
Seasonal Flow	Year
Section of State	NW

Directions   In the town of Steamboat Springs, take 3rd St. east from Lincoln Ave. (US 40). Take a right onto Fish Creek Falls Road and proceed 4 miles to the parking area (last 2 miles are dirt). The upper (north) asphalt trail leads to a viewpoint in 1/8 of a mile. The lower (south) dirt trail leads to the viewpoint at the base of the falls in 1/8 of a mile.

Waterfall Name	Ingram Falls
State	Colorado
Type	Plunge/Cascade
Variant Name	
Height in feet	90
County	San Miguel
Topo Map	Telluride
Geo Coord	375522N1074540W
Map Ref Code	37107-H7
Elevation ft	11000
Water Source	Ingram Creek
Seasonal Flow	Year
Section of State	SW

Directions   See directions for Bridal Veil Falls. Ingram Falls is 1/2 mile further along the trail.

Waterfall Name	Lake Fork Falls East
State	Colorado
Type	Tiered/Horsetail
Variant Name	Upper Lake Fork Falls
Height in feet	35
County	San Miguel
Topo Map	Mount Wilson
Geo Coord	375118N1075245W
Map Ref Code	37107-G8
Elevation ft	8800
Water Source	Lake Fork East
Seasonal Flow	Year
Section of State	SW

Directions   From Telluride, take Hwy. 145 S. towards Ophir and Dolores about 7 miles. Turn right onto the gravel road at the green sign that reads "Ames/Illium". Go 0.9 mile and take the first left turn (very sharp). Go 0.3 mile to the Ames Power Station. From here, only 4WD vehicles are recommended. Continue past the Power Station, veering left at the Y (sign says private road but it is passable). Continue uphill another 0.4 mile to another Y and veer right. Proceed another 100 yards to a turnaround and park. Falls can be viewed from the cliff.

Waterfall Name	Lake Fork Falls West
State	Colorado
Type	Plunge
Variant Name	Lower Lake Fork Falls
Height in feet	200
County	San Miguel
Topo Map	Mount Wilson
Geo Coord	375106N1075212W
Map Ref Code	37107-G8
Elevation ft	8700
Water Source	Lake Fork
Seasonal Flow	Year
Section of State	SW

Directions   Follow the directions to Lake Fork Falls East. Once there, continue on the trail to the top of East Falls, then carefully cross over the creek. Continue on the trail a few hundred feet to the top of West Falls. The trail leads north along the ridge for a better view of the falls. Use CAUTION-steep dropoffs.

Waterfall Name	North Clear Creek Falls
State	Colorado
Type	Segmented/Plunge/Horsetail
Variant Name	Clear Creek Falls North
Height in feet	100
County	Hinsdale
Topo Map	Hermit Lakes
Geo Coord	375057N1070859W
Map Ref Code	37107-G2
Elevation ft	10000
Water Source	North Clear Creek
Seasonal Flow	Year
Section of State	SW

Directions   From Creede, take Hwy 149 N. for approx. 26 miles to FS 510 (on the right just north of Mile Mark 48). Turn right onto 510 (look for sign to North Clear Creek Falls) and go 0.8 mile, then veer left into the parking area and viewpoint. In Rio Grande National Forest.

Waterfall Name	Piedra Falls
State	Colorado
Type	Tiered/Plunge
Variant Name	
Height in feet	60
County	Mineral
Topo Map	Pagosa Peak
Geo Coord	372901N1070539W
Map Ref Code	37107-D1
Elevation ft	8400
Water Source	East Fork Piedra River
Seasonal Flow	Year
Section of State	SW

Directions   From Pagosa Springs, take Hwy. 160 W. to Piedra Road (631). Turn right (north) and go 17.9 miles (pavement ends after 6.2 miles to gravel) to Middle Fork Road (636). Turn right and go about 2 miles to East Toner Rd. (637). Turn right and follow to the end (about 8 miles). Park here and hike about 1/2 mile to the falls (trail well-marked). Use caution on East Toner Rd.; the dirt can be slick if wet. In San Juan National Forest.

Waterfall Name	Potholes
State	Colorado
Type	Punchbowl
Variant Name	The Potholes Falls
Height in feet	15
County	Mesa
Topo Map	Payne Wash
Geo Coord	385718N1085112W
Map Ref Code	38108-H7
Elevation ft	6600
Water Source	Little Dolores River
Seasonal Flow	Year
Section of State	NW

Directions   From Grand Junction, take Road 340 to the East entrance of Colorado National Monument (look for sign). Go uphill to the summit and take the first road on the left towards Glade Park (well-marked, called DS Rd.). On reaching Glade Park Store (on the right), continue straight on DS Road 8 more miles to 9.8 Rd. and turn left (dirt). Go approx. 2.5 miles and turn right just before the second cattle guard. Several roads branch off this road but they all lead to the unmarked parking area. Hike a few hundred feet down the sloping granite rocks to the series of falls.

Waterfall Name	Rifle Falls
State	Colorado
Type	Segmented/Plunge
Variant Name	
Height in feet	70
County	Garfield
Topo Map	Rifle Falls
Geo Coord	394039N1074152W
Map Ref Code	39107-F6
Elevation ft	6600
Water Source	Rifle Creek
Seasonal Flow	Year
Section of State	NE

Directions   From Rifle, take Hwy. 13 N. to Hwy. 325 (just outside of town). Turn right (north); there will be a sign for Rifle Falls here. Go approx. 11 miles to Rifle Falls State Recreation Area Campground (about 6.5 miles past dam). Drive through the camp area to the parking and picnic area. The falls is a short hike from here. Entry fee.

Waterfall Name	Silver Cascade
State	Colorado
Type	Cascade
Variant Name	Spoon Falls
Height in feet	200
County	El Paso
Topo Map	Manitou Springs
Geo Coord	384712N1035421W
Map Ref Code	38103-G8
Elevation ft	7600
Water Source	North Cheyenne Canyon Creek
Seasonal Flow	Sp
Section of State	SE

Directions   In Colorado Springs, take Interstate 25 S. to Exit 140B (Tejon St.). Turn right (south) and go to Cheyenne Blvd. Turn right (west), continue past Seven Falls into North Cheyenne Canyon Park and follow signs to Helen Hunt Falls parking area. Hike up the trail next to Helen Hunt Falls to Silver Cascade. The well-maintained trail is a steep 1/4 mile.

Waterfall Name	Silver Falls
State	Colorado
Type	Plunge/Cascade
Variant Name	
Height in feet	30
County	Mineral
Topo Map	Wolf Creek Pass
Geo Coord	372543N1064642W
Map Ref Code	37106-D7
Elevation ft	8600
Water Source	Waterfall Creek
Seasonal Flow	Year
Section of State	SW

Directions   From Pagosa Springs at the San Juan River Bridge on the east side of town, take Hwy. 160 E. Go 10 miles to East Fork Road (667) and turn right (gravel road). Go about 8 miles to the old Forest Service Guard Station on the left. Park here and hike past the building upstream about 200 yards to the falls. 4WD vehicle recommended on gravel road. In San Juan National Forest.

Waterfall Name	South Clear Creek Falls
State	Colorado
Type	Plunge
Variant Name	Clear Creek Falls South
Height in feet	60
County	Hinsdale
Topo Map	Hermit Lakes
Geo Coord	374931N1070919W
Map Ref Code	37107-G2
Elevation ft	9650
Water Source	South Clear Creek
Seasonal Flow	Year
Section of State	SW

Directions   From Creede, take Hwy. 149 N. for approx 23 miles to FS Silver Thread Campground. It will be on the right between Mile Marks 45 and 46. Drive to the parking area at the end of the campground to the marked trailhead. The trail on the right goes close to the falls (1/8-mile hike). The trail on the left goes along the ridge to a panoramic viewpoint of the falls (1/4-mile hike). In Rio Grande National Forest.

Waterfall Name	Treasure Falls
State	Colorado
Type	Plunge
Variant Name	
Height in feet	100
County	Mineral
Topo Map	Wolf Creek Pass
Geo Coord	372635N1065224W
Map Ref Code	37106-D7
Elevation ft	8560
Water Source	Fall Creek
Seasonal Flow	Year
Section of State	SW

Directions   From Pagosa Springs at the San Juan River Bridge, take Hwy. 160 E. for 15 miles to the large parking area on the right. There is a sign for the falls here. The trail is about 1/4 mile to the base of the falls. The trail to the left of the restrooms is the most maintained. In San Juan National Forest.

Waterfall Name	Twin Falls
State	Colorado
Type	Segmented/Horsetail
Variant Name	
Height in feet	100
County	Ouray
Topo Map	Telluride
Geo Coord	375849N1074520W
Map Ref Code	37107-H7
Elevation ft	11000
Water Source	Sneffles Creek
Seasonal Flow	Year
Section of State	SW

Directions   From Ouray, take Road 361 (dirt) towards Yankee Boy Basin (starts from south end of town). Go about 7 miles to the falls viewpoint. 4WD vehicle recommended.

Waterfall Name	Uncompahgre Falls
State	Colorado
Type	Cascade
Variant Name	Uncompahgre River Falls
Height in feet	200
County	Ouray
Topo Map	Ironton
Geo Coord	375712N1073720W
Map Ref Code	37107-H6
Elevation ft	8800
Water Source	Uncompahgre River
Seasonal Flow	Year
Section of State	SW

Directions   From Ouray, take Hwy. 550 S. Go 3.5 miles to the turnout on the right (on the left is Engineers Pass Road). The falls is on the right, flowing down the cliffside.

Waterfall Name	Yellow Rose Falls
State	Colorado
Type	Segmented/Plunge
Variant Name	
Height in feet	50
County	Ouray
Topo Map	Silverton
Geo Coord	375712N1074031W
Map Ref Code	37107-G6
Elevation ft	10400
Water Source	Imogene Creek
Seasonal Flow	Year
Section of State	SW

Directions   From Ouray, take Road 361 (dirt) towards Yankee Boy Basin (starts at south end of town). Go 6.2 miles to Imogene Pass Road and turn left. Go 1.5 miles to the falls viewpoint on the left. 4WD vehicle recommended.

Waterfall Name	Arch Falls
State	Montana
Type	Plunge
Variant Name	
Height in feet	30
County	Gallatin
Topo Map	Fridley Peak
Geo Coord	452538N1105737W
Map Ref Code	45110-D8
Elevation ft	7400
Water Source	Hyalite Creek
Seasonal Flow	Year
Section of State	SW

Directions   See directions for Palisades Falls. Follow those directions to the Hyalite Reservoir. The mileage count for Arch Falls starts from the parking lot just before the dam. Cross the dam (rough dirt road) and follow the east side of the lake about 4 miles total, continuing straight at the Y towards Hyalite Creek Trailhead (follow sign) and park. Hike on the gradual uphill Hyalite Creek Trail for about 1.25 miles to the falls. A sign marks "Arch Falls" to the right.

Waterfall Name	Black Eagle Falls
State	Montana
Type	Block
Variant Name	
Height in feet	80
County	Cascade
Topo Map	Northwest Great Falls
Geo Coord	473102N1111529W
Map Ref Code	47111-E3
Elevation ft	3300
Water Source	Missouri River
Seasonal Flow	Year
Section of State	NW

Directions   From Great Falls, go north on 15th St., then turn right (east) on River Drive (just before the bridge over the Missouri River). At the top of the hill, turn left into the scenic overlook (across from the baseball stadium).

Waterfall Name	Cataract Falls
State	Montana
Type	Fan
Variant Name	
Height in feet	80
County	Lewis and Clark
Topo Map	Steamboat Mountain
Geo Coord	471919N1123611W
Map Ref Code	47112-C5
Elevation ft	5250
Water Source	Cataract Creek
Seasonal Flow	Year
Section of State	NW

Directions   From Augusta, take Rt. 435 S. and then turn right (west) onto Elk Creek Road (gravel). Go about 10 miles to the parking area at the end of the road. Cross the creek at the trailhead (follow sign towards falls) and go to the gate of private property. Turn left here and follow the trail up the canyon to the base of the falls. Total hike is about 1/4 mile.

Waterfall Name	Champagne Falls
State	Montana
Type	Fan
Variant Name	Champayne Falls
Height in feet	40
County	Gallatin
Topo Map	Fridley Peak
Geo Coord	452428N1105727W
Map Ref Code	45110-D8
Elevation ft	7600
Water Source	Hyalite Creek
Seasonal Flow	Year
Section of State	SW

Directions   See directions to Palisades Falls and Arch Falls. From Arch Falls, continue on the Hyalite Creek Trail to Champagne Falls on the right (marked by sign). Total distance from parking area to falls is about 2.5 miles.

Waterfall Name	Crooked Falls
State	Montana
Type	Block
Variant Name	Horseshoe Falls
Height in feet	30
County	Cascade
Topo Map	Northeast Great Falls
Geo Coord	473210N1111144W
Map Ref Code	47111-E2
Elevation ft	3100
Water Source	Missouri River
Seasonal Flow	Year
Section of State	NW

Directions   From Great Falls, take 15th St. north, and turn right (east) onto River Drive (just before bridge over Missouri River). Turn left onto Giant Springs Road (sign reads Giant Springs State Park). Go to the second scenic overlook at the top of the hill and park. From here, Rainbow Falls can be seen to the left and to the right is Crooked Falls. For a closer look at Crooked Falls, follow the trail on the SE ridge of the river for about 1 mile.

Waterfall Name	Double Falls
State	Montana
Type	Segmented/Cascade
Variant Name	
Height in feet	20
County	Lewis and Clark
Topo Map	Double Falls
Geo Coord	472425N1124323W
Map Ref Code	47112-D6
Elevation ft	5350
Water Source	Ford Creek
Seasonal Flow	Year
Section of State	NW

Directions   From Augusta, take the unnamed road east towards Benchmark (see sign). Go about 15 miles (road starts out paved but turns to gravel) and turn left onto gravel Road 235 (sign reads Benchmark Wilderness Camp). Follow this road to the camping/parking area on the left (just past Mile Mark 4). Follow the trail marked by the sign for Double Falls for a short distance to the falls.

Waterfall Name	Graves Creek Falls
State	Montana
Type	Horsetail/Cascade
Variant Name	
Height in feet	100
County	Sanders
Topo Map	Belknap
Geo Coord	474312N1152240W
Map Ref Code	47115-F4
Elevation ft	3100
Water Source	Graves Creek
Seasonal Flow	Year
Section of State	NW

Directions   From the town of Thompson Falls, take Rt. 200 N. a few miles and turn right (east) onto Blue Slide Road. Stay to the right at the Y and continue 6.4 miles and turn right onto gravel Graves Creek Road 367 (just past Mile Mark 6). Go 2.8 miles to the Graves Creek Falls Overlook parking area on the left. The top of the falls is a short walk from here.

Waterfall Name	Great Falls
State	Montana
Type	Block
Variant Name	Ryan Dam Falls/Big Falls
Height in feet	80
County	Cascade
Topo Map	Morony Dam
Geo Coord	473408N1110720W
Map Ref Code	47111-E1
Elevation ft	3000
Water Source	Missouri River
Seasonal Flow	Year
Section of State	NW

Directions   From Great Falls, take Rt. 87 N. (towards Havre). After crossing the Missouri River Bridge, go 3.5 miles more and turn right (east) onto Ryan Dam Road. Follow the signs for Ryan Dam for 7 miles to the parking area. Walk a short distance across the suspension bridge to the island for a head-on view of the roaring falls. When the falls is viewed in person, it will be clear why the photo was composed this way.

Waterfall Name	Grotto Falls
State	Montana
Type	Fan
Variant Name	
Height in feet	40
County	Gallatin
Topo Map	Fridley Peak
Geo Coord	452609N1105747W
Map Ref Code	45110-D8
Elevation ft	7200
Water Source	Hyalite Creek
Seasonal Flow	Year
Section of State	SW

Directions See directions for Arch Falls. From the parking area, hike on the paved wheelchair access trail for 1.25 miles directly to the falls.

Waterfall Name	Kootenai Falls
State	Montana
Type	Block
Variant Name	
Height in feet	30
County	Lincoln
Topo Map	Kootenai Falls
Geo Coord	482720N1154544W
Map Ref Code	48115-D7
Elevation ft	2100
Water Source	Kootenai River
Seasonal Flow	Year
Section of State	NW

Directions From Libby, take Rt. 2 N. for 10 miles to Kootenai Falls County Park on the right. Hike 1/4 mile on the well-maintained trail to the falls.

Waterfall Name	Lost Creek Falls
State	Montana
Type	Cascade
Variant Name	
Height in feet	40
County	Deer
Topo Map	West Valley
Geo Coord	461232N1130020W
Map Ref Code	46113-B1
Elevation ft	6300
Water Source	Lost Creek
Seasonal Flow	Year
Section of State	SW

Directions   From Anaconda, take Hwy. 10 E. and go north on Rt. 48. Once on Rt. 48, take a quick left (north) onto Galen Road (273). Go 2 miles and turn left (west) onto Lost Creek Road (635). Go 6 miles to Lost Creek State Park. The falls is at the end of the road inside the Park. A very short walk on the asphalt trail leads to the base of the falls.

Waterfall Name	Martin Falls
State	Montana
Type	Cascade
Variant Name	
Height in feet	70
County	Flathead
Topo Map	Radnor
Geo Coord	483401N1144107W
Map Ref Code	48114-E6
Elevation ft	3700
Water Source	Martin Creek
Seasonal Flow	Year
Section of State	NW

Directions   From Olney at the intersection of Rt. 93 and Main St., take Main St. south. Go past the Briggs Mercantile, cross the RR tracks and turn right onto Road 60 at the T intersection (towards Good Creek). Cross the bridge over the river, pass the lumber mill and turn right onto Road 910 (total of 3 miles from T intersection to Rd. 910). Go 4.8 miles on this gravel road and park at the sign for "Martin Falls". The short trail is on the left to the falls.

Waterfall Name	Memorial Falls
State	Montana
Type	Plunge
Variant Name	
Height in feet	30
County	Cascade
Topo Map	Neihart
Geo Coord	465455N1104132W
Map Ref Code	46110-H6
Elevation ft	6200
Water Source	Memorial Creek
Seasonal Flow	Year
Section of State	NW

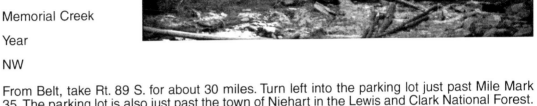

Directions From Belt, take Rt. 89 S. for about 30 miles. Turn left into the parking lot just past Mile Mark 35. The parking lot is also just past the town of Niehart in the Lewis and Clark National Forest. From the well-marked trailhead to the falls is about 1/2 mile.

Waterfall Name	Morrell Falls
State	Montana
Type	Horsetail
Variant Name	
Height in feet	100
County	Powell
Topo Map	Morrell Lake
Geo Coord	471804N1132743W
Map Ref Code	47113-C4
Elevation ft	5000
Water Source	Morrell Creek
Seasonal Flow	Year
Section of State	SW

Directions From the town of Seeley Lake, take Rt. 83 N. and turn right (east) onto unmarked FR 477 (just past town). This road is also called Morrell Creek Road (follow sign to Seeley Creek Hiking Area). Go about 7 miles on this gravel road to the parking area (follow signs to Morrell Falls). The hike is a moderate 2 miles from the parking area.

Waterfall Name	Natural Bridge Falls
State	Montana
Type	Cascade
Variant Name	
Height in feet	30
County	Sweet Grass
Topo Map	McLeod Basin
Geo Coord	453240N1101226W
Map Ref Code	45110-E2
Elevation ft	5100
Water Source	Boulder River
Seasonal Flow	Year
Section of State	SW

Directions   From Big Timber, take Rt. 298 S. Pass the town of McLeod. One mile past Mile Mark 25, turn left into Natural Bridge and Falls State Monument. There are several well-marked trails to the bridge and falls. All trails are less than 1 mile.

Waterfall Name	Ousel Falls
State	Montana
Type	Tiered/Fan
Variant Name	
Height in feet	50
County	Gallatin
Topo Map	Ousel Falls
Geo Coord	451421N1112027W
Map Ref Code	45111-B3
Elevation ft	6600
Water Source	West Fork Gallatin River
Seasonal Flow	Year
Section of State	SW

Directions   From Belgrade, take Rt. 191 S. At Mile Mark 48, go west towards Big Sky Meadow Village. In 2.5 miles, turn left (south) onto the unmarked dirt road. In 1 mile veer right at the Y (soon marked Ousel Falls Road). Go 1.1 miles to the cattle guard and park. Hike down the dirt road to the left and then follow the unmarked trail along the canyon ridge (trail goes in a SW direction). Listen for the sound of the powerful falls and follow the very steep trail to the falls overlook. Total hike from the parking area to the falls is about 1/2 mile.

Waterfall Name	Palisades Falls
State	Montana
Type	Fan
Variant Name	
Height in feet	100
County	Gallatin
Topo Map	Fridley Peak
Geo Coord	452815N1105540W
Map Ref Code	45110-D8
Elevation ft	7300
Water Source	Palisades Creek
Seasonal Flow	Year
Section of State	SW

Directions   From Bozeman, take 19th Road south and turn left (south) onto Hyalite Canyon Road. Follow Hyalite Canyon Road to Hyalite Reservoir (road will change to gravel). Total distance from Bozeman to Reservoir is about 16 miles. Cross the dam and follow the rough dirt road along the east side of the reservoir. In 2 miles veer left at the Y (follow sign to Palisades Falls). Go 1 more mile to the parking area on the left. Hike about 1/2 mile on the asphalt trail to the falls.

Waterfall Name	Pine Creek Falls East
State	Montana
Type	Horsetail
Variant Name	
Height in feet	80
County	Park
Topo Map	Mt. Cowan
Geo Coord	452932N1102956W
Map Ref Code	45110-D4
Elevation ft	6400
Water Source	East Fork Pine Creek
Seasonal Flow	Year
Section of State	SW

Directions   From Livingston, take Interstate 90 E. for 3 miles to Rt. 89 and go south. Go 3 miles and turn left (east) onto East River Road (540). Proceed 7.8 miles and turn left (east) onto Luccock Park Road (sign here reads Pine Creek Campground). Go 1.8 miles and the road changes to gravel. Continue straight another 1.4 miles to the trailhead at the back of Pine Creek Campground. Follow the trail a short walk to both the East and South Falls.

Waterfall Name	Pine Creek Falls South
State	Montana
Type	Fan
Variant Name	South Fork Pine Creek Falls
Height in feet	90
County	Park
Topo Map	Mt. Cowan
Geo Coord	452850N1102958W
Map Ref Code	45110-D4
Elevation ft	6200
Water Source	South Fork Pine Creek
Seasonal Flow	Year
Section of State	SW

Directions	See directions for Pine Creek Falls East.

Waterfall Name	Pintlar Falls
State	Montana
Type	Block
Variant Name	Pintler Falls
Height in feet	100
County	Deer Lodge
Topo Map	Pintlar Lake
Geo Coord	455136N1132641W
Map Ref Code	45113-G4
Elevation ft	6400
Water Source	Pintlar Creek
Seasonal Flow	Year
Section of State	SW

Directions	Near Wisdom at the intersection of Routes 43 and 278, take Rt. 278 W. Go approx. 5 miles. Turn right towards Pintlar Lake Campground. In about 6 miles, park at the falls trailhead in the campground. A short hike leads to the falls viewpoint.

Waterfall Name   Rainbow Falls

State   Montana

Type   Segmented/Block

Variant Name

Height in feet   50

County   Cascade

Topo Map   Northeast Great Falls

Geo Coord   473200N1111217W

Map Ref Code   47111-E2

Elevation ft   3169

Water Source   Missouri River

Seasonal Flow   Year

Section of State   NW

Directions   See directions for Crooked Falls.

Waterfall Name   Skalkaho Falls

State   Montana

Type   Fan

Variant Name

Height in feet   80

County   Ravalli

Topo Map   Burnt Fork Lake

Geo Coord   461527N1134932W

Map Ref Code   46113-C7

Elevation ft   6200

Water Source   Falls Creek

Seasonal Flow   Year

Section of State   SW

Directions   From Hamilton, take Rt. 93 S. for 2.5 miles and turn left (east) onto Rt. 38 (Skalkaho Road). Go 21.4 miles (the last 7 miles on gravel) to the falls on the left.

Waterfall Name	Snowshoe Falls
State	Montana
Type	Fan
Variant Name	
Height in feet	20
County	Missoula
Topo Map	Lolo Hot Springs
Geo Coord	464032N1143413W
Map Ref Code	46114-F5
Elevation ft	4450
Water Source	West Fork Lolo Creek
Seasonal Flow	Year
Section of State	SW

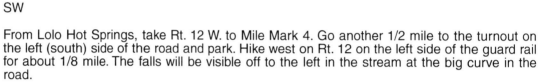

Directions   From Lolo Hot Springs, take Rt. 12 W. to Mile Mark 4. Go another 1/2 mile to the turnout on the left (south) side of the road and park. Hike west on Rt. 12 on the left side of the guard rail for about 1/8 mile. The falls will be visible off to the left in the stream at the big curve in the road.

Waterfall Name	Yaak Falls
State	Montana
Type	Block/Slide
Variant Name	
Height in feet	30
County	Lincoln
Topo Map	Newton Mountain
Geo Coord	483855N1155302W
Map Ref Code	48115-F8
Elevation ft	2400
Water Source	Yaak River
Seasonal Flow	Year
Section of State	NW

Directions   From Troy, take US Rt. 2 N. and turn right (north) onto Rt. 508. Go 6.5 miles to the pullout on the right. The pullout is past Mile Mark 6 and also past Yaak Falls Campground. Walk slightly downstream to see the falls.

Red River

Espanola

Jemez Springs

Santa Fe

Gallup

Ramah

Albuquerque

NEW MEXICO

Cloudcroft

Glenwood

Carlsbad

Las Cruces

Waterfall Name	Bluff Springs Falls
State	New Mexico
Type	Segmented/Horsetail
Variant Name	
Height in feet	20
County	Otero
Topo Map	Bluff Springs
Geo Coord	325002N1054424W
Map Ref Code	32105-G6
Elevation ft	8000
Water Source	Bluff Spring
Seasonal Flow	Year
Section of State	SE

Directions   From Cloudcroft, take Rt. 130 S. Turn right (south) onto Road 6563 (Sunspot Hwy). Go approx. 10 miles and turn left (east) onto Rt. 164 (Upper Penasco River Rd.). There is a sign at this point for Bluff Springs. Go 4 miles (last 2 are on gravel) to the parking area on the right (sign for Bluff Springs). The falls can be seen from here. In Lincoln National Forest.

Waterfall Name	Frijoles Lower Falls
State	New Mexico
Type	Plunge
Variant Name	Lower Frijoles Falls
Height in feet	60
County	Sandoval
Topo Map	Frijoles
Geo Coord	354539N1061530W
Map Ref Code	35106-G3
Elevation ft	5900
Water Source	Frijoles Creek
Seasonal Flow	Year
Section of State	NW

Directions   See directions for Frijoles Upper Falls. Continue hiking on the same trail for another 1/4 mile to the Lower Falls.

Waterfall Name	Frijoles Upper Falls
State	New Mexico
Type	Horsetail
Variant Name	Upper Frijoles Falls
Height in feet	60
County	Sandoval
Topo Map	Frijoles
Geo Coord	354548N1061533W
Map Ref Code	35106-G3
Elevation ft	6000
Water Source	Frijoles Creek
Seasonal Flow	Year
Section of State	NW

Directions   From Santa Fe, take US 285 N. to Pojoaque. Go west on Rt. 502 (follow signs to Bandelier National Monument) and go south on SR 4. Proceed to the Park Visitors Center and obtain a map. The trailhead is at the end of the Backcountry Parking Area. Hike 1.5 miles on the up and down trail through the canyon to the falls viewpoint. Entry fee.

Waterfall Name	Jemez Falls
State	New Mexico
Type	Fan
Variant Name	
Height in feet	40
County	Sandoval
Topo Map	Redondo Peak
Geo Coord	354846N1063621W
Map Ref Code	35106-G5
Elevation ft	7800
Water Source	East Fork Jemez River
Seasonal Flow	Year
Section of State	NW

Directions   From Jemez Springs, take Rt. 4 N. and turn right into Jemez Falls Campground (just past Mile Mark 30). Drive to the end of the road and park in the trailhead parking area. The falls trail is to the right (well-marked with signs). The easy, well-maintained hiking trail is 1/2 mile to the falls viewpoint.

Waterfall Name	Middle Fork Cascades
State	New Mexico
Type	Cascade
Variant Name	
Height in feet	30
County	Taos
Topo Map	Wheeler Peak
Geo Coord	363651N1052440W
Map Ref Code	36105-E4
Elevation ft	10200
Water Source	Middle Fork of the Red River
Seasonal Flow	Sp,Sm
Section of State	NE

Directions　From Red River, take Rt. 38 S. and veer right at the Y onto Rt. 578. Proceed to the end of the pavement (about 1/2 mile past Mile Mark 6) and park. Hike or take a 4WD vehicle on Middle Fork Lake Rd. for 2 miles to the wooden bridge that crosses over Middle Fork Cascades. The first mile of Middle Fork Lake Rd. is a gradual incline with the next mile and beyond being steep switchbacks on rocky terrain. The trail is very well-marked the entire distance.

Waterfall Name	Middle Fork Lake Falls
State	New Mexico
Type	Horsetail
Variant Name	Falls at Middle Fork Lake
Height in feet	100
County	Taos
Topo Map	Wheeler Peak
Geo Coord	363527N1052458W
Map Ref Code	36105-E4
Elevation ft	11000
Water Source	Middle Fork Lake Creek
Seasonal Flow	Sp,Sm
Section of State	NE

Directions　See directions for Middle Fork Cascades. Continue on Middle Fork Lake Road for another mile past the Cascades to the lake. The falls can be seen on the opposite side of the lake flowing down the steep rock cliff.

Waterfall Name	Nambe Falls
State	New Mexico
Type	Tiered/Plunge
Variant Name	Nambe Pueblo Falls
Height in feet	90
County	Sante Fe
Topo Map	Tesuque
Geo Coord	355044N1055421W
Map Ref Code	35105-G8
Elevation ft	6800
Water Source	Nambe River
Seasonal Flow	Year
Section of State	NE

Directions   From Espanola, take Rt. 84 S. and then go east on Rt. 503. Just past Mile Mark 3, turn right (south) onto NP 101 (sign here for Nambe Falls). Go 5.2 miles to the Ranger Station (located on Nambe Pueblo land). At the Ranger Station, turn right and proceed to the end of the campground and park. Hike to the bridge a short distance from the parking area. From here, a sign points to the falls. The hike is a moderately strenuous 10 minutes to the falls. Entry fee.

Waterfall Name	Sitting Bull Falls
State	New Mexico
Type	Horsetail/Fan
Variant Name	
Height in feet	80
County	Eddy
Topo Map	Queen
Geo Coord	321435N1044145W
Map Ref Code	32104-B6
Elevation ft	4700
Water Source	Sitting Bull Springs
Seasonal Flow	Year
Section of State	SE

Directions   From Carlsbad, take Rt. 285 N. for 12 miles and turn left (south) onto Rt. 137 for 39 miles to the end of the road and the parking lot (follow signs to Sitting Bull Falls). The trail to the falls starts at the left side of the parking area. The easy, well-developed trail is 1/8 mile to the falls.

Waterfall Name	Soda Dam Falls
State	New Mexico
Type	Fan
Variant Name	
Height in feet	15
County	Sandoval
Topo Map	Jemez Springs
Geo Coord	354726N1064103W
Map Ref Code	35106-G6
Elevation ft	6300
Water Source	Jemez River
Seasonal Flow	Year
Section of State	NW

Directions   From Jemez Springs, take Rt. 4 N. for about 2.25 miles (past the Ranger Station) to the falls on the right (east) side of the road.

Waterfall Name	The Falls
State	New Mexico
Type	Cascade
Variant Name	Ramah Falls
Height in feet	20
County	Cibola
Topo Map	Ramah
Geo Coord	351228N1082633W
Map Ref Code	35108-B4
Elevation ft	7300
Water Source	Cebolla Creek
Seasonal Flow	Sp
Section of State	NW

Directions   From the Post Office in Ramah, go east on Rt. 53. In 1.3 miles turn left onto FR 157 (also called McGaffey and Timberlake Rd.). A 4WD vehicle is recommended from here. Go 6.4 miles to the Y and veer right staying on FR 157. Continue another 2.2 miles to where a sandy track (2 tire tracks) goes off to the right. Turn here and go about 100 yards on this track (veering right at the Y) and park before the small ravine. Hike due east for about 1/4 mile up and over the ridge to the rock gorge and falls; no defined trail.

Waterfall Name	Water Gate Falls
State	New Mexico
Type	Cascade
Variant Name	
Height in feet	15
County	Otero
Topo Map	Rogers Ruins
Geo Coord	324223N1054430W
Map Ref Code	32105-F6
Elevation ft	7600
Water Source	Sacramento River
Seasonal Flow	Sp
Section of State	SE

Directions	From Cloudcroft, take Rt. 130 S. to Road 6563 (Sunspot Hwy.) and turn right (south). Go about 16 miles to FR 537 (Sacramento Dr.) and turn left (gravel). Go approx. 7 miles to a large pull-out on the right and park. The falls can be seen from here off to the right. In Lincoln National Forest.

Waterfall Name	Whitewater Canyon Lower Falls
State	New Mexico
Type	Plunge
Variant Name	Lower Whitewater Canyon Falls
Height in feet	10
County	Catron
Topo Map	Holt Mountain
Geo Coord	332222N1084910W
Map Ref Code	33108-C7
Elevation ft	5000
Water Source	Whitewater Creek
Seasonal Flow	Sp,Sm
Section of State	SW

Directions	Take Rt. 180 to the north end of Glenwood. Just past Mile Mark 51, turn right (east) onto unmarked Whitewater Rd. Sign here reads "Catwalk 5 miles, Whitewater Picnic Ground". Go the 5 miles and park at the end of the road in the parking area. The hike is 2/3 mile to the falls with some steep and rocky sections. The catwalk is the first 100 yards of the trail.

Waterfall Name	Whitewater Canyon Upper Falls
State	New Mexico
Type	Horsetail
Variant Name	Upper Whitewater Canyon Falls
Height in feet	10
County	Catron
Topo Map	Holt Mountain
Geo Coord	332120N1084740W
Map Ref Code	33108-C7
Elevation ft	5600
Water Source	Whitewater Creek
Seasonal Flow	Sp,Sm
Section of State	SW

Directions   See directions for Whitewater Canyon Lower Falls. Take the same trail, however, the Upper Falls are about a 1-mile hike.

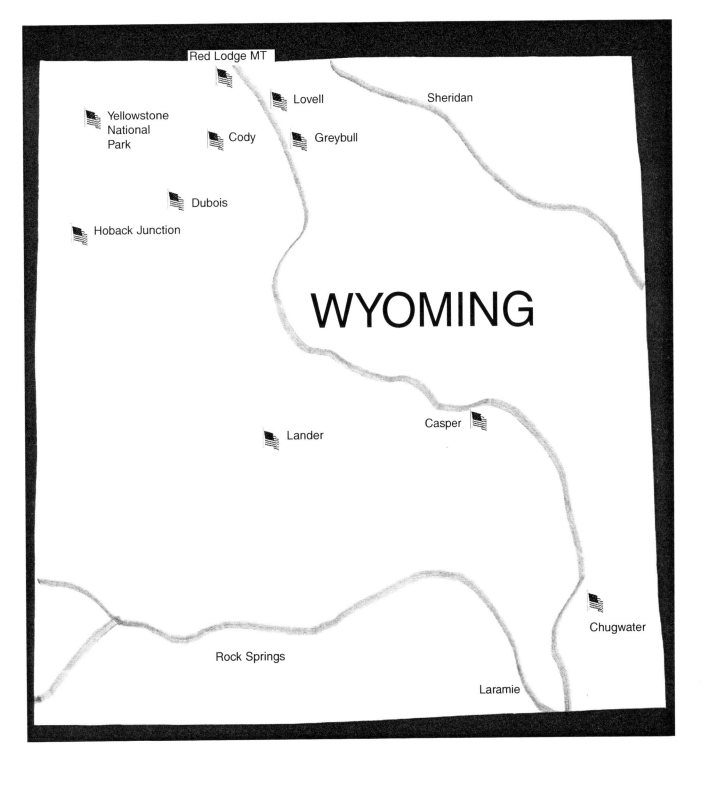

Red Lodge MT

Lovell

Sheridan

Yellowstone
National
Park

Cody

Greybull

Dubois

Hoback Junction

WYOMING

Lander

Casper

Chugwater

Rock Springs

Laramie

Waterfall Name	Beartooth Falls
State	Wyoming
Type	Cascade/Block
Variant Name	
Height in feet	100
County	Park
Topo Map	Beartooth Butte
Geo Coord	445615N1093612W
Map Ref Code	44109-H5
Elevation ft	8800
Water Source	Beartooth Creek
Seasonal Flow	Sp,Sm,F
Section of State	NW

Directions   From Red Lodge, Montana, take Rt. 212 S. Go over the Beartooth Mountains Scenic Byway, pass Beartooth Lake on the right, go another 1/4 mile and then park in the small turnout on the right (north). The falls can be viewed across the canyon on the left (south) side of the road. There is actually no official turnout for the falls. The best view is from the guard rail on the left (south) side of the road. (CAUTION-cars)

Waterfall Name	Bridal Veil Falls
State	Wyoming
Type	Plunge
Variant Name	
Height in feet	100
County	Park
Topo Map	Bald Peak
Geo Coord	445041N1092026W
Map Ref Code	44109-G3
Elevation ft	5400
Water Source	Falls Creek
Seasonal Flow	Year
Section of State	NW

Directions   From Cody, take Rt. 120 W. Go about 30 miles and turn left (west) onto County Road 1AB (also named FS 119) just before Mile Mark 129. Go 3.7 miles and veer left at the Y (sign on right reads Clark Fork Fish Hatchery). Go 8 miles and park where the pavement ends. From here, hike or 4WD on the rough dirt road to the left (follow the Clark Fork of the Yellowstone River) for about 1.5 miles to the first dirt road on the right (north). This road is just before the crossing of Falls Creek (unmarked). Turn right and follow the dirt road uphill to the end. From here, follow the faint trail that continues up the hill through the canyon. Follow this trail up the east side of Falls Creek to the falls. Distance from dirt road at Falls Creek crossing to falls is about 1/2 mile.

Waterfall Name	Brindle Falls
State	Wyoming
Type	Cascade
Variant Name	
Height in feet	30
County	Big Horn
Topo Map	Shell Falls
Geo Coord	443550N1073705W
Map Ref Code	44107-E5
Elevation ft	7000
Water Source	Brindle Creek
Seasonal Flow	Sp,Sm
Section of State	NW

Directions See directions for Shell Falls. Brindle Falls can be seen across the canyon from the NW viewpoint of the Shell Falls Canyon Loop, a short distance from the parking area. There is a 3-mile hike to the falls; ask for directions at the Shell Falls Visitors Center.

Waterfall Name	Brooks Lake Creek Falls
State	Wyoming
Type	Block/Cascade
Variant Name	
Height in feet	200
County	Fremont
Topo Map	Kisinger Lakes
Geo Coord	434214N1095801W
Map Ref Code	43109-F8
Elevation ft	8300
Water Source	Brooks Lake Creek
Seasonal Flow	Year
Section of State	SW

Directions From Dubois, take Rt. 287 N. Just past Mile Mark 33, turn left towards Falls Campground in the Shoshone National Forest. Go 1/2 mile to the trailhead (veer left after the campground entrance). Follow the well-marked trail a short distance to the falls viewpoint.

Waterfall Name	Crazy Creek Falls
State	Wyoming
Type	Cascade
Variant Name	Crazy Creek Cascade
Height in feet	200
County	Park
Topo Map	Jim Smith Peak
Geo Coord	445612N1094650W
Map Ref Code	44109-H7
Elevation ft	7000
Water Source	Crazy Creek
Seasonal Flow	Year
Section of State	NW

Directions   Start at the junction of Routes 212 and 296 (Chief Joseph Scenic Highway) about 50 miles NW of Cody. Take Rt. 212 W. Go 2.5 miles and park in the parking area on the north side of the road across from Crazy Creek Campground. Follow the trail at the west end of the parking area upstream (north) for a few hundred yards to the falls.

Waterfall Name	Diamond Falls
State	Wyoming
Type	Punchbowl
Variant Name	Private
Height in feet	10
County	Platte
Topo Map	
Geo Coord	
Map Ref Code	
Elevation ft	
Water Source	
Seasonal Flow	Sp
Section of State	SE

Directions   Private land. Permission can be granted to see the falls through the Diamond Ranch Horse Stables. The ranch is near the town of Chugwater.

Waterfall Name	Five Springs Falls
State	Wyoming
Type	Plunge/Cascade
Variant Name	
Height in feet	80
County	Bighorn
Topo Map	Medicine Wheel
Geo Coord	444802N1075735W
Map Ref Code	44107-G8
Elevation ft	7000
Water Source	Five Springs Creek
Seasonal Flow	Year
Section of State	NW

Directions   From Lovell, take Rt. 14A to the east. Turn left (north) towards Five Springs Falls Camp-ground between Mile Marks 22 and 23. Go 2 miles and park at the upper campground parking area on the left side of the creek. Follow the well-marked trail for about 1/8 mile up the creekside to the falls.

Waterfall Name	Garden Creek Falls
State	Wyoming
Type	Horsetail
Variant Name	
Height in feet	60
County	Natrona
Topo Map	Casper
Geo Coord	424558N1061957W
Map Ref Code	42106-G3
Elevation ft	6500
Water Source	Garden Creek
Seasonal Flow	Sp,Sm
Section of State	SE

Directions   From Casper, take Poplar St. to the south. At the junction with Rt. 220, continue straight anoth-er 6 miles (road name changes to Garden Creek Road) and turn right (south) onto Rt. 251 towards Rotary Park. Go 0.6 mile and park in the parking area at the end of the road. Follow the trail upstream a short distance to the falls.

Waterfall Name	Granite Falls
State	Wyoming
Type	Block
Variant Name	
Height in feet	40
County	Teton
Topo Map	Granite Falls
Geo Coord	432155N1102634W
Map Ref Code	43110-F7
Elevation ft	7000
Water Source	Granite Creek
Seasonal Flow	Year
Section of State	NW

Directions   From Hoback Junction, take Rt. 189/191 S. Turn east onto FR 30500 (gravel) towards Granite Recreation Area. The turn is before the Hoback River Bridge and before Mile Mark 152. Go 9 miles (stay on the road towards the Hot Springs) and park in the parking area for the falls on the right (follow sign). The falls can be seen from here.

Waterfall Name	Lake Creek Falls
State	Wyoming
Type	Cascade
Variant Name	
Height in feet	60
County	Park
Topo Map	Muddy Creek
Geo Coord	445531N1094221W
Map Ref Code	44109-H6
Elevation ft	7500
Water Source	Lake Creek
Seasonal Flow	Year
Section of State	NW

Directions   Start at the junction of Routes 212 and 296 (Chief Joseph Scenic Highway) about 50 miles NW of Cody. From the junction, take Rt. 212 E. Go about 3/4 mile and park on the north side of the road near the bridge over Lake Creek. From here, paths lead a short distance to the falls.

Waterfall Name	Lower Falls of Yellowstone River
State	Wyoming
Type	Plunge
Variant Name	Yellowstone Falls
Height in feet	120
County	Park
Topo Map	Canyon Village
Geo Coord	444420N1102956W
Map Ref Code	44110-F4
Elevation ft	7700
Water Source	Yellowstone River
Seasonal Flow	Year
Section of State	NW

Directions	Located in Yellowstone National Park. Obtain directions from the Park Office.

Waterfall Name	Popo Agie Falls
State	Wyoming
Type	Segmented/Cascade
Variant Name	
Height in feet	200
County	Fremont
Topo Map	Cony Mountain
Geo Coord	424318N1085254W
Map Ref Code	42108-F8
Elevation ft	7600
Water Source	Middle Fork Popo Agie River
Seasonal Flow	Year
Section of State	SW

Directions	From Lander, take Rt. 131 S. (Sinks Canyon Road) towards Sinks Canyon State Park. Pass the Park and turn left onto FS 300. Go 1/4 mile (just past the single-lane bridge) and park in the parking area for the falls. Take the Middle Fork Trail (well-marked) for about 1.5 miles to the falls (follow signs).

Waterfall Name	Shell Falls
State	Wyoming
Type	Plunge
Variant Name	
Height in feet	50
County	Big Horn
Topo Map	Shell Falls
Geo Coord	443511N1073646W
Map Ref Code	44107-E5
Elevation ft	6300
Water Source	Shell Creek
Seasonal Flow	Year
Section of State	NW

Directions   From Greybull, take Rt. 14 E. Park at the Shell Falls Scenic Area just past Mile Mark 26. Hike the Scenic Loop Trail for a short distance to the several viewpoints.

Waterfall Name	Tower Falls
State	Wyoming
Type	Plunge
Variant Name	
Height in feet	200
County	Park
Topo Map	Tower Junction
Geo Coord	445338N1102311W
Map Ref Code	44110-H4
Elevation ft	6400
Water Source	Tower Creek
Seasonal Flow	Year
Section of State	NW

Directions   Located in Yellowstone National Park. Obtain directions from the Park Office.

CHAPTER 3

The Plains States

Iowa
Kansas
Minnesota
Missouri
Nebraska
Oklahoma
South Dakota
Texas

Dripping Springs
OKLAHOMA

Decorah

McGregor

Sioux City

Otho

IOWA

Des Moines

Iowa City

Waterfall Name	Beulah Spring Falls
State	Iowa
Type	Fan
Variant Name	Beulah Springs
Height in feet	20
County	Clayton
Topo Map	Giard
Geo Coord	430210N0911752W
Map Ref Code	43091-A3
Elevation ft	920
Water Source	Bloody Run Creek
Seasonal Flow	Year
Section of State	NE

Directions   About halfway between McGregor and Monona is the junction of Routes 18 and 52 S. Take 18 E. for 1/2 mile to Spook Cave Road and turn left (north). Go 2 miles to Spook Cave and Campground and turn left into the driveway. The Springs can be seen on the right in about 50 yards.

Waterfall Name	Bridal Veil Falls
State	Iowa
Type	Plunge/Horsetail
Variant Name	
Height in feet	20
County	Clayton
Topo Map	Clayton
Geo Coord	425958N0911001W
Map Ref Code	42091-H2
Elevation ft	950
Water Source	Pikes Peak Springs
Seasonal Flow	Sp
Section of State	NE

Directions   From McGregor at the intersection of Business Rt. 18 and Rt. 340, go south on 340 (uphill) to Pike's Peak State Park (follow signs about 3 miles). The trailhead to the falls is behind the stone concession building, which is at the end of the parking lot for the picnic area. A short hike about 0.3 mile leads to the falls along a wood platform trail.

Waterfall Name   Dunning's Spring Falls

State   Iowa

Type   Cascade

Variant Name   Dunning's Spring

Height in feet   40

County   Winneshiek

Topo Map   Decorah

Geo Coord   431807N0914730W

Map Ref Code   43091-C7

Elevation ft   900

Water Source   Dunning's Spring

Seasonal Flow   Year

Section of State   NE

Directions   From Decorah at the intersection of College Dr. and Quarry Rd., go east on Quarry Rd. 0.4 mile. Turn left onto the single-lane road marked by a small sign "Dunning's Spring". The parking and picnic area is 0.1 mile ahead. The falls can be seen from here.

Waterfall Name   Malanaphy Spring Falls

State   Iowa

Type   Segmented/Fan

Variant Name   Malanaphy Spring

Height in feet   30

County   Winneshiek

Topo Map   Decorah

Geo Coord   432130N0915001W

Map Ref Code   43091-C7

Elevation ft   1100

Water Source   Malanaphy Spring

Seasonal Flow   Year

Section of State   NE

Directions   From Decorah, go north on Rt. 52 to Pole Line Road and turn to the west (left). Go 2.2 miles to Bluffton Road and turn right. Go 0.7 mile to dirt road and small parking area on the right (this is just before the bridge over the Upper Iowa River). Hike down the old dirt road about 1 mile to the spring and falls (paralleling the Upper Iowa River walking in an upstream direction).

Waterfall Name	Woodman Hollow Falls
State	Iowa
Type	Cascade
Variant Name	Falls at Woodman Hollow
Height in feet	20
County	Webster
Topo Map	Evanston
Geo Coord	422502N0940610W
Map Ref Code	42094-D1
Elevation ft	1100
Water Source	Woodman Hollow Creek
Seasonal Flow	Sp
Section of State	NW

No
Photo
Available

Directions From Otho, take Nelson Ave. for about 1.5 miles to Woodman Hollow Road (gravel). Follow Woodman Hollow Road towards the power lines, then look for the sign for "Falls at Woodman Hollow". The hike to the falls is about 1/2 mile. The falls flow into the Des Moines River. Once in the park, follow the trail that parallels the Des Moines River in a southerly direction. Then follow Woodman Hollow Creek upstream to the falls.

Waterfall Name	Bourbon Lake Falls
State	Kansas
Type	Block
Variant Name	Bourbon Falls
Height in feet	60
County	Bourbon
Topo Map	Moran SE
Geo Coord	374736N0950303W
Map Ref Code	37095-G1
Elevation ft	940
Water Source	Bourbon Lake Creek
Seasonal Flow	Sp
Section of State	SE

Directions   From Moran at the junction of Routes 54 and 59, take Rt. 59 S. for 9 miles and turn left onto Rt. 203 (towards Elsmore). Go 5 miles (road will turn to gravel) to a T intersection near the lake. Turn left at the T and go 1/2 mile to the stop sign. Turn right and proceed a short distance to the bridge over the creek. The falls can be seen to the right through the trees.

Waterfall Name	Butcher Falls
State	Kansas
Type	Plunge
Variant Name	
Height in feet	15
County	Chautauqua
Topo Map	Elgin NE
Geo Coord	370850N0961604W
Map Ref Code	37096-B3
Elevation ft	850
Water Source	Caney Creek
Seasonal Flow	Year
Section of State	SE

Directions   From Sedan, take Rt. 99 N. At the junction with Rt.166, continue to the right on Rt. 99 N. Proceed 1.2 miles from that junction to Staats Ranch Road and turn left (gravel). Go 4 miles and veer right at the Y; go another 0.1 mile to the gate on the right (if the gate is locked, continue straight up the road to Staats Ranch and get permission to see the falls). If the gate is open, the falls can be viewed from the gated road in about 100 yards just before the bridge over the creek.

Waterfall Name	Chase Lake Falls
State	Kansas
Type	Tiered/Cascade
Variant Name	Chase Falls
Height in feet	40
County	Chase
Topo Map	Cottonwood Falls
Geo Coord	382215N0963440W
Map Ref Code	38096-C5
Elevation ft	1200
Water Source	Prather Creek
Seasonal Flow	Year
Section of State	SE

Directions   Near Strong City at the junction of Routes 50 and 177, take 177 S. (towards Cottonwood Falls town) for about 3 miles. Turn right (west) towards Chase State Fishing Lake (look for sign). Go 2.5 miles to the gravel road at the entrance to the lake and turn left. Follow this road to the earthen dam on the left and park off to the left. Hike across the dam and follow the trail to the left at the other end of the dam. This leads to the top of the falls.

Waterfall Name	Chatauqua Falls
State	Kansas
Type	Tiered /Block
Variant Name	Sedan Lake Falls
Height in feet	15
County	Chatauqua
Topo Map	Sedan
Geo Coord	370952N0961241W
Map Ref Code	37096-B2
Elevation ft	900
Water Source	Deer Creek
Seasonal Flow	Sp
Section of State	SE

Directions   From Sedan, take Rt. 99 N. At the junction of Rt. 166, continue straight on Rt. 99 for 3.4 miles to City Lake Park on right (white arch says City Lake). Turn right (gravel) and go 0.4 mile to the park entrance gate and then veer right (the lake will be on the left). Proceed past the last building on the right and park. The falls is to the left a short distance.

Waterfall Name	Elk Falls
State	Kansas
Type	Block
Variant Name	
Height in feet	10
County	Elk
Topo Map	Elk Falls
Geo Coord	372228N0961050W
Map Ref Code	37096-C2
Elevation ft	900
Water Source	Elk River
Seasonal Flow	Year
Section of State	SE

Directions   From the town of Elk Falls, follow the wood signs on Rt. 160 to the historic bridge and falls, very well-marked.

Waterfall Name	Eureka Lake Falls
State	Kansas
Type	Block
Variant Name	Falls at Eureka Lake
Height in feet	30
County	Greenwood
Topo Map	Eureka NE
Geo Coord	375305N0961721W
Map Ref Code	37096-H3
Elevation ft	1150
Water Source	Bachelor Creek
Seasonal Flow	Sp
Section of State	SE

Directions   In Eureka at the intersection of Rt. 54 and N. Main St., go north 1 mile on N. Main St. Turn right onto 13th St. Look for sign saying (Airport/City Lake). Proceed 0.3 mile and turn left onto N. State St. In 4 miles, the Eureka Lake entrance will be on left (marked by stone pillars); continue past the pillars a short distance to the bridge over the creek. The falls can be seen from here on the left.

Waterfall Name	Falls at the Hollow
State	Kansas
Type	Tiered/Plunge
Variant Name	The Hollow Falls
Height in feet	12
County	Chautauqua
Topo Map	Chautauqua
Geo Coord	370726N0961155W
Map Ref Code	37096-A2
Elevation ft	900
Water Source	Deer Creek
Seasonal Flow	Sp
Section of State	SE

Directions   In Sedan at the intersection of E. Main St. and Sherman St., go down the hill on Sherman St. to the parking area. Take the wood walkway 100 feet to the falls.

Waterfall Name	Liddle Biddle Falls
State	Kansas
Type	Tiered/Block
Variant Name	Swinging Bridge Falls
Height in feet	4
County	Elk
Topo Map	Moline
Geo Coord	372207N0961742W
Map Ref Code	37096-C3
Elevation ft	1050
Water Source	Wildcat Creek
Seasonal Flow	Year
Section of State	SE

Directions   In the town of Moline at the intersection of 5th St. and Biddle St., look for the Swinging Bridge and falls.

Waterfall Name	Osro Falls
State	Kansas
Type	Block
Variant Name	
Height in feet	2
County	Chautauqua
Topo Map	Cedar Vale East
Geo Coord	370322N0962637W
Map Ref Code	37096-A4
Elevation ft	850
Water Source	Caney River
Seasonal Flow	Year
Section of State	SE

Directions   Ask for directions from the Chamber of Commerce in Cedar Vale. Several gravel county roads will lead to the falls access point. The half-mile hike to the falls is through a wheat field on a tractor trail.

Waterfall Name	Pillsbury Crossing Falls
State	Kansas
Type	Block
Variant Name	Falls at Pillsbury Crossing
Height in feet	5
County	Riley
Topo Map	St. George
Geo Coord	390737N0962605W
Map Ref Code	39096-B4
Elevation ft	1040
Water Source	Deep Creek
Seasonal Flow	Year
Section of State	NE

Directions   From Manhattan, take Rt. 177 S. a couple miles to Deep Creek Road and turn left. Go 3.8 miles to Pillsbury Crossing Road veering left at the Y (gravel road). Go 2.2 miles to Pillsbury Crossing Lane and turn right. Continue a short distance to the parking area on right. To get the best view of the falls, cross over the creek (low-water bridge-4WD vehicle recommended).

Waterfall Name	Tuttle Creek Falls
State	Kansas
Type	Tiered/Block
Variant Name	Tuttle Falls
Height in feet	10
County	Pottawatomie
Topo Map	Tuttle Creek Dam
Geo Coord	391506N0963310W
Map Ref Code	39096-C5
Elevation ft	1050
Water Source	Tuttle Creek
Seasonal Flow	Sp
Section of State	NE

No
Photo
Available

Directions   From Manhattan, take Rt. 24 W. Follow signs to Tuttle Creek State Park. Falls can be seen at the natural rocky dam overflow outlet. Very seasonal.

MINNESOTA

Duluth

Minneapolis/St. Paul

Redwood Falls

Mankato

Pipestone

Waterfall Name	Baptism Falls
State	Minnesota
Type	Block
Variant Name	High Falls/Illgen Falls
Height in feet	60
County	Lake
Topo Map	Illgen City
Geo Coord	472110N0911240W
Map Ref Code	47091-C2
Elevation ft	900
Water Source	Baptism River
Seasonal Flow	Year
Section of State	NE

Directions   From Duluth, take Rt. 61 N. to Mile Mark 58.5. Turn right into the Tettegouche State Park parking area. The trailhead is just past the Ranger Station to the right. A 1.5-mile moderate hike leads to the falls.

Waterfall Name	Brule River Upper Falls
State	Minnesota
Type	Cascade
Variant Name	Upper Falls Brule River
Height in feet	40
County	Cook
Topo Map	Marr Island
Geo Coord	474937N0900250W
Map Ref Code	47090-G1
Elevation ft	850
Water Source	Brule River
Seasonal Flow	Year
Section of State	NE

Directions   From Duluth, take Rt. 61 N. for 123.8 miles and turn left into Judge Magney State Park. Go to the picnic/trail parking area. A 7/8-mile hike, with some steep stairs, leads to the falls. Entry fee.

Waterfall Name	Caribou Falls
State	Minnesota
Type	Tiered/Fan
Variant Name	
Height in feet	70
County	Lake
Topo Map	Little Marias
Geo Coord	472808N0910155W
Map Ref Code	47091-D8
Elevation ft	900
Water Source	Caribou River
Seasonal Flow	Year
Section of State	NE

Directions From Duluth, take Rt. 61 N. for 71.3 miles to the bridge over the Caribou River. Cross over the bridge and park in the parking lot on the left. The trailhead is at the end of the lot. Take the moderate 1/2-mile hike to the falls.

Waterfall Name	Cascade Falls
State	Minnesota
Type	Tiered/Cascade
Variant Name	Upper Cascade Falls
Height in feet	50
County	Cook
Topo Map	Deer Yard Lake
Geo Coord	474231N0903126W
Map Ref Code	47090-F5
Elevation ft	700
Water Source	Cascade River
Seasonal Flow	Year
Section of State	NE

Directions From Duluth, take Rt. 61 N. for 99.8 miles to Cascade River State Park. Park in the turnout on the right just before the bridge (before main entrance to the Park). The trail starts on the other side of the road and makes a loop, so begin on either side of the river. Several falls can be viewed along the way with Upper Cascade Falls being the most impressive. Upper Cascade is at the 1/2 way point (about 1/4 mile from parking area); the viewpoint is from the bridge over the river.

Waterfall Name	Cross River Falls
State	Minnesota
Type	Cascade
Variant Name	
Height in feet	80
County	Cook
Topo Map	Schroeder
Geo Coord	473236N0905301W
Map Ref Code	47090-E8
Elevation ft	750
Water Source	Cross River
Seasonal Flow	Year
Section of State	NE

Directions   From Duluth, take Rt. 61 N. for 80.2 miles to the bridge over the Cross River. Park just before the bridge. The falls can be viewed from here. Also walk along the cliffside ledge downstream (next to the cabin rentals) to view the lower falls and gorge.

Waterfall Name	Devil's Kettle Falls
State	Minnesota
Type	Tiered/Block
Variant Name	
Height in feet	50
County	Cook
Topo Map	Marr Island
Geo Coord	474942N0900240W
Map Ref Code	47090-G1
Elevation ft	900
Water Source	Brule River
Seasonal Flow	Year
Section of State	NE

Directions   See directions for Brule River Upper Falls. Devil's Kettle is on the same trail 700 feet further on.

Waterfall Name	Gooseberry Lower Falls
State	Minnesota
Type	Segmented/Tiered/Block
Variant Name	Lower Gooseberry Falls
Height in feet	80
County	Lake
Topo Map	Split Rock Point
Geo Coord	470834N0912804W
Map Ref Code	47091-B4
Elevation ft	700
Water Source	Gooseberry River
Seasonal Flow	Year
Section of State	NE

Directions   From Duluth, take Rt. 61 N. for 39.5 miles to Gooseberry Falls State Park. The Upper Falls is near the bridge over Gooseberry River on the west side of Rt. 61. The Lower Falls is on the east side of Rt. 61. A 1-mile, well-maintained loop trail, with some stairs, goes to the bottom of the falls.

Waterfall Name	Gooseberry Upper Falls
State	Minnesota
Type	Block/Cascade
Variant Name	Upper Gooseberry Falls
Height in feet	30
County	Lake
Topo Map	Split Rock Point
Geo Coord	470835N0912803W
Map Ref Code	47091-B4
Elevation ft	750
Water Source	Gooseberry River
Seasonal Flow	Year
Section of State	NE

Directions   See directions for Gooseberry Lower Falls.

Waterfall Name	Hidden Falls
State	Minnesota
Type	Cascade
Variant Name	
Height in feet	20
County	Cook
Topo Map	Tofte
Geo Coord	473324N0905227W
Map Ref Code	47090-E7
Elevation ft	750
Water Source	Temperance River
Seasonal Flow	Year
Section of State	NE

Directions   From Duluth, take Rt. 61 N. for 81.4 miles to Temperance River State Park. Park in the parking area on the west side of the road (just before the entrance to the park). Take the Cauldron/Hidden Falls Trail (located on the west side of Rt. 61) for a few hundred feet to the main falls viewpoint. Continue up the boulder trail for more views of the falls, higher cascades, and gorge.

Waterfall Name	Minnehaha Falls
State	Minnesota
Type	Plunge
Variant Name	
Height in feet	50
County	Hennepin
Topo Map	Saint Paul West
Geo Coord	445453N0931235W
Map Ref Code	44093-H2
Elevation ft	800
Water Source	Minnehaha Creek
Seasonal Flow	Year
Section of State	SE

Directions   In Minneapolis at the junction of Rt. 55 and Minnehaha Parkway, go south on the Minnehaha Parkway to Minnehaha Park (on the west side of the Mississippi River). A very short walk on the asphalt trail from the parking lot leads to the falls.

Waterfall Name   Minneopa Falls

State   Minnesota

Type   Block

Variant Name

Height in feet   40

County   Blue Earth

Topo Map   Mankato West

Geo Coord   440809N0940512W

Map Ref Code   44094-B1

Elevation ft   900

Water Source   Minneopa Creek

Seasonal Flow   Year

Section of State   SE

Directions   From Mankato, take Rt. 60/169 S.W. for about 6 miles to Minneopa State Park. A sign marks the way to the falls which is a very short distance from the parking/picnic area.

Waterfall Name   Pigeon Falls

State   Minnesota

Type   Segmented/Plunge

Variant Name   High Falls

Height in feet   120

County   Cook

Topo Map   Pigeon Point

Geo Coord   480017N0893552W

Map Ref Code   48089-A5

Elevation ft   700

Water Source   Pigeon River

Seasonal Flow   Year

Section of State   NE

Directions   From Duluth, take Rt. 61 N. for 151 miles to Grand Portage State Park (just before the Canadian border). Turn left into the parking area. The trail starts near the Ranger Station. The falls is a 1/2-mile easy hike. Entry fee.

Waterfall Name	Ramsey Falls
State	Minnesota
Type	Segmented/Plunge
Variant Name	Redwood Falls
Height in feet	40
County	Redwood
Topo Map	Delhi
Geo Coord	443237N0950732W
Map Ref Code	44095-E2
Elevation ft	1000
Water Source	Ramsey Creek
Seasonal Flow	Year
Section of State	SW

Directions   On the west side of the town of Redwood Falls, at the intersection of Rt. 19 and Grove St., take Grove St. north into Alexander Ramsey Park (follow signs). The overlook of the falls is next to the parking lot (follow signs).

Waterfall Name	Temperance River Falls
State	Minnesota
Type	Cascade
Variant Name	
Height in feet	40
County	Cook
Topo Map	Tofte
Geo Coord	473440N0905405W
Map Ref Code	47090-E7
Elevation ft	800
Water Source	Temperance River
Seasonal Flow	Year
Section of State	NE

Directions   See directions for Hidden Falls. Temperance Falls is further upstream (about 1/2 mile) via the same trail.

Waterfall Name	Winnewissa Falls
State	Minnesota
Type	Block
Variant Name	Pipestone Falls
Height in feet	15
County	Pipestone
Topo Map	Pipestone North
Geo Coord	440055N0961912W
Map Ref Code	44096-A3
Elevation ft	1700
Water Source	Pipestone Creek
Seasonal Flow	Sp
Section of State	SW

Directions   From Pipestone, take Rt. 75 N. to NE 9th St. Go west on NE 9th St. for 1/2 mile to Pipestone National Monument (follow signs). Obtain a map at the Visitors Center. A 3/4-mile circular loop trail passes by the falls.

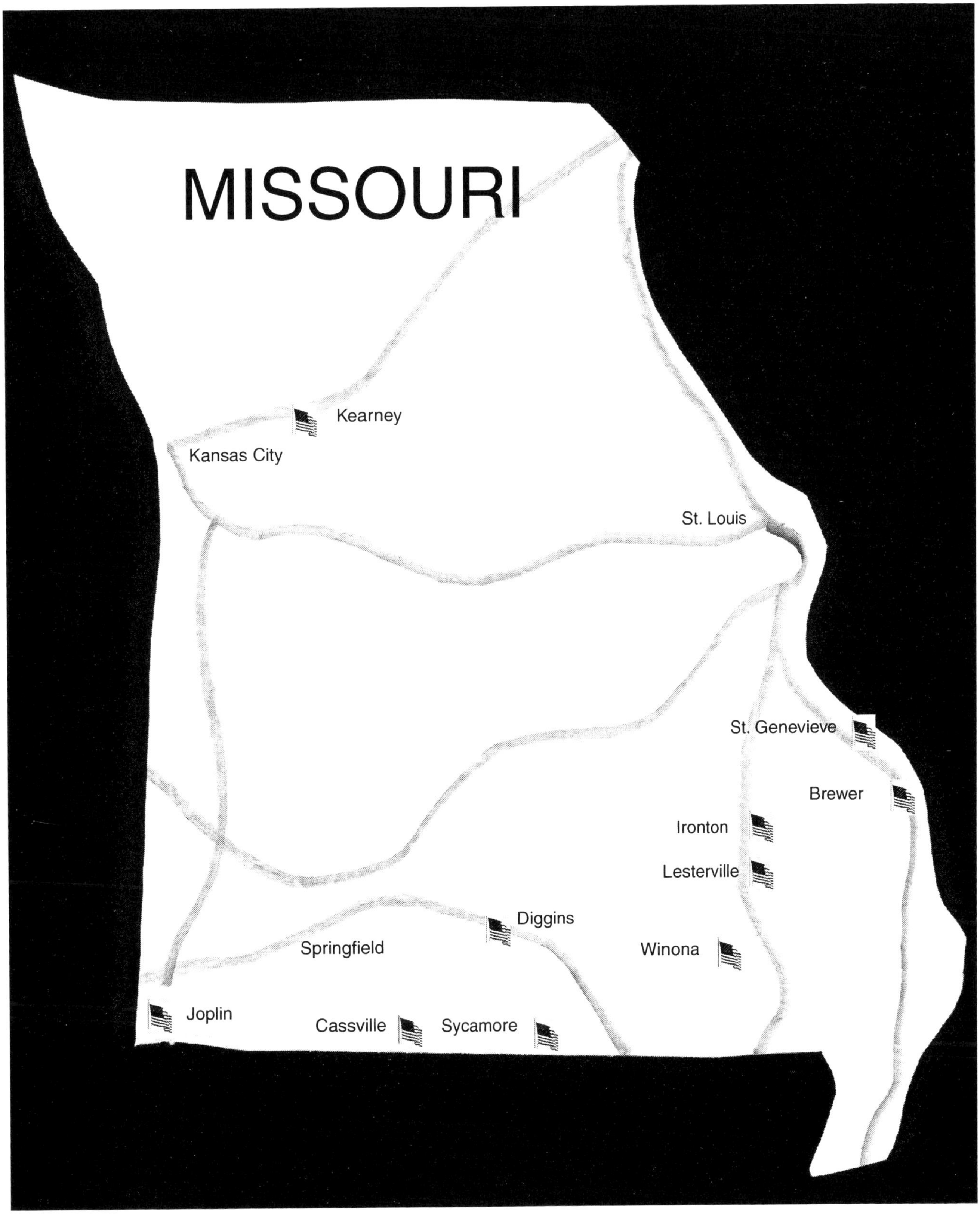

MISSOURI

Kearney

Kansas City

St. Louis

St. Genevieve

Brewer

Ironton

Lesterville

Diggins

Winona

Springfield

Joplin

Cassville   Sycamore

Waterfall Name	Fall Creek Falls
State	Missouri
Type	Tiered/Plunge
Variant Name	Fall Branch Falls
Height in feet	20
County	Perry
Topo Map	Lithium
Geo Coord	374855N0895510W
Map Ref Code	37089-G8
Elevation ft	400
Water Source	Fall Branch
Seasonal Flow	Sp
Section of State	SE

Directions — From Brewer at the junction of Routes 61 N. and M, go east on Rt. M for 1.6 miles to the Y. Go left at the Y onto Perry County Road 910 (gravel). Go 1.8 miles to Fall Branch Drive across the creek and park. Hike to the right (downstream) about 100 yards to the falls and cavern.

Waterfall Name	Falling Springs Falls
State	Missouri
Type	Plunge
Variant Name	
Height in feet	20
County	Oregon
Topo Map	Greer
Geo Coord	365221N0911733W
Map Ref Code	36091-G3
Elevation ft	600
Water Source	Falling Springs
Seasonal Flow	Year
Section of State	SE

Directions — From Winona at the junction of Routes 60 and 19 S., go south on Rt. 19 for about 9.6 miles to FR 3170 (gravel). Turn left (sign reads "Falling Springs 3 miles") and then left again onto FR 3164 for 2.4 miles to the parking/picnic area on the right. The falls can be seen next to the old mill. In Mark Twain National Forest.

Waterfall Name	Finley Falls
State	Missouri
Type	Segmented/Block
Variant Name	
Height in feet	7
County	Webster
Topo Map	Seymour
Geo Coord	370340N0925012W
Map Ref Code	37092-B7
Elevation ft	1500
Water Source	Little Finley Creek
Seasonal Flow	Sp
Section of State	SW

Directions   In Diggins at the intersection of Routes 60 and NN, take Rt. NN south for 2.1 miles to Road 325. Turn left and go 0.3 mile. Continue straight as the road turns to gravel and is now called Road 326. Go another 0.6 mile and turn right onto unnamed gravel road. Go 0.2 mile to the falls on the right.

Waterfall Name	Grand Falls
State	Missouri
Type	Block
Variant Name	
Height in feet	15
County	Newton
Topo Map	Joplin West
Geo Coord	370210N0943230W
Map Ref Code	37094-A5
Elevation ft	1100
Water Source	Shoal Creek
Seasonal Flow	Year
Section of State	SW

Directions   From Interstate 44, take the Joplin exit (6) and go south on Rt. 86. Turn right at the first street (Glendale) and go 0.8 mile to Jackson St. and turn left. Cross over Shoal Creek bridge and then immediately turn right onto Riverside Rd. Go 1.1 miles to the pullout on the right. The falls can be seen to the right from here.

Waterfall Name	Hickory Canyon Falls
State	Missouri
Type	Horsetail
Variant Name	Falls at Hickory Canyon
Height in feet	40
County	St. Genevieve
Topo Map	Sprott
Geo Coord	375220N0901750W
Map Ref Code	37090-G3
Elevation ft	800
Water Source	Hickory Creek
Seasonal Flow	Sp
Section of State	SE

Directions   From Exit 150 off of Interstate 55, take Rt. 32 W. for 8.6 miles and turn right onto Road C. Go 3.3 miles to Sprott Rd. (gravel) and turn left. Go 1.8 miles to turnout parking area on the left. The 1/4-mile trail starts from the parking area and is well-marked.

Waterfall Name	Hodgson Mill Spring Falls
State	Missouri
Type	Block/Cascade
Variant Name	Man-Made
Height in feet	5
County	Ozark
Topo Map	Sycamore
Geo Coord	364231N0921602W
Map Ref Code	36092-F3
Elevation ft	800
Water Source	Hodgson Spring
Seasonal Flow	Year
Section of State	SW

Directions   Near Sycamore at the junction of Routes 181 S. and H, take Rt. 181 S. for 4 miles to the mill and falls.

Waterfall Name	Johnson's Shut-Ins Cascades
State	Missouri
Type	Cascade
Variant Name	Johnson Shut-Ins
Height in feet	100
County	Reynolds
Topo Map	Johnson's Shut-ins
Geo Coord	373228N0905005W
Map Ref Code	37090-E7
Elevation ft	800
Water Source	East Fork Black River
Seasonal Flow	Year
Section of State	SE

Directions   From Lesterville, take Rt. 49/72 W. for 2 miles. Turn north on County Road N and go 6 miles to Johnson Shut-Ins State Park. Turn right into the Park and go to the parking lot near the Park Office and Store. The trailhead is at the end of the road. Take the 1/4-mile easy walk to the main viewpoint of the falls.

Waterfall Name	Mina Sauk Falls
State	Missouri
Type	Horsetail
Variant Name	
Height in feet	130
County	Iron
Topo Map	Ironton
Geo Coord	373345N0904428W
Map Ref Code	37090-E6
Elevation ft	1300
Water Source	Taum Sauk Creek
Seasonal Flow	Sp
Section of State	SE

Directions   From Ironton, take Rt. 21/49 S. and turn right onto Road CC (follow signs for Taum Sauk Mountain State Park, about 9 miles total). Go to the trailhead at the High Point parking area (follow signs). The trail is a rocky 1.2-mile descent to the falls. The trail is a section of the Ozark Trail.

Waterfall Name	Roaring River Spring Falls
State	Missouri
Type	Plunge
Variant Name	Roaring Hollow Falls
Height in feet	90
County	Barry
Topo Map	Eagle Rock
Geo Coord	363527N0934955W
Map Ref Code	36093-E7
Elevation ft	1500
Water Source	Roaring River Hollow
Seasonal Flow	Sp
Section of State	SW

Directions   From Cassville, take Rt. 112 S. about 7 miles to Roaring River State Park. Follow signs to Fish Hatchery and Spring Lake. The falls and cave are a short walk from the parking lot at the far side of the small lake.

Waterfall Name	Rocky Falls
State	Missouri
Type	Cascade
Variant Name	Rocky Creek Falls
Height in feet	40
County	Shannon
Topo Map	Steggall Mountain
Geo Coord	370536N0911234W
Map Ref Code	37091-A2
Elevation ft	850
Water Source	Rocky Creek
Seasonal Flow	Sp
Section of State	SE

Directions   From Winona at the junction of Routes 19 and H (Casey's General Store on the corner), take Rt. H north for 8.7 miles to Rt. NN. Turn right (east) and go 2 miles to NN 526 (gravel) and turn right. There is a sign here for Rocky Falls. Go 0.3 mile to the unmarked gravel road (sign for Rocky Falls) and turn left. Go 0.1 mile to the parking area. The falls is a short distance from the parking area.

Waterfall Name	Tryst Falls
State	Missouri
Type	Block
Variant Name	
Height in feet	8
County	Clay
Topo Map	Kearney
Geo Coord	392226N0941658W
Map Ref Code	39094-C3
Elevation ft	820
Water Source	Williams Branch
Seasonal Flow	Sp
Section of State	NW

Directions   From Kearney at the junction of Routes 92 and 33, take Rt. 92 E. for 5.2 miles to Tryst Falls Park on the right. The falls can be viewed from the parking area.

Waterfall Name	Berry Falls
State	Nebraska
Type	Block
Variant Name	
Height in feet	10
County	Cherry
Topo Map	Sparks
Geo Coord	425405N1002216W
Map Ref Code	42100-H3
Elevation ft	2310
Water Source	Berry Bridge Creek
Seasonal Flow	Sp
Section of State	NW

Directions   From Valentine, take Rt. 12 E. for 13 miles and turn right (just past Mile Mark 13) onto the unmarked gravel road (school on the SW corner). Go approx 3.5 miles and park just before the metal bridge. The falls can be seen from here across the Niobrara River.

Waterfall Name	Fort Falls
State	Nebraska
Type	Horsetail
Variant Name	
Height in feet	60
County	Cherry
Topo Map	Cornell Dam
Geo Coord	425400N1002800W
Map Ref Code	42100-H4
Elevation ft	2460
Water Source	Fort Creek
Seasonal Flow	Sp
Section of State	NW

Directions   From Valentine, take Rt. 12 E. for 4 miles to Fort Niobrara Wildlife Refuge. Turn right into the refuge and follow the signs to the falls. From the parking area, take the 100-yard walk (some stairs) down to the falls base.

Waterfall Name	Little Cedar Falls
State	Nebraska
Type	Plunge
Variant Name	
Height in feet	10
County	Cherry
Topo Map	Sparks
Geo Coord	425232N1001540W
Map Ref Code	42100-H3
Elevation ft	2250
Water Source	Brewer Bridge Creek
Seasonal Flow	Sp
Section of State	NW

Directions   In the town of Sparks off of Rt. 12, take the gravel road south past Sharps Campground. Go 7.6 miles total to a sandy road on the right and park. At this point, the river will be on the right and a pasture will be on the left. Hike on the sandy road a short distance to a grassy area with picnic tables. The falls can be seen from here across the Niobrara River. 4WD vehicle recommended.

Waterfall Name	Nature Falls
State	Nebraska
Type	Fan
Variant Name	
Height in feet	15
County	Brown
Topo Map	Muleshoe Creek
Geo Coord	424822N1000752W
Map Ref Code	42100-G2
Elevation ft	2160
Water Source	Nature Creek
Seasonal Flow	Sp
Section of State	NW

Directions   In the town of Sparks off of Rt. 12, take the gravel road south for 15.5 miles (past Rocky Ford Campground) to the Y intersection. Veer right at the Y towards Rock Barn Camp. Go 0.7 mile to the cattle guard. Cross the cattle guard and park. Hike to the right along the barbed wire fence to the Niobrara River. The falls will be off to the left across the river. 4WD vehicle recommended.

Waterfall Name	North Loup Falls
State	Nebraska
Type	Block
Variant Name	Big Falls
Height in feet	15
County	Cherry
Topo Map	Big Falls
Geo Coord	422504N1011344W
Map Ref Code	42101-D2
Elevation ft	3200
Water Source	North Loup River
Seasonal Flow	Sp
Section of State	NW

Directions   From Merritt Lake, take Rt. 97 S. Between Mile Marks 93 and 94, turn right (west) onto the sandy gravel road (look for sign to God's Cattle Country). Go 11 miles and veer left (south) at the Y intersection. Go another 1.4 miles to the bridge over the North Loup River, cross the bridge and park. Hike downstream (east) on the south side of the river about 1/4 mile to the falls. 4WD vehicle recommended for last 1.4 miles of drive.

Waterfall Name	Smith Falls
State	Nebraska
Type	Fan
Variant Name	
Height in feet	70
County	Cherry
Topo Map	Sparks
Geo Coord	425317N1001857W
Map Ref Code	42100-H3
Elevation ft	2450
Water Source	Smith Springs
Seasonal Flow	Sp
Section of State	NW

Directions   From Valentine, take Rt. 12 E. for 15 miles and turn right onto the gravel road towards Smith Falls State Park (follow signs). Go 4 miles to the Park Headquarters. From here, canoes are available to cross the 50-foot wide Niobrara River. Once on the other side, a short walk leads to the falls.

Waterfall Name	Snake River Falls
State	Nebraska
Type	Block
Variant Name	Snake Falls
Height in feet	40
County	Cherry
Topo Map	Snake River Falls
Geo Coord	424030N1005124W
Map Ref Code	42100-F7
Elevation ft	2800
Water Source	Snake River
Seasonal Flow	Year
Section of State	NW

Directions　　From Valentine, take Rt. 97 S. towards Merritt Lake. In about 20 miles, turn right towards Snake Falls and Snake Falls Canyon Restaurant (follow signs). Go about 1/2 mile to the restaurant and park. Pay the small admission fee and follow the well-marked trail about 1/4 mile to the falls.

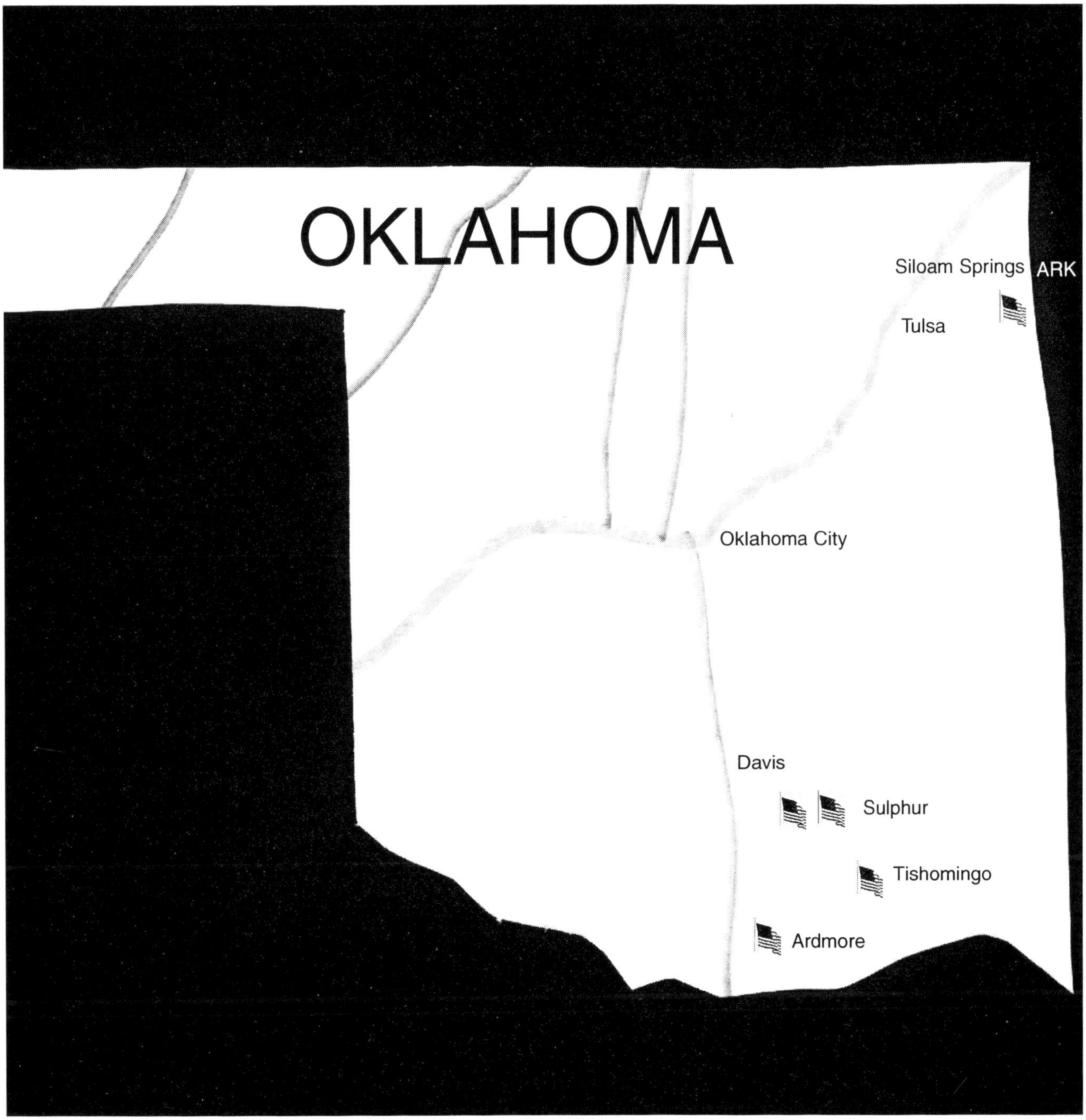

OKLAHOMA

Siloam Springs ARK

Tulsa

Oklahoma City

Davis

Sulphur

Tishomingo

Ardmore

Waterfall Name	Blue Horseshoe Falls
State	Oklahoma
Type	Horseshoe/Cascade
Variant Name	Falls on Blue River
Height in feet	6
County	Johnston
Topo Map	Connerville SE
Geo Coord	341905N0963522W
Map Ref Code	34096-C5
Elevation ft	750
Water Source	Blue River
Seasonal Flow	Year
Section of State	SE

Directions   From Tishomingo, take Rt. 78 E. Go 3.8 miles and turn left into the Blue River Public Fishing and Hunting Area (follow sign). Go 6 miles to the Fishing Area entrance. Pass the entrance and follow the gravel road to the Area 1 Camping Loop. The falls can be seen from the road off to the left about 3/4 of the way around the loop.

Waterfall Name	Bridal Veil Falls
State	Oklahoma
Type	Block
Variant Name	
Height in feet	10
County	Murray
Topo Map	Turner Falls
Geo Coord	342528N0970859W
Map Ref Code	34097-D2
Elevation ft	1040
Water Source	Honey Creek
Seasonal Flow	Year
Section of State	SE

Directions   See directions to Turner Falls. Once in Turner Falls Park, follow the signs up to Arbuckle Camp. Park in the parking lot on the left and walk a short distance to the falls viewpoint. The falls are slightly upstream to the right.

Waterfall Name	Dripping Springs Falls
State	Oklahoma
Type	Plunge
Variant Name	Swinging Bridge Falls
Height in feet	70
County	Adair
Topo Map	Siloam Springs NW
Geo Coord	361019N0943957W
Map Ref Code	36094-B6
Elevation ft	1000
Water Source	Dripping Springs Branch
Seasonal Flow	Year
Section of State	NE

Directions   From Siloam Springs, Arkansas, take Rt. 412 W. Go 3.3 miles and turn left onto New Line Ranch Road. Take the first right hand turn onto unmarked Old Route 33. Continue 1.8 miles to the State Park on the left. Obtain a map. The falls is a short walk from the parking lot.

Waterfall Name	Hickory Falls
State	Oklahoma
Type	Block
Variant Name	
Height in feet	30
County	Carter
Topo Map	Milo
Geo Coord	342133N0971731W
Map Ref Code	34097-C3
Elevation ft	1000
Water Source	Hickory Creek
Seasonal Flow	Year
Section of State	SE

Directions   From Ardmore, take Interstate 35 N. In about 10 miles, turn left onto Rt. 53. Follow Rt. 53 W. and turn right (north) onto Mountain Lake Rd. Go 2.3 miles and cross over Hickory Creek, then park on the roadside near the large gate to the Arbuckle Ranch. The falls can be seen from the road at this point off to the right (on private property).

Waterfall Name   Little Dripper Falls

State   Oklahoma

Type   Fan

Variant Name

Height in feet   30

County   Adair

Topo Map   Siloam Springs NW

Geo Coord   361018N0943956W

Map Ref Code   36094-B6

Elevation ft   1000

Water Source   Dripping Springs

Seasonal Flow   Year

Section of State   NE

Directions   See directions to Dripping Springs Falls. Little Dripper is on the same trail as the main falls.

Waterfall Name   Little Niagara Falls

State   Oklahoma

Type   Tiered/Cascade

Variant Name   Chickasaw Falls

Height in feet   10

County   Murray

Topo Map   Sulphur North

Geo Coord   343030N0965700W

Map Ref Code   34096-E8

Elevation ft   1080

Water Source   Travertine Creek

Seasonal Flow   Year

Section of State   SE

Directions   From Sulphur, take Rt. 177 S. Follow the signs to Chickasaw National Recreation Area. Obtain a map from the Visitors Center. A well-marked trail leads from the Visitors Center to the falls.

Waterfall Name	Price Falls
State	Oklahoma
Type	Tiered/Block
Variant Name	
Height in feet	40
County	Murray
Topo Map	Dougherty
Geo Coord	342534N0970624W
Map Ref Code	34097-D1
Elevation ft	900
Water Source	Falls Creek
Seasonal Flow	Year
Section of State	SE

Directions   From Davis, take Rt. 77 S. Turn left onto Rt. 77D just before the junction with Interstate 35. Go past Arbuckle Wilderness Park on the right. Continue straight until reaching the sign for Oddfellows and Rebekahs Price Falls Youth Camp sign on the right. Turn right. Follow the road as it curves to the right; the falls can be seen off to the right.

Waterfall Name	Turner Falls
State	Oklahoma
Type	Segmented/Fan
Variant Name	
Height in feet	77
County	Murray
Topo Map	Turner Falls
Geo Coord	352531N0970854W
Map Ref Code	34097-D2
Elevation ft	960
Water Source	Honey Creek
Seasonal Flow	Year
Section of State	SE

Directions   From Ardmore, take Interstate 35 N. towards Davis. In about 10 miles, take Rt. 77 S. towards Turner Falls Park (follow signs). Follow the signs in the Park to the falls. Entry fee.

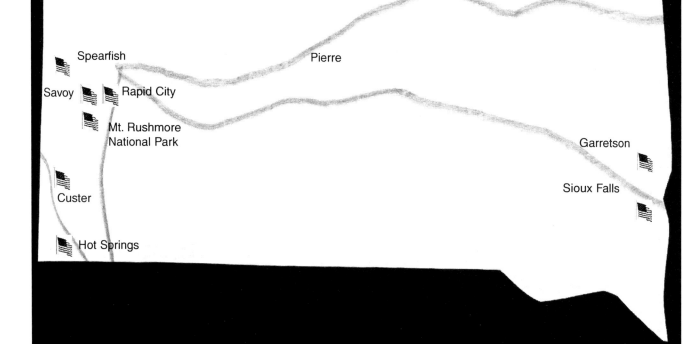

SOUTH DAKOTA

Aberdeen

Spearfish

Savoy

Rapid City

Mt. Rushmore
National Park

Pierre

Garretson

Sioux Falls

Custer

Hot Springs

Waterfall Name	Bridal Veil Falls
State	South Dakota
Type	Horsetail/Plunge
Variant Name	
Height in feet	100
County	Lawrence
Topo Map	Maurice
Geo Coord	442501N1035250W
Map Ref Code	44103-D8
Elevation ft	4000
Water Source	Branch of Spearfish Creek
Seasonal Flow	Year
Section of State	SW

Directions   From Spearfish, take Rt. 14A to the south. Go 5.8 miles to view the falls off to the left (east) side of the road.

Waterfall Name	Cascade Falls
State	South Dakota
Type	Cascade
Variant Name	
Height in feet	10
County	Fall River
Topo Map	Cascade Springs
Geo Coord	431910N1033348W
Map Ref Code	43103-C5
Elevation ft	3300
Water Source	Cascade Springs
Seasonal Flow	Year
Section of State	SW

Directions   From Hot Springs town, take Rt. 71 S. Go about 10 miles and turn right (west) into well-marked Cascade Falls Picnic Area. A short stairway from the parking area leads to the falls.

Waterfall Name	Devil's Falls
State	South Dakota
Type	Cascade
Variant Name	
Height in feet	20
County	Minnehaha
Topo Map	Garretson West
Geo Coord	434403N0963002W
Map Ref Code	43096-F5
Elevation ft	1400
Water Source	Split Rock Creek
Seasonal Flow	Year
Section of State	SE

Directions From Garretson, take Rt. 11 N. Follow signs to Devil's Gulch. A hiking map is available at the Visitors Center. A short loop trail leads from the Visitors Center to the falls.

Waterfall Name	Fall River Falls
State	South Dakota
Type	Cascade
Variant Name	
Height in feet	200
County	Fall River
Topo Map	Hot Springs
Geo Coord	432408N1032503W
Map Ref Code	43103-D4
Elevation ft	3200
Water Source	Fall River
Seasonal Flow	Year
Section of State	SW

Directions At the junction of Routes 385/18/79 (near Hot Springs), take Rt. 385 N. Go 1 mile and turn right onto Road 79F (Fall River Vet Clinic on corner). Go 0.4 mile, pass under the overpass, and park in the pullout next to the small snow fence on the left. Walk downstream on the worn path along the rocks for a few hundred feet to view the roaring cascades.

Waterfall Name	Grizzly Bear Falls
State	South Dakota
Type	Horsetail/Plunge
Variant Name	
Height in feet	10
County	Pennington
Topo Map	Iron Mountain
Geo Coord	435150N1032748W
Map Ref Code	43103-G4
Elevation ft	4960
Water Source	Grizzly Bear Creek
Seasonal Flow	Year
Section of State	SW

Directions   From the parking lot of Mt. Rushmore, walk due south across the road. At the left end of the guard rail, walk up the hillside to the left to reach the main trail. Hike the main trail downhill for about 3/4 mile to the intersection with Centennial Trail (look for the trees marked with the numbers 3/89). Follow the trail towards Iron Creek Horse Camp. When two streams merge into one, stay on the right (west) side of the right stream. Go upstream following the faint trail next to the streambed. The falls is about an 8-minute hike from the sign "Iron Creek Horse Camp".

Waterfall Name	Remington Falls
State	South Dakota
Type	Cascade
Variant Name	
Height in feet	10
County	Custer
Topo Map	Iron Mountain
Geo Coord	434955N1032730W
Map Ref Code	43103-G4
Elevation ft	5000
Water Source	Iron Creek Branch
Seasonal Flow	Sp
Section of State	SW

Directions   At the junction of Routes 87 and 16A near Custer, take Rt. 87 N. Go 5.8 miles and turn right onto the gravel road at the Camp Remington sign. Go 0.9 mile and park just before the second bridge. Hike on the west (left) side of the stream in a northerly direction (upstream). Upon reaching a small cabin, continue on the foot trail upstream for about 1/4 mile to the falls. More cascades can be viewed by climbing the large boulders to the left.

Waterfall Name	Roughlock Falls
State	South Dakota
Type	Segmented/Plunge
Variant Name	
Height in feet	50
County	Lawrence
Topo Map	Savoy
Geo Coord	442100N1035633W
Map Ref Code	44103-C8
Elevation ft	5140
Water Source	Little Spearfish Creek
Seasonal Flow	Year
Section of State	SW

Directions From Savoy at the intersection of Rt. 14A and FR 222 (gravel), take FR 222 S.W. Go 1 mile and park in the Roughlock Falls picnic area (follow signs). Follow the loop trail around the falls for a total hike of about 1/4 mile.

Waterfall Name	Sioux Falls
State	South Dakota
Type	Tiered/Cascade
Variant Name	
Height in feet	100
County	Minnehaha
Topo Map	Sioux Falls East
Geo Coord	433320N0964322W
Map Ref Code	43096-E6
Elevation ft	1320
Water Source	Big Sioux River
Seasonal Flow	Year
Section of State	SE

Directions In the town of Sioux Falls at the intersection of Falls Park Drive and Phillips Ave., park in the lot of Sioux Falls Park. The falls can be seen a short distance from the parking lot.

Waterfall Name	Spearfish Falls
State	South Dakota
Type	Plunge
Variant Name	
Height in feet	60
County	Lawrence
Topo Map	Savoy
Geo Coord	442110N1035545W
Map Ref Code	44103-C8
Elevation ft	5000
Water Source	Little Spearfish Creek
Seasonal Flow	Sp,Sm
Section of State	SW

Directions   From Spearfish, take Rt. 14A to the south. Go about 12.8 miles and park in the parking area on the left (east) side of the road (near the Latchstring Restaurant/Village). Follow the Spearfish Canyon Nature Trail from behind the building. The improved gravel trail leads about 1/4 mile gently downhill and across the river to the falls viewpoint.

Waterfall Name	Sylvan Lake Lower Falls
State	South Dakota
Type	Cascade
Variant Name	Sylvan Lake Falls #3
Height in feet	50
County	Custer
Topo Map	Custer
Geo Coord	435040N1033434W
Map Ref Code	43103-G5
Elevation ft	5940
Water Source	Sylvan Lake Creek
Seasonal Flow	Year
Section of State	SW

Directions   See directions for Sylvan Lake Upper Falls.

Waterfall Name	Sylvan Lake Middle Falls
State	South Dakota
Type	Cascade
Variant Name	Sylvan Lake Falls #2
Height in feet	50
County	Custer
Topo Map	Custer
Geo Coord	435044N1033432W
Map Ref Code	43103-G5
Elevation ft	5970
Water Source	Sylvan Lake Creek
Seasonal Flow	Year
Section of State	SW

Directions   See directions for Sylvan Lake Upper Falls.

Waterfall Name	Sylvan Lake Upper Falls
State	South Dakota
Type	Cascade
Variant Name	Sylvan Lake Falls #1
Height in feet	50
County	Custer
Topo Map	Custer
Geo Coord	435048N1033430W
Map Ref Code	43103-G5
Elevation ft	6000
Water Source	Sylvan Lake Creek
Seasonal Flow	Year
Section of State	SW

Directions   From Custer, take Rt. 16 E. Go 1 mile and turn left (north) onto Rt. 89. Go 6 miles (follow signs to Sylvan Lake) and park in the parking area for Sylvan Lake. Hike the Sunday Gulch Trail to the back side of the dam. Follow the gorge trail along the creek. There are stairs to navigate and some boulder hopping involved for several hundred yards to view all three falls and numerous cascades. Entry fee.

Waterfall Name	Thunderhead Falls
State	South Dakota
Type	Block
Variant Name	
Height in feet	30
County	Pennington
Topo Map	Pactola Dam
Geo Coord	440301N1032451W
Map Ref Code	44103-A4
Elevation ft	4400
Water Source	Rapid Creek
Seasonal Flow	Year
Section of State	SW

Directions   From Rapid City, take Rt. 44 W. Go about 9 miles and turn left (south) onto Thunderhead Falls Road. Follow the road and signs for about 1 mile to the end of the road and parking area. The falls are a short walk from the parking area. There are two falls here. The first one is inside the cave and an entrance fee is required. The second one can be viewed from the trail leading to the cave. No fee is charged for the second falls.

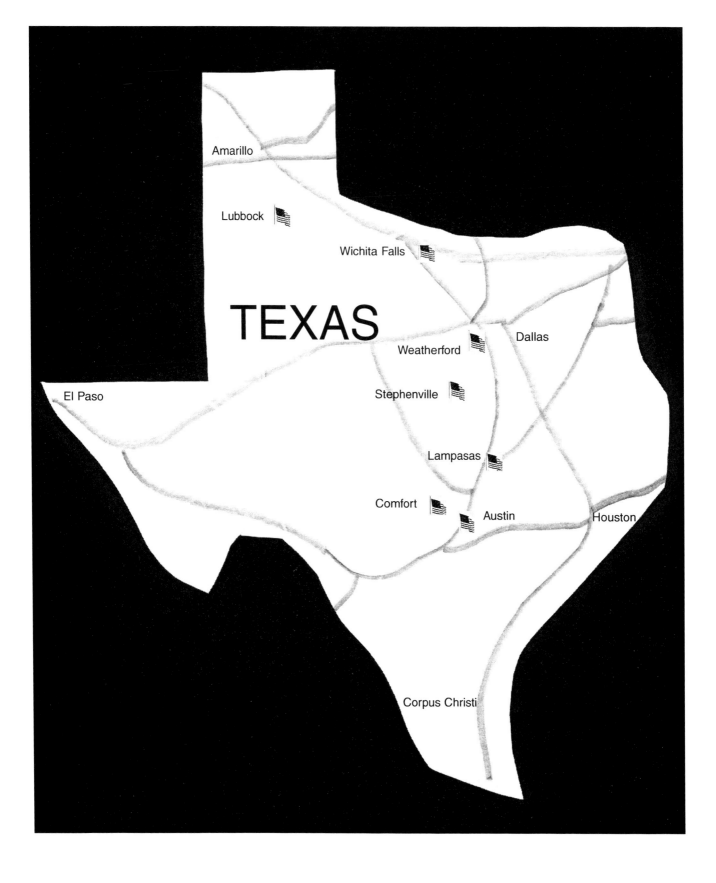

TEXAS

Amarillo

Lubbock

Wichita Falls

Dallas

Weatherford

Stephenville

El Paso

Lampasas

Comfort

Austin

Houston

Corpus Christi

Waterfall Name	Big Joshua Creek Falls
State	Texas
Type	Block
Variant Name	
Height in feet	20
County	Kendall
Topo Map	Waring
Geo Coord	295440N0984953W
Map Ref Code	29098-H7
Elevation ft	1420
Water Source	Big Joshua Creek
Seasonal Flow	Sp
Section of State	SE

Directions   From Comfort at the intersection of Interstate 10 and Business Rt. 87, take the frontage road east (on the south side of Interstate 10). Go 5.5 miles and park near the bridge over Big Joshua Creek (sign). The falls can be viewed off to the right from the bridge (on private property).

Waterfall Name	Gorman Falls
State	Texas
Type	Plunge/Cascade
Variant Name	
Height in feet	100
County	San Saba
Topo Map	Gorman Falls
Geo Coord	310329N0982855W
Map Ref Code	31098-A4
Elevation ft	1110
Water Source	Gorman Creek
Seasonal Flow	Year
Section of State	SE

Directions   From Lampasas, take Rt. 580 W. to the town of Bend. Go 4 miles on the gravel road to the Colorado Bend State Park entrance. Go another 6 miles on the gravel road to the Park Headquarters (follow signs). To visit the falls, a ranger-guided tour must be arranged. The tours are held every Saturday and Sunday or prearranged mid-week in advance. The hike to the falls is on a rocky 3/4-mile trail.

Waterfall Name	Hamilton Pools
State	Texas
Type	Plunge
Variant Name	Hamilton Pool Falls
Height in feet	80
County	Travis
Topo Map	Shingle Hills
Geo Coord	301910N0980655W
Map Ref Code	30098-C1
Elevation ft	960
Water Source	Hamilton Creek
Seasonal Flow	Sp
Section of State	SE

Directions   From Austin, take Rt. 71 W. Go approx. 16 miles and turn left (south) onto Hamilton Pools Road, near the town of Bee Cave. Go about 13 miles and turn right into the parking area (follow sign). A short walk leads to the falls and large lagoon. Entry fee.

Waterfall Name	Kickapoo Falls
State	Texas
Type	Tiered/Plunge
Variant Name	
Height in feet	10
County	Hood
Topo Map	Dennis
Geo Coord	323243N0975915W
Map Ref Code	32097-E8
Elevation ft	800
Water Source	Kickapoo Creek
Seasonal Flow	Sp
Section of State	NE

Directions   From Stephenville, take Rt. 281 N. At Morgan Mill, take Rt. 1189 N. towards Lipan. At about 3.7 miles past Lipan, turn left onto Falls Road (gravel). Go about 1/2 mile and park near where the road crosses over Kickapoo Creek. Hike downstream about 200 feet to the rock slabs to view the falls.

Waterfall Name	McKinney Lower Falls
State	Texas
Type	Segmented/Block
Variant Name	Lower McKinney Falls
Height in feet	12
County	Travis
Topo Map	Montopolis
Geo Coord	301050N0974238W
Map Ref Code	30097-B6
Elevation ft	500
Water Source	Onion and Williamson Creeks
Seasonal Flow	Year
Section of State	SE

Directions   From Interstate 35 in Austin, take Rt. 71 E. Turn right (south) onto Rt. 183 (follow sign to McKinney Falls State Park) and go 3 miles to the Park entrance. Obtain map and directions to falls at the Visitors Center. The falls is a short hike from the parking area. Entry fee.

Waterfall Name	McKinney Upper Falls
State	Texas
Type	Segmented/Plunge
Variant Name	Upper McKinney Falls
Height in feet	8
County	Travis
Topo Map	Montopolis
Geo Coord	301059N0974230W
Map Ref Code	30097-B6
Elevation ft	550
Water Source	Onion Creek
Seasonal Flow	Year
Section of State	SE

Directions   See directions to McKinney Lower Falls.

Waterfall Name	Mystery Falls
State	Texas
Type	Plunge
Variant Name	Private
Height in feet	60
County	Kendall
Topo Map	Kendalia
Geo Coord	
Map Ref Code	
Elevation ft	
Water Source	
Seasonal Flow	Year
Section of State	SE

Directions This falls is on private land. It once was open for public use due to the landowners' kindness and willingness to share the falls beauty with others. However, several years ago the public became abusive of the falls area and the surrounding property by throwing trash there, breaking tree branches and displaying other miscreant behavior. The owners then decided to close the falls to public use, since the natural beauty of the area was being severely compromised. We include this waterfall here to encourage people visiting these areas of natural beauty and uniqueness to help take care of them and keep them in their natural state for all to enjoy.

Waterfall Name	Pedernales Falls
State	Texas
Type	Tiered/Cascade
Variant Name	
Height in feet	100
County	Blanco
Topo Map	Pedernales Falls
Geo Coord	302022N0981516W
Map Ref Code	30098-C3
Elevation ft	800
Water Source	Pedernales River
Seasonal Flow	Year
Section of State	SE

Directions From Austin, take Rt. 71 W. In about 26 miles turn left (south) onto Rt. 281 towards Johnson City. Turn left (east) onto Road 2766 and proceed 9 miles to Pedernales State Park (follow signs). Obtain a map and directions at Park Headquarters. Entry fee.

Waterfall Name	Rock Falls
State	Texas
Type	Plunge
Variant Name	Private
Height in feet	20
County	Parker
Topo Map	Anneta
Geo Coord	323820N0974235W
Map Ref Code	32097-F6
Elevation ft	1100
Water Source	Bear Creek
Seasonal Flow	Sp
Section of State	NE

Directions From Weatherford at the junction of Interstate 20/80 and Rt. 171, take Rt. 171 S. Continue straight at the junction with Rt. 51, then turn left at Bearcreek Rd. (sign here reads Moncrief Ranch). Go 1.6 miles and park near the brown pipe fence on the left. The falls can be viewed from the bridge over the creek. The falls is on private land (the Moncrief Ranch) that is a sanctuary for exotic wild animals from around the world. The animals and the falls can be seen from the road through the fence.

Waterfall Name	Silver Falls
State	Texas
Type	Segmented/Plunge
Variant Name	
Height in feet	8
County	Crosby
Topo Map	Crosbyton
Geo Coord	333958N1010936W
Map Ref Code	33101-F2
Elevation ft	2700
Water Source	White River
Seasonal Flow	Sp
Section of State	NW

Directions From Lubbock, take Rt. 82 E. Go about 35 miles and pass through Crosbyton. About 4 miles to the east of Crosbyton on Rt. 82, park in the roadside rest (on the south side of the road). The falls is located on the right (west) side of the rest area in a small gorge under the Rt. 82 bridge. A trail leads to the base of the falls.

Waterfall Name	Spicewood Springs
State	Texas
Type	Horsetail/Plunge
Variant Name	
Height in feet	5
County	San Saba
Topo Map	Gorman Falls
Geo Coord	310320N982850W
Map Ref Code	31098-A4
Elevation ft	1299
Water Source	Spicewood Springs
Seasonal Flow	Sp
Section of State	SE

Directions See directions for Gorman Falls. Spicewood Springs is located a short distance from the Park Headquarters. A small trail leads to the falls.

Waterfall Name	Wichita Falls
State	Texas
Type	Tiered/Block
Variant Name	
Height in feet	40
County	Wichita
Topo Map	Wichita Falls West
Geo Coord	335510N0983040W
Map Ref Code	33098-H5
Elevation ft	900
Water Source	Wichita River
Seasonal Flow	Year
Section of State	NE

Directions From Wichita Falls, take Rt. 277 S. towards Abilene. Turn right onto Sunset Dr. (sign here reads Lucy Park). Park in the first parking area on the left. Follow the signs along the River Walk for about 0.4 mile to the falls. The falls are man-made replacing those that were washed away 100 years ago in a flood.

CHAPTER 4

The Midwestern States

Illinois

Indiana

Kentucky

Michigan

Ohio

Wisconsin

St. Louis Canyon Falls
ILLINOIS

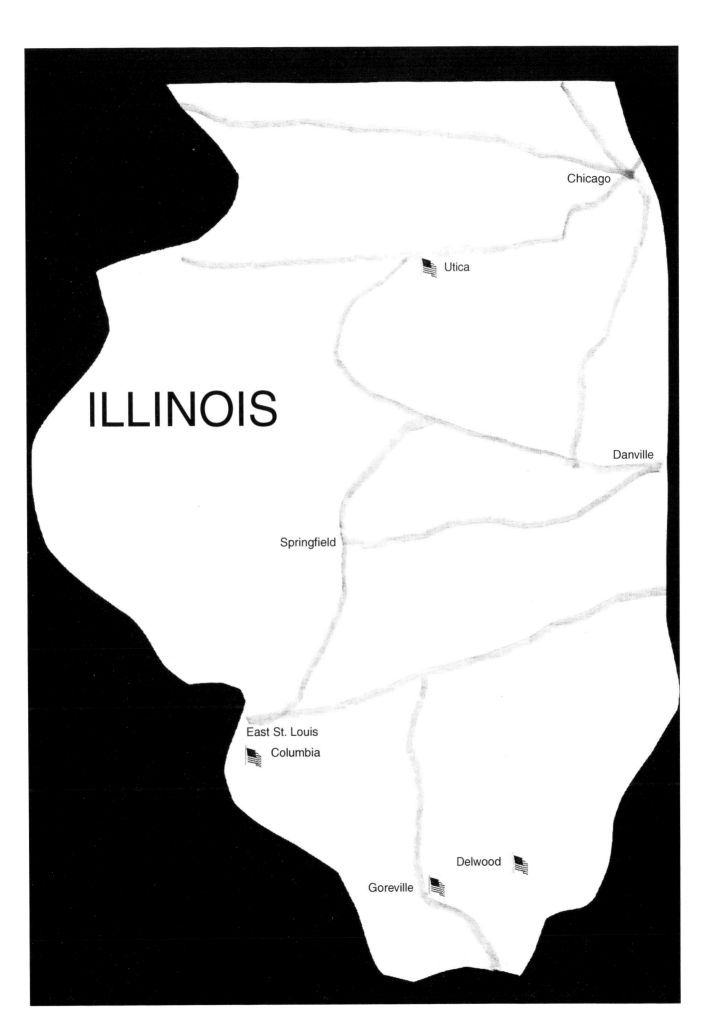

ILLINOIS

Chicago

Utica

Danville

Springfield

East St. Louis

Columbia

Delwood

Goreville

Waterfall Name	Burden Falls
State	Illinois
Type	Tiered/Plunge
Variant Name	
Height in feet	40
County	Pope
Topo Map	Stonefork
Geo Coord	373349N0883831W
Map Ref Code	37088-E6
Elevation ft	550
Water Source	Burden Creek
Seasonal Flow	Sp
Section of State	SE

Directions   From Delwood at the intersection of Rt. 145 and FS 402, go west on FS 402 (gravel). There will be a sign for Bell Smith Springs near the intersection. Once on FS 402, there will be a sign for Burden Falls. Go 4.6 miles, cross over the creek and park on the right in the gravel parking area. Sign says "Burden Falls Wilderness". From the parking area, the trail leads along the left side of the bluff for about 100 yards to the top of the falls.

Waterfall Name	Cascade Falls
State	Illinois
Type	Plunge
Variant Name	
Height in feet	50
County	La Salle
Topo Map	La Salle
Geo Coord	411736N0890203W
Map Ref Code	41089-C1
Elevation ft	500
Water Source	Deer Park Creek
Seasonal Flow	Sp
Section of State	NE

Directions   From Interstate 80, take the Utica exit. Go south on Hwy. 178 for about 4 miles (past junction with Rt. 71). Follow signs to Dells Area, Matthiessen State Park. Turn right into the Park and go about 1 mile to the parking area. From the trailhead near the parking area, take 200 stairs down to the overlook at the brink of the falls.

Waterfall Name	Cave Falls
State	Illinois
Type	Segmented/Plunge
Variant Name	Regent Falls
Height in feet	50
County	Johnson
Topo Map	Lick Creek
Geo Coord	373230N0891008W
Map Ref Code	37089-E1
Elevation ft	600
Water Source	Regent Creek
Seasonal Flow	Sp
Section of State	SE

Directions   At Exit 40 off of Interstate 57 near Goreville, take Goreville Road east. Go about 0.6 mile to Regent Lane and turn right (gravel). Go 1.1 miles to where the creek flows over the road and park. The brink of the falls is to the left of the road. A trail along the the left side of the bluff leads to the base of the falls (use CAUTION).

Waterfall Name	Falling Springs Falls
State	Illinois
Type	Plunge/Fan
Variant Name	
Height in feet	50
County	St. Clair
Topo Map	Columbia
Geo Coord	382955N0901203W
Map Ref Code	38090-D2
Elevation ft	500
Water Source	Falling Springs
Seasonal Flow	Year
Section of State	SW

Directions   Traveling north on Interstate 255 from Columbia, take the Dupo Exit (9). At the stop sign, continue straight across S. Main St. onto Industrial Drive (this is a frontage road that goes by a large quarry). Follow Industrial Dr. for 2.4 miles (it will curve to the right and become Falling Springs Drive). Continue straight another 0.4 mile to Falling Springs Park. The falls can be seen from the parking area in the Park.

Waterfall Name	Ferne Clyffe Falls
State	Illinois
Type	Horsetail/Plunge
Variant Name	Happy Hollow Falls
Height in feet	50
County	Johnson
Topo Map	Goreville
Geo Coord	373150N0885906W
Map Ref Code	37088-E8
Elevation ft	520
Water Source	Happy Hollow Creek
Seasonal Flow	Sp
Section of State	SE

Directions   From Goreville, take Hwy. 37 S. for 1.5 miles to Ferne Clyffe State Park. Turn right into the Park. The trailhead to the falls is located in the Deer Ridge Campground. The hike is about 1 mile round trip. For more details, acquire a Park map.

Waterfall Name	La Salle Canyon Falls
State	Illinois
Type	Tiered/Cascade
Variant Name	
Height in feet	40
County	La Salle
Topo Map	Starved Rock
Geo Coord	411804N0885642W
Map Ref Code	41088-C8
Elevation ft	560
Water Source	La Salle Canyon Creek
Seasonal Flow	Sp
Section of State	NE

Directions   Take the Utica exit off of Interstate 80. Follow Rt. 178 S. for 2.75 miles to Rt. 71 (past Starved Rock State Park entrance). Go left (east) on Rt. 71 for 2.7 miles to the Trail Parking area. This is the Owl/La Salle/Tonti Canyons Trailheads parking area. There is a map at the start of trail. The hike is 3/4 mile to the falls with some stairs on the way.

Waterfall Name	St. Louis Canyon Falls
State	Illinois
Type	Plunge
Variant Name	
Height in feet	50
County	La Salle
Topo Map	La Salle
Geo Coord	411903N0890310W
Map Ref Code	41089-C1
Elevation ft	520
Water Source	St. Louis Canyon Creek
Seasonal Flow	Sp
Section of State	NE

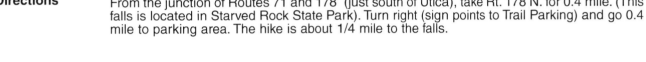

Directions   From the junction of Routes 71 and 178 (just south of Utica), take Rt. 178 N. for 0.4 mile. (This falls is located in Starved Rock State Park). Turn right (sign points to Trail Parking) and go 0.4 mile to parking area. The hike is about 1/4 mile to the falls.

Waterfall Name	Tonti Canyon Falls
State	Illinois
Type	Twin/Plunge
Variant Name	Tonti Falls
Height in feet	60
County	La Salle
Topo Map	Starved Rock
Geo Coord	411810N0885745W
Map Ref Code	41088-C8
Elevation ft	600
Water Source	Tonti Canyon Creek
Seasonal Flow	Sp
Section of State	NE

Directions   See directions for La Salle Canyon Falls. Tonti Falls is on the same trail but 1/4 mile further along. A true twin falls.

INDIANA

Gary

Lafayette

 Williamsport

Indianapolis

Greencastle

Muncie

Bridgeton

 Gosport

Hartsville

Cataract

Madison

Hanover

Sulphur

Evansville

Waterfall Name	Anderson Falls
State	Indiana
Type	Block
Variant Name	
Height in feet	15
County	Bartholomew
Topo Map	Grammer
Geo Coord	391420N0854222W
Map Ref Code	39085-B6
Elevation ft	700
Water Source	Fall Fork
Seasonal Flow	Year
Section of State	SE

Directions   In Hartsville at the junction of S.R. 46 and Washington St., go west on S.R. 46 for 1.8 miles to Road 300N. Turn left (south) and go 0.4 mile to Road 1100E and turn right. Go 1 mile to Bartholomew County Park parking area on the right. The falls is directly across the road.

Waterfall Name	Big Clifty Falls
State	Indiana
Type	Plunge
Variant Name	Clifty Falls
Height in feet	60
County	Jefferson
Topo Map	Clifty Falls
Geo Coord	384559N0852611W
Map Ref Code	38085-G4
Elevation ft	800
Water Source	Clifty Creek
Seasonal Flow	Sp
Section of State	SE

Directions   From the junction of Routes 7 and 62, just north of Madison, take Rt. 62 W. for 1.1 miles to the north entrance to Clifty Falls State Park. Turn left into the Park. The trailhead is close to the entrance (obtain a Park map). The hike is short to the overlook and an additional few hundred stairs to the base of the falls.

Waterfall Name	Bridgeton Bridge Falls
State	Indiana
Type	Block
Variant Name	Bridgeton Falls
Height in feet	20
County	Parke
Topo Map	Catlin
Geo Coord	393840N0871018W
Map Ref Code	39087-F2
Elevation ft	560
Water Source	Big Racoon Creek
Seasonal Flow	Year
Section of State	SW

Directions   Located in Bridgeton. Cross over the covered bridge to the parking lot and falls.

Waterfall Name	Cataract Lower Falls
State	Indiana
Type	Block
Variant Name	Lower Cataract Falls
Height in feet	30
County	Owen
Topo Map	Cataract
Geo Coord	392633N0864910W
Map Ref Code	39086-D7
Elevation ft	670
Water Source	Old Mill Creek
Seasonal Flow	Year
Section of State	SW

Directions   Take Exit 37 off of Interstate 70 and go south on Rt. 243 to the town of Cataract. Continue on Rt. 243 until reaching Rt. 42, then turn left. Cross the bridge, take the first left (unmarked) and follow this for about 8 miles to Cataract Falls Park. The falls is a short distance from the parking lot.

photo by Judi Moodie

Waterfall Name	Cataract Upper Falls
State	Indiana
Type	Tiered/Block
Variant Name	Upper Cataract Falls
Height in feet	50
County	Owen
Topo Map	Cataract
Geo Coord	392604N0864848W
Map Ref Code	39086-D7
Elevation ft	720
Water Source	Old Mill Creek
Seasonal Flow	Year
Section of State	SW

Directions   Follow the directions to Cataract Lower Falls. From the parking lot exit, turn left, cross the covered bridge, and then take the first road to the left (downhill and dirt). Just before crossing the creek, the falls can be seen off to the left.   photo by Judi Moodie

Waterfall Name	Clinton Falls
State	Indiana
Type	Block
Variant Name	
Height in feet	20
County	Putnam
Topo Map	Clinton Falls
Geo Coord	394255N0865740W
Map Ref Code	39086-F8
Elevation ft	750
Water Source	Little Walnut Creek
Seasonal Flow	Sp
Section of State	SW

Directions   In Greencastle at the junction of Routes 240 and 231, go north on Rt. 231 for 5 miles to the small viilage of Brick Chapel. In the village, go left (west) on Road 350N. Proceed about 6 miles following the signs to Clinton Falls. This is the heart of Indiana's covered bridge country; obtain a map at the Greencastle Visitors Center.

Waterfall Name   Harts Falls

State   Indiana

Type   Tiered/Cascade

Variant Name

Height in feet   30

County   Jefferson

Topo Map   Madison West

Geo Coord   384037N0852730W

Map Ref Code   38085-F4

Elevation ft   750

Water Source   Harts Falls Creek

Seasonal Flow   Sp

Section of State SE

Directions   From Hanover at the intersection of Main and Madison Streets, take Main St. east for 0.1 mile to Hanover Beach Hill Road. Turn right (south) and go down the steep hill veering right to stay on the main road. Go past the sewage treatment plant; continue straight as the road becomes gravel and turns into (unmarked) River Rd. Harts Falls Creek crosses over the road; park here (the distance from Main St. to Harts Falls Creek is about 3.3 miles). Walk upstream boulder hopping for about 1/8 mile to the falls.

Waterfall Name   Hemlock Cliff Falls

State   Indiana

Type   Plunge

Variant Name

Height in feet   50

County   Crawford

Topo Map   Taswell

Geo Coord   381608N0863226W

Map Ref Code   38086-C5

Elevation ft   650

Water Source   Hemlock Creek

Seasonal Flow   Sp

Section of State SW

Directions   From the junction of Interstate 64 and Rt. 37 (Exit 86 near Sulphur and English), go south on Rt. 37 for 6.6 miles. Turn right (west) onto the unnamed county road (sign says "Union Chapel, National Forest Scenic Trail, and Hemlock Cliffs"). Go 2.6 miles (turns to gravel) to the gravel road on the right (sign for "Hemlock Cliffs"). Turn right and go 1.7 miles to another gravel road on the right (sign for "NF Scenic Trail, Hemlock Cliffs") and turn right. Go 0.5 mile to the parking area. The trailhead is at the far end of the roundabout. Once on the trail, veer right at the Y. The hike is an easy 1/4 mile to the falls.

Waterfall Name	Porter's Cave Falls
State	Indiana
Type	Plunge
Variant Name	Cave Falls
Height in feet	40
County	Owen
Topo Map	Quincy
Geo Coord	392548N0863737W
Map Ref Code	39086-D6
Elevation ft	750
Water Source	Butler Creek
Seasonal Flow	Year
Section of State	SW

Directions　　From Gosport, go north on Rt. 67 (mileage count starts at Gilley's Truck Stop) for 1.8 miles to unmarked Road 700E. (700E is the first road on the left and is just past the big metal grain storage containers which are on the right). Turn left and go 4.2 miles to the T intersection (Road 950N). Turn right onto 950N and go 1/2 mile to Porter's Cave Store and entrance. The falls is about 100 yards down the trail. This is private property but open to the public; there may be an entry fee.

Waterfall Name	Tunnel Falls
State	Indiana
Type	Plunge
Variant Name	
Height in feet	80
County	Jefferson
Topo Map	Clifty Falls
Geo Coord	384540N0852542W
Map Ref Code	38085-G4
Elevation ft	800
Water Source	Deans Branch
Seasonal Flow	Sp
Section of State	SE

Directions　　See directions to Big Clifty Falls. Obtain Park map for specific directions. There are some stairs on the trail down to the falls overlook.

Waterfall Name	Williamsport Falls
State	Indiana
Type	Plunge
Variant Name	
Height in feet	90
County	Warren
Topo Map	Williamsport
Geo Coord	401710N0871730W
Map Ref Code	40087-C3
Elevation ft	550
Water Source	Fall Branch
Seasonal Flow	Sp
Section of State	NW

Directions   From Williamsport at the junction of Rt. 28 and N. Monroe St., go south on N. Monroe St. In a short distance, cross over Railroad St. and look for the sign for the falls on the left (the sign is just before the bridge and next to the fire department). From here, follow the gravel driveway to the left along the fence line to the viewing platform.

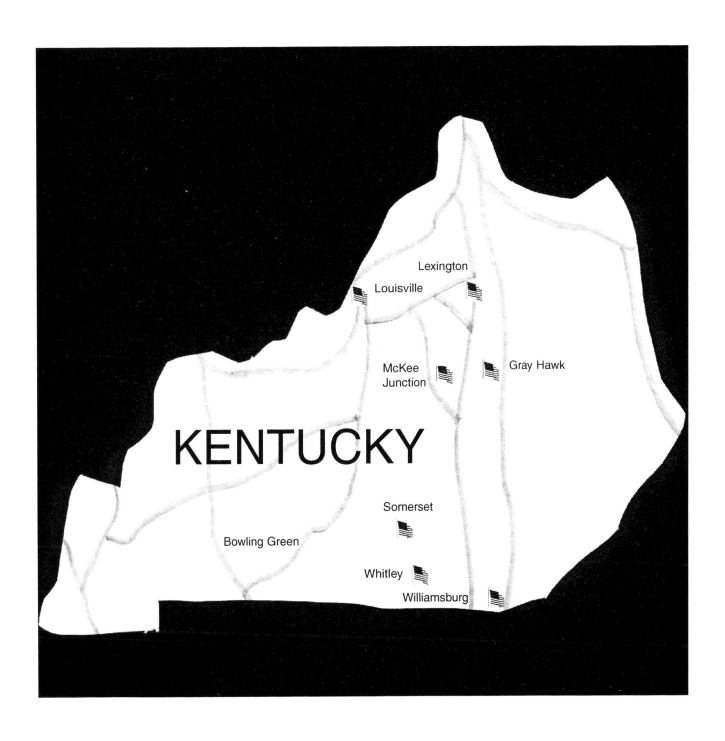

Waterfall Name	Cumberland Falls
State	Kentucky
Type	Block
Variant Name	
Height in feet	70
County	McCreary
Topo Map	Cumberland Falls
Geo Coord	365020N0842043W
Map Ref Code	36084-G3
Elevation ft	825
Water Source	Cumberland River
Seasonal Flow	Year
Section of State	SE

Directions   From Williamsburg, take Interstate 75 N. to Exit 15. Go north on Rt. 25W to Rt. 90 and turn left (west). Follow signs to Cumberland Falls State Resort Park. In 8 miles (past the Dupont Lodge), park in the Cumberland Falls parking lot on the right. The falls is 200 yards away via a well-developed pathway.

Waterfall Name	Dog Slaughter Falls
State	Kentucky
Type	Block
Variant Name	
Height in feet	15
County	Whitley
Topo Map	Cumberland Falls
Geo Coord	365136N0841804W
Map Ref Code	36084-G3
Elevation ft	800
Water Source	Little Dog Slaughter Creek
Seasonal Flow	Sp
Section of State	SE

Directions   Follow directions to Cumberland Falls. However, before reaching Cumberland Falls, look for the sign for "Daniel Boone National Forest" on the right and soon thereafter FR 195 (gravel); turn right and go 3 miles to a small pullout on the left. Park here. There is a trail going down to the creek (unsigned). Follow the trail across the bridge over the creek and turn right. Follow the trail downstream for 1.5 miles to the falls.

Waterfall Name	Eagle Falls
State	Kentucky
Type	Plunge
Variant Name	
Height in feet	35
County	McCreary
Topo Map	Cumberland Falls
Geo Coord	365034N0842039W
Map Ref Code	36084-G3
Elevation ft	825
Water Source	Eagle Creek
Seasonal Flow	Sp
Section of State	SE

Directions   See directions for Cumberland Falls. From the parking area at Cumberland Falls State Resort Park, take Rt. 90 W. (right), proceed across the bridge and park in the first pullout (about 0.6 mile) on the right. (This is on the opposite side of the river from CFSRP.) The trailhead is at the north end of the pullout. Follow Trail 9 for about 1 mile to Eagle Falls, well-marked, steep in some areas with sharp dropoffs, use CAUTION.

Waterfall Name	Falls of the Ohio
State	Kentucky
Type	Block
Variant Name	
Height in feet	10
County	Jefferson
Topo Map	New Albany (IN)
Geo Coord	381617N0854552W
Map Ref Code	38085-C7
Elevation ft	460
Water Source	Ohio River
Seasonal Flow	W,Sp
Section of State	NW

No
Photo
Available

Directions   Follow signs in Louisville, from the intersection of Interstate 64, Interstate 264 and the Sherman Minton Bridge to Falls of the Ohio State Park, Clarksville, Indiana.

Waterfall Name	Flat Lick Falls
State	Kentucky
Type	Plunge
Variant Name	
Height in feet	40
County	Jackson
Topo Map	Tyner
Geo Coord	372225N0835603W
Map Ref Code	37083-C8
Elevation ft	1200
Water Source	Flat Lick Creek
Seasonal Flow	Year
Section of State	SE

Directions From the town of Gray Hawk, take Rt. 421 S. to Mile Mark 8. Proceed another 1/2 mile to the unmarked road on the right (road is directly across from Road 1071 E. and just before the gas station). Turn right and make a quick left on the first road to the left. Follow this road for about 1 mile and veer right at the Y (gravel road and trailer home on left). Go about 1/2 mile and turn left onto the dirt road just past the large pond. This road can be very bumpy and muddy. Hike or drive down this road (going in a southerly direction) and continue along it as it turns SW (right). The road ends in a parking area. The total distance on the dirt road is about 1/4 mile. Follow the faint trail at the end of the parking area for about 200 feet through the woods and to the brink of the falls. Follow the rim of the cavern (with CAUTION) around to the right for a full view of the falls.

Waterfall Name	Mark Branch Falls
State	Kentucky
Type	Plunge
Variant Name	
Height in feet	80
County	McCreary
Topo Map	Bell Farm
Geo Coord	363735N0844120W
Map Ref Code	36084-F6
Elevation ft	1000
Water Source	Mark Branch
Seasonal Flow	Sp
Section of State	SE

Directions From Whitley, take Rt. 92 W. Cross the Big South Fork Cumberland River and immediately turn left at Road 1363 (sign here points to Bell Farm and Great Meadow). Go about 11 miles to the T intersection (paved road ends). Turn left towards Bell Farm Horse Camp and go 0.1 mile. Turn right at the fork continuing towards Bell Farm Horse Camp. Go 1.2 miles and turn right again at the fork now heading towards Peters Mountain, Road 139. Go 3.8 miles to the parking area for Peters Mountain Big South Fork Trailhead. Roads 139, 569 and 6101 meet here. Diagonally across the road from the parking area is the trailhead for the Sheltowee Trail. This trail goes in a northwesterly direction for approx. 3/4 mile to the falls.

Waterfall Name	McCammon Falls
State	Kentucky
Type	Tiered/Plunge
Variant Name	
Height in feet	50
County	Jackson
Topo Map	McKee
Geo Coord	372304N0835718W
Map Ref Code	37083-D8
Elevation ft	1200
Water Source	McCammon Branch
Seasonal Flow	Year
Section of State	SE

Directions　From Mckee Junction at the intersection of Routes 421 and 290, take Rt. 421 S. for 5.3 miles and turn right onto the paved road marked by the sign reading "Gray Hawk Community Park and Fairgrounds". Go 0.1 mile and turn left onto the first paved road on the left (unmarked). Go 0.7 mile to the Park and Fairgrounds; the road ends here. Walk past the horse ring and down the gravel road on the right side of the picnic shelter. Cross over the grassy area to the barbed wire fence. Turn right and follow the fence line down to the wooded cliffside. Follow the faint, steep trail through the woods to the gorge. Falls is to the left and can be heard before it is seen. Some boulder hopping required.

Waterfall Name	Mill Cascades
State	Kentucky
Type	Twin/Cascade
Variant Name	Raven Run Falls
Height in feet	20
County	Fayette
Topo Map	Cole Town
Geo Coord	375319N0842302W
Map Ref Code	37084-H4
Elevation ft	850
Water Source	Raven Run Creek
Seasonal Flow	Year
Section of State	NE

Directions　The mileage count starts from the junction of Routes 418/25/421 to the southeast of Lexington (near Jacobson Park). Go south on 25/421 (Richmond Road) for 3.4 miles to Road 1975 (Jacks Creek Road) and turn right. Go 3.8 miles to Road 1976E and continue straight ahead for 1.4 miles to Raven Run Nature Sanctuary. Turn left into the Sanctuary and proceed 0.4 mile to the parking lot. Hike 1/4 mile to the Nature Center and obtain a map of the park and directions to The Mill. Several trails lead there with the most direct one being about 2 miles round trip.

Waterfall Name	Pounder Branch Falls
State	Kentucky
Type	Tiered/Plunge
Variant Name	Pounder Falls
Height in feet	70
County	Laurel
Topo Map	Ano
Geo Coord	370040N0841712W
Map Ref Code	37084-A3
Elevation ft	1000
Water Source	Pounder Branch
Seasonal Flow	Sp
Section of State	SE

Directions   See directions to Vanhook Falls. Follow the trail for about 2 miles (don't go all the way to Cane Creek); listen for the sound of rushing water off to the right-hand side. A short spur trail shoots off the main trail for about 30 feet to a cliffside view of the falls on the opposite side of the gorge.

Waterfall Name	Vanhook Falls
State	Kentucky
Type	Plunge
Variant Name	
Height in feet	50
County	Laurel
Topo Map	Ano
Geo Coord	370151N0841710W
Map Ref Code	37084-A3
Elevation ft	1000
Water Source	Vanhook Branch
Seasonal Flow	Sp
Section of State	SE

Directions   From Somerset, take Rt. 192 S. for about 19 miles to the junction with Road 1193. Park at the Daniel Boone National Forest Sheltowee Trace parking area. Take the Sheltowee Trace Trail to the north (located on the opposite side of Rt. 192 from the parking area) to Cane Creek. In about 2.5 miles, cross over the second bridge (goes over Cane Creek) and continue on the trail for another 1/4 mile to the falls.

Waterfall Name	Yahoo Falls
State	Kentucky
Type	Plunge
Variant Name	
Height in feet	115
County	McCreary
Topo Map	Nevelsville
Geo Coord	364602N0843050W
Map Ref Code	36084-G5
Elevation ft	900
Water Source	Yahoo Creek
Seasonal Flow	Sp
Section of State	SE

Directions   From Whitley, at the north end of town, Rt. 27 will intersect with a street called 700 Business. Go left (west) on 700 Business for approx. 4 miles to gravel Road 660 and turn right (sign for Yahoo Falls). Go 1.5 miles to the picnic/parking area. The hike is about 1/4 mile to the falls; some stair climbing is required to the falls base.

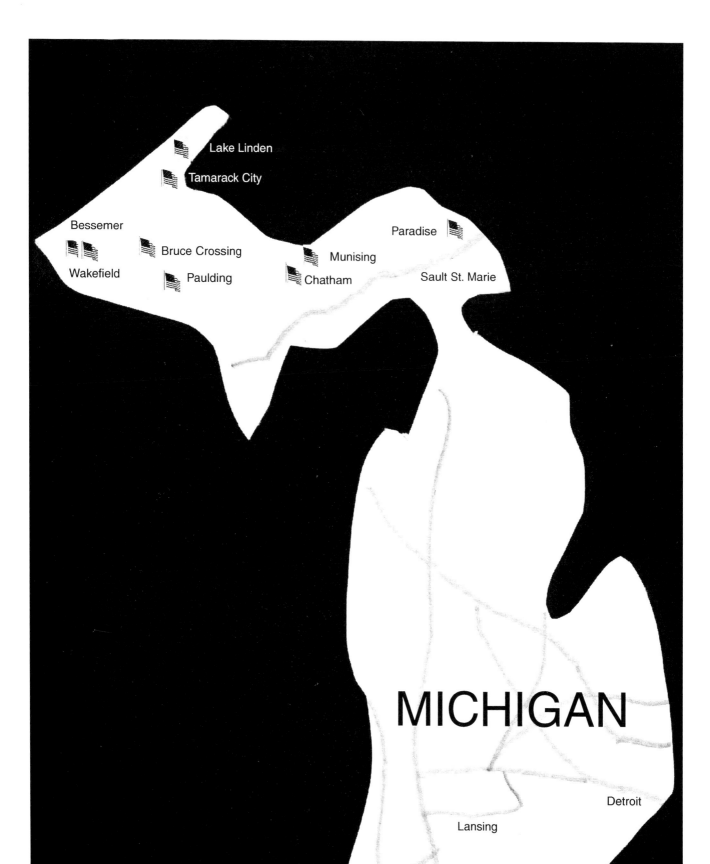

Waterfall Name	Agate Falls
State	Michigan
Type	Block
Variant Name	
Height in feet	50
County	Ontonagon
Topo Map	Trout Creek
Geo Coord	462851N0890527W
Map Ref Code	46089-D1
Elevation ft	900
Water Source	Ontonagon River
Seasonal Flow	Year
Section of State	NW

Directions From Bruce Crossing at the junction of Routes 45 and 28, go east on Rt. 28 for 7 miles to Joseph Oravec Roadside Park (on the south side of the road just past the bridge that goes over the Middle Branch Ontonagon River). Hike from here through the tunnel under the bridge and go about 1000 feet downstream to the base of the falls (very steep, rocky).

Waterfall Name	Bond Falls
State	Michigan
Type	Block/Cascade
Variant Name	
Height in feet	50
County	Ontonagon
Topo Map	Paulding
Geo Coord	462432N0890758W
Map Ref Code	46089-D2
Elevation ft	1320
Water Source	Mid Branch Ontonagon River
Seasonal Flow	Year
Section of State	NW

Directions From Paulding at the junction of Rt. 45 and Bond Falls Road, take Bond Falls Road east for 4 miles to Bond Falls Park. A sign on the north side of the road points the way to the falls trail. The falls is several hundred yards downstream via some steep sections and stairs.

Waterfall Name	Bridal Veil Falls
State	Michigan
Type	Horsetail
Variant Name	
Height in feet	100
County	Alger
Topo Map	Wood Island SE
Geo Coord	463020N0863103W
Map Ref Code	46086-E5
Elevation ft	700
Water Source	Bridal Veil Creek
Seasonal Flow	Sp
Section of State	NE

Directions　From Munising at the junction of Routes 28 and H58, take H58 N. for 5.3 miles to Miners Castle Road and turn left (sign here for Miners Castle). Go 6 miles to the parking area. Hike a short distance to the Miners Castle viewing platform. Looking to the NE across Lake Superior, the falls can be seen sliding into the lake. Bring binoculars. Best seen by boat.

Waterfall Name	Douglas Houghton Falls
State	Michigan
Type	Segmented/Horsetail
Variant Name	Houghton Falls
Height in feet	120
County	Houghton
Topo Map	Laurium
Geo Coord	471226N0882538W
Map Ref Code	47088-B4
Elevation ft	900
Water Source	Hammell Creek
Seasonal Flow	Sp
Section of State	NW

Directions　From Lake Linden, take M26 N. to the blinking light at the north end of town and turn left (west) following M26. Go 1.5 miles to large pullout on the right. Hike on the unmarked trail off to the right to the stream. Cross over the stream on the concrete bridge to access the trail on the other side. Follow the trail downstream a few hundred yards to the clifftop viewpoint of the falls and deep gorge below (use CAUTION).

Waterfall Name	Gabbro Falls
State	Michigan
Type	Segmented/Tiered
Variant Name	
Height in feet	60
County	Gogebic
Topo Map	Thomaston
Geo Coord	463008N0895929W
Map Ref Code	46089-E8
Elevation ft	1200
Water Source	Black River
Seasonal Flow	Year
Section of State	NW

Directions   From the traffic signal in Wakefield, go west on Rt. 2 for 2.2 miles to Blackjack Road and turn right (north). Go 1.5 miles and follow the road as it curves sharply to the left at the Blackjack Ski Area sign. Cross the Black River through the covered bridge. Turn left and go up the hill on the gravel road for about 0.4 mile, then make a U-turn at the lumber yard on the right. Park here. A short trail leads through the woods to the brink of the falls.

Waterfall Name	Gorge Falls
State	Michigan
Type	Block
Variant Name	
Height in feet	30
County	Gogebic
Topo Map	Black River Harbor
Geo Coord	463825N0900301W
Map Ref Code	46090-F1
Elevation ft	950
Water Source	Black River
Seasonal Flow	Year
Section of State	NW

Directions   From Bessemer at the junction of Routes 2 and 513 (N. Moore Rd.), go north on Rt. 513 towards Black River Harbor. Follow Rt. 513 (National Scenic Byway) for 14 miles to Ottawa National Forest/Gorge Falls/Potawatomi Falls Area. Turn right and follow the signs to the parking area. A very short walk leads to the viewing platform.

Waterfall Name	Laughing Whitefish Falls
State	Michigan
Type	Plunge/Cascade
Variant Name	
Height in feet	90
County	Alger
Topo Map	Sand River
Geo Coord	462302N0870406W
Map Ref Code	46087-D1
Elevation ft	900
Water Source	Laughing Whitefish River
Seasonal Flow	Sp
Section of State	NE

Directions   From Chatham at the junction of Routes 94 and H01, take Rt. 94 W. for 7.8 miles to N. Sundell Rd. (sign says Laughing Whitefish Falls State Park). Turn right (north) and go about 2.2 miles to the State Park entrance. From the parking area, the hike is 1/3 mile to the falls and viewing platform (there are a few stairs on the way).

Waterfall Name	Lower Hungarian Falls
State	Michigan
Type	Fan
Variant Name	
Height in feet	100
County	Houghton
Topo Map	Larium
Geo Coord	471001N0882725W
Map Ref Code	47088-B4
Elevation ft	900
Water Source	Hungarian Creek
Seasonal Flow	Sp
Section of State	NW

Directions   From Tamarack City (S. of Hubbell) at the intersection of 6th St. and M26, take 6th St. west (sign points to the Calumet Golf Club). Go 0.1 mile and veer left at the Y. Go uphill (gravel road) for 0.2 mile to the second dirt road on the left. Turn left and go a short distance to the end of the road and park. Follow the small trail to the west about 1/4 mile to view the falls from the top of the ravine through the trees.

Waterfall Name	Manabezho Falls
State	Michigan
Type	Block
Variant Name	
Height in feet	20
County	Gogebic
Topo Map	Tiebel Creek
Geo Coord	464228N0895818W
Map Ref Code	46089-F8
Elevation ft	650
Water Source	Presque Isle River
Seasonal Flow	Year
Section of State	NW

Directions   From Wakefield at the junction of Routes 2 and M28, take M28 north for 2 miles to County Road 519. Turn left and go 17 miles to the sign for Presque Isle Unit/Falls Campground, Porcupine Mountains Wilderness State Park. Continue 1 more mile on 519 to the falls parking area (well-marked). The viewing platform is a short walk from the parking area.

Waterfall Name	Munising Falls
State	Michigan
Type	Plunge
Variant Name	
Height in feet	50
County	Alger
Topo Map	Munising
Geo Coord	462503N0863702W
Map Ref Code	46086-D6
Elevation ft	600
Water Source	Munising Creek
Seasonal Flow	Sp
Section of State	NE

Directions   From Munising at the junction of Routes 28 and 58 (NPS and USFS Info Center located here), take Rt. 58 N. Veer left at the Y (sign here for Munising Falls) and go about 2 miles to the falls parking area on the right. The asphalt trail is about 1/8 mile to the base of the falls.

Waterfall Name	Potawatomi Falls
State	Michigan
Type	Slide/Cascade
Variant Name	Pottawatomie Falls
Height in feet	30
County	Gogebic
Topo Map	Black River Harbor
Geo Coord	463815N0900305W
Map Ref Code	46090-F1
Elevation ft	900
Water Source	Black River
Seasonal Flow	Year
Section of State	NW

Directions   See directions for Gorge Falls. Potawatomi Falls is along the same trail but seen before Gorge Falls. Has wheelchair access.

Waterfall Name	Rainbow Falls
State	Michigan
Type	Block
Variant Name	
Height in feet	30
County	Gogebic
Topo Map	Black River Harbor
Geo Coord	463932N0900237W
Map Ref Code	46090-F1
Elevation ft	890
Water Source	Black River
Seasonal Flow	Year
Section of State	NW

Directions   See directions for Gorge Falls. Rainbow Falls is on the same trail a short distance before Gorge Falls.

Waterfall Name	Upper Tahquamenon Falls
State	Michigan
Type	Block
Variant Name	Upper Falls/Big Falls
Height in feet	50
County	Luce
Topo Map	Betsy Lake South
Geo Coord	463430N0851526W
Map Ref Code	46085-E3
Elevation ft	700
Water Source	Tahquamenon River
Seasonal Flow	Year
Section of State	NE

Directions   From Paradise, take M123 W. for 15 miles to the parking area for Upper Tahquamenon Falls on the left. The 1/4-mile asphalt trail takes in several viewpoints.

Waterfall Name	Amphitheater Falls
State	Ohio
Type	Horsetail/Plunge
Variant Name	
Height in feet	40
County	Greene
Topo Map	Clifton
Geo Coord	394720N0835020W
Map Ref Code	39083-G7
Elevation ft	950
Water Source	Little Miami River Branch
Seasonal Flow	Sp
Section of State	SW

Directions   From Clifton at the junction of Water St. and Rt. 72, take Water St. west. Go past the Clifton Mill and in about 0.2 mile, turn right onto Jackson St., then immediately turn left into the parking lot of Clifton Gorge. Hike along the trail paralleling the Little Miami River. Take the lower trail to the left when it branches off the cliff trail. Pass Steamboat Rock and continue a short distance to the falls on the right. There is a map at the trailhead; distance to falls is 1/2 mile. In John Bryan State Park.

Waterfall Name	Ash Cave Falls
State	Ohio
Type	Plunge
Variant Name	
Height in feet	100
County	Hocking
Topo Map	South Bloomingville
Geo Coord	392315N0823237W
Map Ref Code	39082-D5
Elevation ft	900
Water Source	Ash Cave Creek
Seasonal Flow	W,Sp
Section of State	SE

Directions   In Hocking Hills State Park. Obtain a detailed map at the Visitors Center. The Visitors Center is located at the junction of Rt. 664 and Interstate 33 near Logan. The falls is located near the intersection of Routes 374 and 56.

Waterfall Name	Berea Falls
State	Ohio
Type	Cascade
Variant Name	
Height in feet	25
County	Cuyahoga
Topo Map	North Olmsted
Geo Coord	412305N0815237W
Map Ref Code	41081-D8
Elevation ft	850
Water Source	E. Branch Rocky River
Seasonal Flow	Year
Section of State	NE

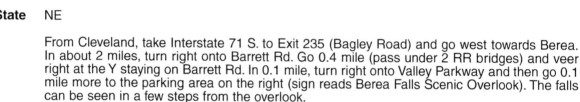

Directions   From Cleveland, take Interstate 71 S. to Exit 235 (Bagley Road) and go west towards Berea. In about 2 miles, turn right onto Barrett Rd. Go 0.4 mile (pass under 2 RR bridges) and veer right at the Y staying on Barrett Rd. In 0.1 mile, turn right onto Valley Parkway and then go 0.1 mile more to the parking area on the right (sign reads Berea Falls Scenic Overlook). The falls can be seen in a few steps from the overlook.

Waterfall Name	Big Lyons Falls
State	Ohio
Type	Plunge
Variant Name	
Height in feet	40
County	Ashland
Topo Map	Jelloway
Geo Coord	403612N0821820W
Map Ref Code	40082-E3
Elevation ft	1000
Water Source	Lyons Creek
Seasonal Flow	Sp
Section of State	NE

Directions   From Butler at the intersection of Rt. 97 and Grant Rd., take Rt. 97 E. Go 4.7 miles and turn left (north) onto McCurdy Rd. Go 1.8 miles and turn right onto Goon Rd. (3006). Sign here reads Mohican Lodge/Pleasant Hill Lake. Go 1.5 miles to the Pleasant Hill Lake Dam parking area on the right. The trailhead is at the far east end of the parking area. Follow the main trail about 1/4 mile and veer right at the Y. In another 1/4 mile, the falls can be seen on the right. In Mohican State Park.

Waterfall Name   Big Spring Hollow Falls

State   Ohio

Type   Plunge

Variant Name

Height in feet   100

County   Hocking

Topo Map   South Bloomingville

Geo Coord   392721N0823305W

Map Ref Code   39082-D5

Elevation ft   800

Water Source   Big Spring

Seasonal Flow   Sp

Section of State   SE

Directions   See directions for Conkle's Hollow Falls. Pass the parking area for Conkle's Hollow and in 0.9 mile, park in the parking area on the left. Obtain a map at the info station. Cross the road to the trailhead for the Hocking State Forest Rock Climbing Area. Cross the bridge over Pine Creek and take the farthest right trail. In about 100 yards, the trail will veer away from the creek and then follow another creek up to Big Spring Hollow. The hike is about a 1/2 mile.

Waterfall Name   Brandywine Falls

State   Ohio

Type   Cascade

Variant Name

Height in feet   60

County   Summit

Topo Map   Northfield

Geo Coord   411614N0813227W

Map Ref Code   41081-C5

Elevation ft   900

Water Source   Brandywine Creek

Seasonal Flow   Year

Section of State   NE

Directions   From Northfield at the junction of Rt. 82 (Aurora Rd.) and Brandywine Rd., take Brandywine Rd. to the south. Go 2 miles and turn right onto Stanford Rd. (just past the Brandywine Inn). In a short distance, turn left into the parking lot for Brandywine Falls. A short boardwalk trail leads to the falls overlooks. In Cuyahoga Valley National Recreation Area.

Waterfall Name	Bridal Veil Falls
State	Ohio
Type	Cascade
Variant Name	
Height in feet	30
County	Cuyahoga
Topo Map	Shaker Heights
Geo Coord	412234N0813251W
Map Ref Code	41081-D5
Elevation ft	800
Water Source	Tinkers Creek
Seasonal Flow	Sp
Section of State	NE

Directions From the Cuyahoga Valley National Recreation Area at the junction of Interstate 271 and Rt. 14 (Broadway), take Rt. 14 N. Go 0.4 mile and veer left at the Y (traffic light) onto Union St. Go 0.7 mile and turn left onto Egbert Rd. Go 0.4 mile and turn right onto Gorge Parkway. Go 1.9 miles and turn left into Bridal Veil Falls parking area (follow signs). The trail is on the right and goes about 1/8 mile (with some stairs) to the falls.

Waterfall Name	Buttermilk Falls
State	Ohio
Type	Fan
Variant Name	
Height in feet	35
County	Summit
Topo Map	Northfield
Geo Coord	411530N0813503W
Map Ref Code	41081-C5
Elevation ft	860
Water Source	Buttermilk Spring
Seasonal Flow	Sp
Section of State	NE

Directions From Northfield at the intersection of Rt. 82 (Aurora Rd.) and Brandywine Rd., take Brandywine Rd. to the south. Go 2 miles and turn right (west) onto Stanford Rd. When Stanford Rd. ends, veer right onto Boston Mills Rd. In 2.5 miles, cross over Riverview Rd. and veer left to stay on Boston Mills Rd. Go 1 more mile and turn right into the parking area (sign reads Blue Hen Falls). Follow the trail (past Blue Hen Falls) in a downstream direction for about 3/4 mile to the falls. Do not take the Buckeye Trail that veers left off the main trail near Blue Hen Falls. In Cuyahoga Valley National Recreation Area.

Waterfall Name	Cedar Falls
State	Ohio
Type	Segmented/Horsetail
Variant Name	
Height in feet	50
County	Hocking
Topo Map	South Bloomingville
Geo Coord	392510N0823125W
Map Ref Code	39082-D5
Elevation ft	840
Water Source	Queer Creek
Seasonal Flow	Sp
Section of State	SE

Directions SW of Logan at the junction of Routes 374 and 56, take Rt. 374 N. Go 2 miles to the Cedar Falls parking area on the left (follow sign). A loop trail from the parking area to the falls takes about 15 minutes (some stairs). In Hocking Hills State Park Region.

Waterfall Name	Conkle's Hollow Falls
State	Ohio
Type	Plunge
Variant Name	
Height in feet	25
County	Hocking
Topo Map	South Bloomingville
Geo Coord	392733N0823456W
Map Ref Code	39082-D5
Elevation ft	920
Water Source	Conkle's Spring
Seasonal Flow	Sp
Section of State	SE

Directions Near Gibisonville at the intersection of Routes 374 and 678, take Rt. 374 S. Go 3.4 miles and turn left onto Big Pine Rd. Go 0.2 mile and turn left into Conkle's Hollow State Preserve and park. Hike the Gorge Trail (it follows the creekbed) to the falls at the end (about 1/2 mile).

Waterfall Name	Hidden Valley Falls
State	Ohio
Type	Horsetail/Fan
Variant Name	
Height in feet	30
County	Lake
Topo Map	Thompson
Geo Coord	414432N0810320W
Map Ref Code	41081-F1
Elevation ft	800
Water Source	Hidden Valley Creek
Seasonal Flow	Sp
Section of State	NE

Directions At Exit 212 off of Interstate 90 (near Painesville), take Rt. 528 S. Go 1.5 miles and turn right onto Klasen Rd. (follow sign to Hidden Valley Park). Go 0.3 mile and park in the parking area on the left. The trailhead is at the west end of the parking area between the restrooms and the sledding hill. Follow the Grand River west for about 3/4 mile. Now climb the dirt stairway over the ridge to the creekbed. Continue up the creekbed about 50 yards to the falls. In the Grand River Reservation.

Waterfall Name	Old Man's Cave Lower Falls
State	Ohio
Type	Horsetail/Plunge
Variant Name	Lower Falls Old Man's Cave
Height in feet	50
County	Hocking
Topo Map	South Bloomingville
Geo Coord	392551N0823235W
Map Ref Code	39082-D5
Elevation ft	900
Water Source	Old Man's Creek
Seasonal Flow	Sp
Section of State	SE

Directions See directions to Old Man's Cave Upper Falls. Go to the west from the Visitors Center for about 1/4 mile (pass Old Man's Cave) to the falls. There are some stairs involved.

Waterfall Name	Old Man's Cave Upper Falls
State	Ohio
Type	Horsetail
Variant Name	Upper Falls Old Man's Cave
Height in feet	50
County	Hocking
Topo Map	South Bloomingville
Geo Coord	392540N0822325W
Map Ref Code	39082-D5
Elevation ft	950
Water Source	Old Man's Creek
Seasonal Flow	Sp
Section of State	SE

Directions   SW of Logan at the junction of Routes 374 and 56, take Rt. 374 N. Go 3.8 miles and turn left (west) onto Rt. 664. In 1/2 mile, park in the parking lot on the right for Old Man's Cave. Obtain a map at the Visitors Center. Hike upstream (east) from the Visitors Center a short distance to the falls. In the Hocking Hills State Park Region.

Waterfall Name	Paine Falls
State	Ohio
Type	Tiered/Block
Variant Name	Payne Falls
Height in feet	30
County	Lake
Topo Map	Painesville
Geo Coord	414240N0810801W
Map Ref Code	41081-F2
Elevation ft	850
Water Source	Paine Creek
Seasonal Flow	Year
Section of State	NE

Directions   At Exit 212 off of Interstate 90 (near Painesville), take Rt. 528 S. Go 2.5 miles and turn right onto Ford Rd. (6). Go 4.7 miles and turn left at the T intersection onto Blair Rd. Go 0.4 mile and turn left onto Paine Rd. Proceed 0.2 mile to the Paine Falls parking area on the right. There is a short boardwalk and gravel path to the falls viewpoints.

Waterfall Name	Sunderland Falls
State	Ohio
Type	Plunge
Variant Name	
Height in feet	40
County	Montgomery
Topo Map	Tipp City
Geo Coord	395301N0841005W
Map Ref Code	39084-H2
Elevation ft	860
Water Source	Sunderland Creek
Seasonal Flow	Sp
Section of State	SW

Directions   From Dayton, take Interstate 75 N. At Exit 63 (Vandalia), go right (east) on E. National Rd. (Rt. 40). Go 0.6 mile and turn right onto Cassel Rd./Clubhouse Way (towards golf course). Go 0.1 mile and turn left onto Old Falls Rd. Go 0.1 mile and park near the Historic Rock and sign reading "Pathway to Waterfall". A short path leads to the brink of the falls.

Waterfall Name	The Cascades
State	Ohio
Type	Plunge
Variant Name	Glen Helen Falls
Height in feet	15
County	Greene
Topo Map	Yellow Springs
Geo Coord	394738N0835234W
Map Ref Code	39083-G8
Elevation ft	950
Water Source	Birch Creek
Seasonal Flow	Year
Section of State	SW

Directions   From Yellow Springs at the junction of Rt. 68 and Corry St., take Corry St. east. In about 1/2 mile, park at the Glen Helen Nature Preserve on the left. Obtain a park map and directions to the falls at the Museum/Visitors Center. The hike to the falls is less than 1 mile.

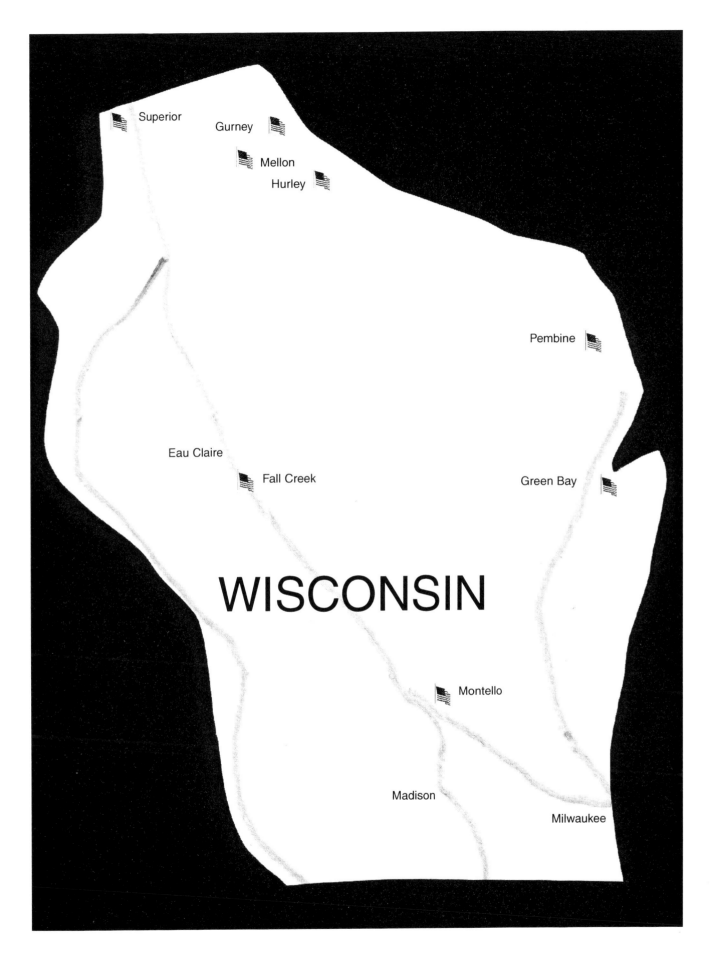

Superior
Gurney
Mellon
Hurley

Pembine

Eau Claire
Fall Creek
Green Bay

WISCONSIN

Montello

Madison
Milwaukee

Waterfall Name	Big Falls
State	Wisconsin
Type	Cascade
Variant Name	
Height in feet	15
County	Eau Claire
Topo Map	Fall Creek
Geo Coord	444915N0911739W
Map Ref Code	44091-G3
Elevation ft	850
Water Source	Eau Claire River
Seasonal Flow	Year
Section of State	NW

Directions   From Fall Creek at the junction of Routes 12 and K, take Rt. K to the north. Go 4 miles and turn left (west) onto Rt. Q. Go 1.9 miles and turn left onto Rt. UN (follow sign to Big Falls County Park). Go 0.8 mile and park in the parking area for Big Falls. Follow the flat, easy trail for about 100 yards to the falls.

Waterfall Name	Big Manitou Falls
State	Wisconsin
Type	Horsetail
Variant Name	Manitou Falls
Height in feet	165
County	Douglas
Topo Map	Sunnyside
Geo Coord	463210N0920716W
Map Ref Code	46092-E1
Elevation ft	1000
Water Source	Black River
Seasonal Flow	Year
Section of State	NW

Directions   From Superior at the junction of Routes 105 and 35, take Rt. 35 S. Go about 9 miles and turn left into Pattison State Park. Obtain a map of the park and falls at the office. From the parking area to the falls is a very short walk. There are several viewpoints.

Waterfall Name	Copper Falls
State	Wisconsin
Type	Segmented/Horsetail
Variant Name	
Height in feet	30
County	Ashland
Topo Map	Mellen
Geo Coord	462223N0903823W
Map Ref Code	46090-C6
Elevation ft	1000
Water Source	Bad River
Seasonal Flow	Year
Section of State	NW

Directions From Mellen at the junction of Routes 13 and 169, take Rt.169 NE. Go 2 miles and turn left into Copper Falls State Park. Go 1.6 miles and park in the last parking area. The falls is a short walk from the parking area. Entry fee.

Waterfall Name	Devil's River Falls
State	Wisconsin
Type	Cascade
Variant Name	Devil's Falls
Height in feet	10
County	Manitowoc
Topo Map	Bellevue
Geo Coord	442705N0875508W
Map Ref Code	44087-D8
Elevation ft	750
Water Source	Devil's River
Seasonal Flow	Sp
Section of State	SE

Directions From Green Bay, take Interstate 43 S. At Exit 164, go east for 1/4 mile and turn left (north) onto County Road R. Go 1.25 miles and park at Devil's River Camper Park on the left. Get permission at the office to view the falls. The falls are a short walk from the parking area.

Waterfall Name	Eighteen Foot Falls
State	Wisconsin
Type	Cascade
Variant Name	
Height in feet	18
County	Marinette
Topo Map	Twelve Foot Falls
Geo Coord	453515N0880747W
Map Ref Code	45088-E2
Elevation ft	1000
Water Source	North Branch Pike River
Seasonal Flow	Year
Section of State	NE

Directions   From Pembine at the junction of Routes 141 and 8 W., take Rt. 8 W. Go 5.8 miles and turn left onto Lilly Lake Road (sign here for Twelve Foot Falls County Park). Go 1.6 miles and turn right onto Twin Lake Road (follow sign to County Park). Go 0.4 mile (road changes to gravel) and turn left onto Twelve Foot Falls Road. Go 2 miles and turn left onto the unnamed dirt road towards Eighteen Foot Falls. Go 0.3 mile and park in the parking area for Eighteen Foot Falls. The falls is a few hundred yards from here.

Waterfall Name	Granite Falls
State	Wisconsin
Type	Segmented/Cascade
Variant Name	Man-Made
Height in feet	25
County	Marquette
Topo Map	Montello
Geo Coord	434733N0891952W
Map Ref Code	43089-G3
Elevation ft	800
Water Source	Fox River
Seasonal Flow	Year
Section of State	SE

Directions   From Montello at the junction of Routes 22 and 23, the falls are located in the old quarry on the corner. The falls are pump assisted, but still make a beautiful sight.

Waterfall Name	Long Slide Falls
State	Wisconsin
Type	Cascade
Variant Name	
Height in feet	40
County	Marinette
Topo Map	Pembine
Geo Coord	454100N0875600W
Map Ref Code	45087-F8
Elevation ft	950
Water Source	N. Branch Pemebonwon River
Seasonal Flow	Year
Section of State	NE

Directions   From Pembine, take Rt. 141 N. Go about 5 miles and turn right onto Morgan Park Road (follow sign to Long Slide Falls Park). Go 1.6 miles and turn right onto Long Slide Road. Go 0.3 mile and park in the parking area. A short walk from here leads to the ridgetop view of the falls. Small entry fee.

Waterfall Name	Potato River Falls
State	Wisconsin
Type	Tiered/Cascade
Variant Name	Potato Falls
Height in feet	30
County	Iron
Topo Map	Gurney
Geo Coord	462740N0903144W
Map Ref Code	46090-D5
Elevation ft	1060
Water Source	Potato River
Seasonal Flow	Year
Section of State	NW

Directions   Near Gurney at the junction of Routes 169 and 2, take Rt. 169 S. Go 2.8 miles and turn right onto Rowe Farm Road (gravel, follow sign to Potato River Falls). Go 1.6 miles and park at the end of the road near the picnic area. Hike on the trail heading south along the ridge and then down the steep steps to the falls viewpoint. Total hike is approx. 1/8 mile.

Waterfall Name	Upper Amnicon Falls
State	Wisconsin
Type	Cascade
Variant Name	Upper Falls
Height in feet	25
County	Douglas
Topo Map	South Range
Geo Coord	463636N0915332W
Map Ref Code	46091-E8
Elevation ft	1000
Water Source	Amnicon River
Seasonal Flow	Year
Section of State	NW

Directions   SE of Superior at the junction of Routes 53 and 2, take Rt. 2 E. Go 0.9 mile and turn left onto Road U (follow sign to Amnicon Falls State Park). Go 0.3 mile and turn left into the Park. Check the posted Park map for directions to the falls. From the parking area, the viewpoint is a short walk. Small entry fee.

Waterfall Name	Upson Falls
State	Wisconsin
Type	Tiered/Block
Variant Name	
Height in feet	20
County	Iron
Topo Map	Upson
Geo Coord	462225N0902457W
Map Ref Code	46090-C4
Elevation ft	1480
Water Source	Potato River
Seasonal Flow	Year
Section of State	NW

Directions   From Hurley at the junction of Routes 2/77/51, take Rt. 77 W. Go 12.8 miles and turn right onto Hoyt Ave. in Upson (follow sign to Upson Park). Go 0.3 mile and turn left onto Upson Park Road. Go 0.2 mile and turn left into Upson Park. The falls can be seen from the left end of the parking area.

Waterfall Name	Wequiok Falls
State	Wisconsin
Type	Plunge
Variant Name	
Height in feet	25
County	Brown
Topo Map	Hilbert
Geo Coord	441241N0880802W
Map Ref Code	44088-B2
Elevation ft	810
Water Source	Wequiok Creek
Seasonal Flow	Sp
Section of State	SE

Directions   From the junction of Rt. 57 and Rt. K South (east of Green Bay), go west on Rt. 57 for 0.4 mile to Wequiock Falls County Park on the north side of the road (follow sign). The falls is located on the north side of the parking area flowing under the concrete bridge.

CHAPTER 5

The South Eastern States

Alabama
Arkansas
Florida
Georgia
Louisiana
Mississippi
North Carolina
South Carolina
Tennessee
Virginia
West Virginia

Noccalula Falls
ALABAMA

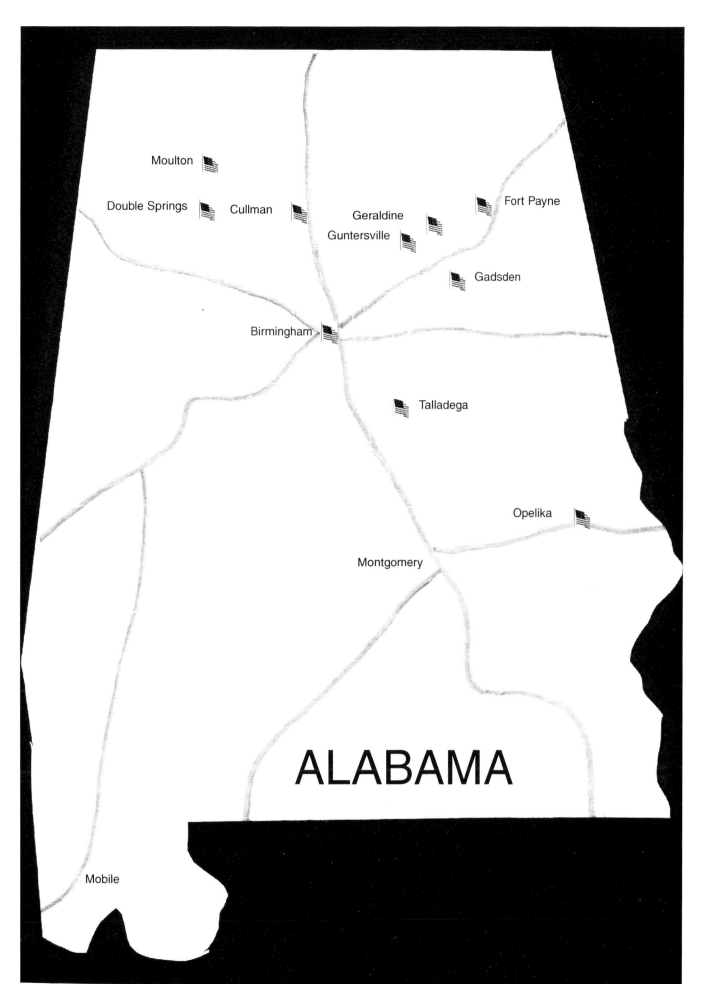

Moulton

Double Springs   Cullman   Geraldine   Fort Payne

Guntersville

Gadsden

Birmingham

Talladega

Opelika

Montgomery

ALABAMA

Mobile

Waterfall Name	Catoma Lake Falls
State	Alabama
Type	Tiered/Cascade
Variant Name	Lake Catoma Falls
Height in feet	120
County	Cullman
Topo Map	Cullman
Geo Coord	341102N0864742W
Map Ref Code	34086-B7
Elevation ft	780
Water Source	Eight Mile Creek
Seasonal Flow	Year
Section of State	NE

Directions From downtown Cullman, take 278E (3rd St. SE) to just beyond the water treatment plant on the right (about 2 miles). Turn left on Larkwood Dr. and go to bottom of the hill (about 1/2 mile). Pass the bridge and the falls will be on the left in a short distance.

Waterfall Name	DeSoto Falls
State	Alabama
Type	Plunge
Variant Name	
Height in feet	120
County	De Kalb
Topo Map	Valley Head
Geo Coord	343256N0853526W
Map Ref Code	34085-E5
Elevation ft	500
Water Source	West Fork Little River
Seasonal Flow	Year
Section of State	NE

Directions From Fort Payne, take Rt. 89 N. for approx. 8 miles. Follow signs to DeSoto State Park.

Waterfall Name	High Falls
State	Alabama
Type	Tiered/Block
Variant Name	Natural Bridge Falls
Height in feet	50
County	De Kalb
Topo Map	Grove Oak
Geo Coord	342400N0860406W
Map Ref Code	34086-D1
Elevation ft	900
Water Source	Town Creek
Seasonal Flow	Year
Section of State	NE

Directions   From the junction of Rt. 75 and Rt. 227 N. in Geraldine, go north on 227 about 4 miles. Turn left onto County Rd. 356 (look for High Falls Park sign). Go past Flat Rock Baptist Church to County Rd. 144 (dirt) and turn left (about 1.5 miles). Veer left at the Y intersection (still on CR 144) to park entrance (about 0.7 mile).

Waterfall Name	High Falls-Lower
State	Alabama
Type	Block
Variant Name	Lower High Falls
Height in feet	25
County	Talladega
Topo Map	Lineville West
Geo Coord	332225N0855018W
Map Ref Code	33085-C7
Elevation ft	1200
Water Source	High Falls Branch of Talladega Creek
Seasonal Flow	W,Sp
Section of State	NE

Directions   From the intersection of Rt. 77 S. and Rt. 21 in Talladega, take 77 S. for 10.3 miles to County Road 209. Go left (east) on 209 towards Chandler Springs approx. 3.4 miles to County Road 12 (look for Lower Odum Scout Trail sign). Turn left on Rt. 12; go 9.2 miles to Road 650 (gravel). Turn left and go 0.3 mile to parking lot. Hike up the wide dirt path on the right of the parking lot (yellow triangle painted on tree marks the trail). Continue a few hundred yards to trailhead sign and map of area. The falls is upstream another 200 yards, with some boulder hopping. In Talladega National Forest.

Waterfall Name	High Falls-Upper
State	Alabama
Type	Tiered
Variant Name	Upper High Falls
Height in feet	25
County	Talladega
Topo Map	Lineville West
Geo Coord	332228N0855015W
Map Ref Code	33085-C7
Elevation ft	1400
Water Source	High Falls Branch of Talladega Creek
Seasonal Flow	W,Sp
Section of State	NE

Directions   Follow directions to High Falls-Lower. Getting to Upper Falls requires being on the left side of the stream. There is a stairway that leads up the rocks on the left side of Lower Falls to Upper Falls.

Waterfall Name	Kinlock Falls
State	Alabama
Type	Tiered
Variant Name	
Height in feet	40
County	Lawrence
Topo Map	Kinlock Spring
Geo Coord	341821N0873004W
Map Ref Code	34087-C5
Elevation ft	900
Water Source	Hubbard Creek
Seasonal Flow	F,W,Sp
Section of State	NW

Directions   From Double Springs, take I95 N. about 8 miles to County Road 23. Turn right (north) on 23 (Rabbittown sign on right). Go 1.2 miles, then veer left at the Y (Sipsey and Brushy Recreation sign goes to right). Continue on 23 for about 2.6 miles (last 1/2 mile is dirt) to turnout on right (before bridge) and park. Follow the blufftop trail to view the falls from above.

Waterfall Name	Little Uchee Creek Falls
State	Alabama
Type	Block/Cascade
Variant Name	Great Falls/We-tum-cau Falls
Height in feet	15
County	Lee
Topo Map	Bleeker
Geo Coord	323030N0851104W
Map Ref Code	32085-E2
Elevation ft	390
Water Source	Little Uchee Creek
Seasonal Flow	Year
Section of State	SE

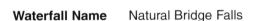

Directions From Opelika, take Rt. 169 S. about 12 miles and veer left onto Rt. 240 east (just past Mile Mark 17). Continue 4 miles to Road 206 (just before overpass bridge). Turn right. The falls will be on the left in a short distance.

Waterfall Name	Natural Bridge Falls
State	Alabama
Type	Plunge
Variant Name	
Height in feet	60
County	Marshall
Topo Map	Mount Carmel
Geo Coord	342729N0861952W
Map Ref Code	34086-D3
Elevation ft	700
Water Source	Ricketts Gap Creek
Seasonal Flow	W,Sp
Section of State	NE

Directions From the Guntersville Welcome Center at the north end of town, take Rt. 431 N. about 11 miles. Just past Sunrise Marina (on the left), turn right onto Cottonville Road (stone house on corner). Go up the hill about 1/2 mile to a row of large boulders on the left. Park in small turnout on right. The natural bridge and falls is a short distance from the boulders. This is private property, but the falls can be seen from the road.

Waterfall Name	Noccalula Falls
State	Alabama
Type	Block/Plunge
Variant Name	Black Creek Falls
Height in feet	90
County	Etowah
Topo Map	Gadsden West
Geo Coord	340229N0860116W
Map Ref Code	34086-A1
Elevation ft	700
Water Source	Black Creek
Seasonal Flow	Year
Section of State	NE

Directions   Take Interstate 59 to Gadsden Exit 188 (County Road 211). Look for Noccalula Falls sign. Follow 211 S. (Noccalula Road) for several miles until you pass the bridge over Black Creek. The falls Visitors Center and parking lot are on the right (look for sign, very well-marked).

Waterfall Name	Peavine Falls
State	Alabama
Type	Horsetail
Variant Name	
Height in feet	35
County	Shelby
Topo Map	Helena
Geo Coord	331820N0864525W
Map Ref Code	33086-C7
Elevation ft	840
Water Source	Peavine Branch
Seasonal Flow	Sp
Section of State	NE

Directions   From Birmingham, take Interstate 65 S. to Exit 246 (Hwy. 119). Turn right (west) and get in the left lane. Turn left onto State Park Road (brown sign for Oak Mountain State Park on right). Follow this a couple miles to Park entrance. Obtain map and directions to falls, taking the blue-blaze trail 0.4 mile from the trailhead. Entry fee.

Waterfall Name	Turkeyfoot Falls
State	Alabama
Type	Fan
Variant Name	
Height in feet	30
County	Winston
Topo Map	Bee Branch
Geo Coord	341720N0872427W
Map Ref Code	34087-C4
Elevation ft	700
Water Source	Turkeyfoot Creek
Seasonal Flow	W,Sp
Section of State	NW

Directions From Moulton, take Rt. 33 S. about 15 miles to County Road 60. Turn right (west) on 60. Go about 3 miles to the Sipsey River Picnic Grounds. Cross over the bridge and continue another 0.4 mile to turnout on left (south) side of road and park (do not go on dirt road). Cross the roadway to the faint trail that goes down the hillside, veering right along the bluff. In a few hundred yards, the falls can be viewed through the trees or follow the trail a bit further to the rock opening. Grab the rappelling rope and clamber down to the streambed for a closer look. In Bankhead National Forest.

Waterfall Name	Welcome Falls
State	Alabama
Type	Block/Plunge
Variant Name	
Height in feet	60
County	Morgan
Topo Map	Lawrence Cove
Geo Coord	341857N0863953W
Map Ref Code	34086-C6
Elevation ft	900
Water Source	Fall Creek
Seasonal Flow	W,Sp
Section of State	NE

Directions From Cullman, take 69 N. about 14 miles to Baileyton. Turn left (north) at Larry's Deli (on right, green Baileyton City Offices sign on left). This is County Road 1564 (no sign). Continue 4.7 miles, then turn right (just before Welcome Church). This is County Road 1578 (no sign). Go 1.4 miles and turn right (look for concrete water valve post on right). This is Welcome Falls Road (no sign). Go downhill for 0.3 mile and park in the pullout on right (just past the stream). Take the dirt trail on the right side of the road a few hundred yards to the falls.

Waterfall Name	Yellow Creek Falls
State	Alabama
Type	Block/Cascade
Variant Name	
Height in feet	30
County	De Kalb
Topo Map	Fort Payne
Geo Coord	342230N0853720W
Map Ref Code	34085-D6
Elevation ft	1300
Water Source	Yellow Creek
Seasonal Flow	Sp
Section of State	NE

Directions   From Gadsden, take Lookout Mountain Parkway for about 18 miles. Turn left at the sign for Little River Canyon. Go 14 miles to Yellow Creek Falls on the right .

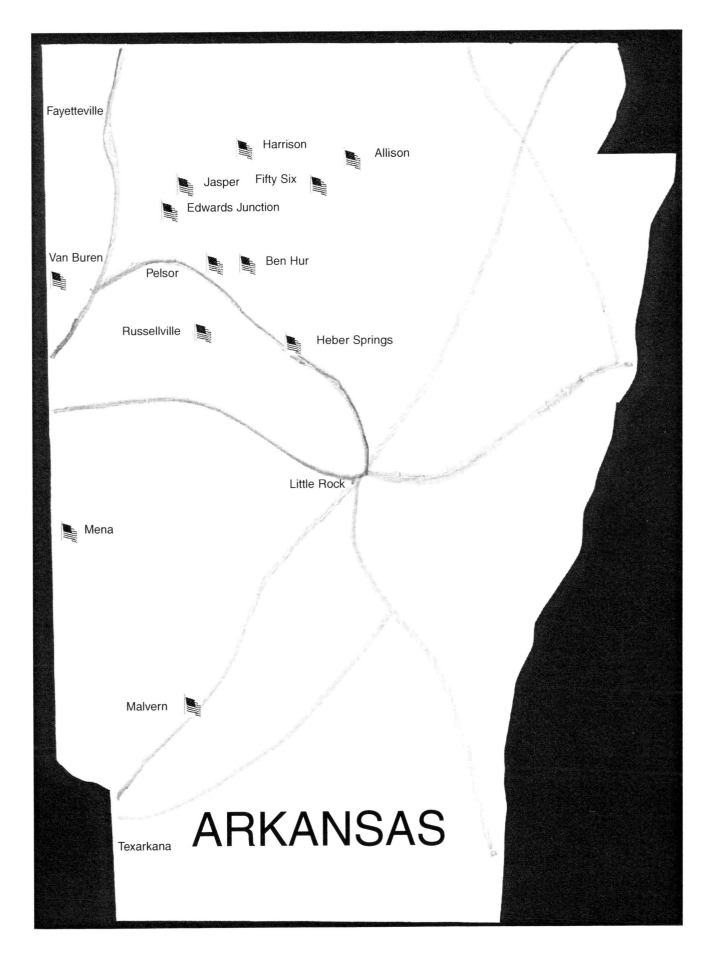

Fayetteville

Harrison

Allison

Jasper   Fifty Six

Edwards Junction

Van Buren

Pelsor   Ben Hur

Russellville

Heber Springs

Little Rock

Mena

Malvern

Texarkana   ARKANSAS

Waterfall Name	Blanchard Springs Falls
State	Arkansas
Type	Segmented/Fan
Variant Name	
Height in feet	10
County	Stone
Topo Map	Fifty Six
Geo Coord	355728N0921040W
Map Ref Code	35092-H2
Elevation ft	600
Water Source	Blanchard Springs
Seasonal Flow	Year
Section of State	NW

Directions   From the intersection of Routes 5/9/14 in Allison, take 14 W. about 6 miles to Blanchard Springs Caverns and turn right (look for sign). Follow sign to the Springs. Take the short walk from the parking area to the falls viewpoint.

Waterfall Name	Bridal Veil Falls
State	Arkansas
Type	Plunge/Cascade
Variant Name	
Height in feet	30
County	Cleburne
Topo Map	Heber Springs
Geo Coord	352739N0920230W
Map Ref Code	35092-D1
Elevation ft	600
Water Source	Bridal Veil Creek
Seasonal Flow	W,Sp
Section of State	NE

Directions   From the junction of 25/5 and 25B at the south end of Heber Springs, take 25/5 S. Go 1/2 mile to Bridal Veil Falls Road on the right (just past Southside Baptist Church). Turn right and go 0.3 mile to pullout on the right (where a red stop sign is hanging from a cable between 2 trees). Hike down this drive to what used to be a picnic area and proceed straight ahead down the cliffside. The falls is to the left. Total hike is about 1/8 mile.

Waterfall Name	Cedar Falls
State	Arkansas
Type	Plunge
Variant Name	
Height in feet	95
County	Conway
Topo Map	Adona
Geo Coord	350717N0925601W
Map Ref Code	35092-A8
Elevation ft	800
Water Source	Cedar Creek
Seasonal Flow	W,Sp,Sm
Section of State	NW

Directions   From Russellville at the junction of Interstate 40 and Rt. 7, take 7 S. for about 13 miles to Centerville. Turn left (east) on Rt. 154 to Petit Jean State Park (about 16 miles). In the Park, look for a sign to Cedar Falls Overlook on the left. The overlook is a short distance from the parking lot.

Waterfall Name	Eden Falls
State	Arkansas
Type	Tiered/Horsetail
Variant Name	
Height in feet	40
County	Newton
Topo Map	Osage SW
Geo Coord	360108N0932237W
Map Ref Code	36093-A4
Elevation ft	1600
Water Source	Clark Creek
Seasonal Flow	Year
Section of State	NW

Directions   At the junction of Routes 7 and 74 in Jasper, take 74 W. about 14 miles to Rt. 43. Turn left (south) on 43 and go 1 mile. Turn right at sign for Lost Valley Campground, Buffalo National River. Proceed 0.4 mile to the camping area and parking lot. The trailhead is at the end of the parking lot. The hike to the falls is about 1.5 miles and passes an interesting Natural Bridge Falls on the way.

Waterfall Name	Falling Water Falls
State	Arkansas
Type	Segmented/Block
Variant Name	
Height in feet	10
County	Pope
Topo Map	Smyrna
Geo Coord	354246N0925710W
Map Ref Code	35092-F8
Elevation ft	1400
Water Source	Falling Water Creek
Seasonal Flow	Sp
Section of State	NW

Directions   From Pelsor (35 miles N. of Russellville at the junction of Routes 7/123/16), take 16 E. about 8 miles to Ben Hur. From the Free Will Baptist Church in Ben Hur, continue on Rt.16 E. for 1.4 miles to FR 1205 (look for sign saying Falling Water Church on left). Turn left (dirt road) and go 2.4 miles to the small pullout on the right. The falls can be seen from here. In Ozark National Forest.

Waterfall Name	Falls Creek Falls
State	Arkansas
Type	Segmented/Plunge/Horsetail
Variant Name	
Height in feet	15
County	Hot Springs
Topo Map	Lake Catherine
Geo Coord	342521N0925434W
Map Ref Code	34092-D8
Elevation ft	400
Water Source	Falls Creek
Seasonal Flow	Sp
Section of State	SW

Directions   From Interstate 30 near Malvern, take Exit 97 and go 12 miles north on Rt. 171. The road ends at Lake Catherine State Park (follow signs). Pick up a trail map at the Visitors Center. Follow the "Waterfall Trail" (red blaze) for a moderate 2-mile loop.

Waterfall Name	Glory Hole Falls
State	Arkansas
Type	Doughnut/Plunge
Variant Name	
Height in feet	25
County	Newton
Topo Map	Fallsville
Geo Coord	354904N0932234W
Map Ref Code	35093-G4
Elevation ft	1920
Water Source	Newton Spring
Seasonal Flow	Sp
Section of State	NW

Directions   From the junction of Routes 21 N. and 16 (Edwards Junction, northeast portion of the Ozark National Forest), take 16 W. Go 2.4 miles to unmarked dirt road on left (south) side of 16. A landmark is a lone farmhouse directly across the road with the name Pierce on the mailbox and a metal driveway gate. Park on the south side of 16 in the slanted grassy shoulder. Hike down the dirt road to the fork, veer right, and continue as the road becomes a trail. The trail crosses a couple small streams and leads to a rocky dropoff. View the Glory Hole (carefully) from the top where the stream shoots through the hole into the cavern below. Continue down the trail to the right to view from the bottom. About a 1-mile hike downhill.

Waterfall Name	Hemmed in Hollow Falls
State	Arkansas
Type	Plunge
Variant Name	Hemmed in Falls
Height in feet	175
County	Newton
Topo Map	Ponca
Geo Coord	360493N0931756W
Map Ref Code	36093-A3
Elevation ft	1500
Water Source	Hemmed in Hollow Creek
Seasonal Flow	Sp
Section of State	NW

Directions   From Harrison at the junction of Routes 7 and 43 S., take 43 S. Go 16.5 miles to the first dirt road on the left after the Compton City sign (this is Road 19 but is unmarked; it goes past a school). Turn left and go 0.8 mile straight south (follow brown "Trails" sign). Turn right at Hemmed in Hollow sign and park on the left (at the trailhead parking area). Take the Compton Trail, following the Hemmed in Hollow signs (well-marked). About a 2.5-mile, strenuous, rocky hike. In Ponca Wilderness Area, Buffalo National River.

Waterfall Name   Kings Bluff Falls

State   Arkansas

Type   Plunge

Variant Name

Height in feet   90

County   Pope

Topo Map   Sand Gap

Geo Coord   354251N0930110W

Map Ref Code   35093-F1

Elevation ft   1600

Water Source   Pedestal Creek

Seasonal Flow   Sp

Section of State NW

Directions   From Pelsor (35 miles N. of Russellville) at the junction of Routes 7/123/16, take 16 E. Go 5.9 miles to Pedestal Rocks Scenic Area on the right. There are two loop trails. The left goes to Arch Rock and Pedestal Rocks. The right goes to Kings Bluff (unmarked at trailhead). To see the falls, take the right-hand trail. Hike the 2-mile loop with a well-developed overlook at the brink of the falls. In Ozark National Forest.

Waterfall Name   Little Missouri Falls

State   Arkansas

Type   Tiered/Cascade

Variant Name

Height in feet   30

County   Montgomery

Topo Map   Big Fork

Geo Coord   342512N0935456W

Map Ref Code   34093-D8

Elevation ft   1240

Water Source   Little Missouri River

Seasonal Flow   Year

Section of State SW

Directions   From the junction of Routes 71/59/88 and 8 in Mena, take Rt. 8 E. Go 24.5 miles to FR 43 (gravel). The signs on right say Little Missouri Falls 6, also Caney Creek Wildlife Management Unit. Turn right here and go about 5 miles to FR 25 and turn right (sign for Little Missouri Falls). Go 0.8 mile to FR 539 and turn left (sign for falls). Go 0.4 mile to the trailhead and picnic area. The falls is an easy 100-yard hike. In Quachita National Forest.

Waterfall Name	Mud Springs Falls
State	Arkansas
Type	Plunge
Variant Name	
Height in feet	50
County	Stone
Topo Map	Calico Rock
Geo Coord	360055N0921025W
Map Ref Code	36092-A2
Elevation ft	800
Water Source	Mud Springs
Seasonal Flow	W,Sp
Section of State	NE

Directions From the town of Fifty-Six on Rt. 14, take 14 W. about 1 mile to Gunner Road 1102 (gravel, sign for Gunner Pool Recreation Area). Turn right and go about 5 miles (pass Gunner Pool Campground) to Green Road 1113 (gravel). Turn right and go 0.9 mile to Sylamore Horsetrail sign and Branscomb Road 1140 on left (gated). Park in the pullout. Hike down the horsetrail about 1 mile. Cross the creek and go up a short marked trail to the falls (about 1/2 mile). In Ozark National Forest.

Waterfall Name	Natural Bridge Falls
State	Arkansas
Type	Fan
Variant Name	
Height in feet	25
County	Newton
Topo Map	Osage SW
Geo Coord	360040N0932230W
Map Ref Code	36093-A4
Elevation ft	1300
Water Source	Clark Creek
Seasonal Flow	Year
Section of State	NW

Directions See directions for Eden Falls.

Waterfall Name	Natural Dam Falls
State	Arkansas
Type	Block
Variant Name	Natural Dam
Height in feet	8
County	Crawford
Topo Map	Natural Dam
Geo Coord	353804N0942302W
Map Ref Code	35094-F4
Elevation ft	640
Water Source	Mountain Fork
Seasonal Flow	Year
Section of State	NW

Directions   From Van Buren, take Rt. 59 N. about 16 miles to the small community of Natural Dam (0.1 mile north of Lee Creek Bridge). Turn left (west) at the sign for Natural Dam 600 ft. (across from the gas station). The parking area is on the left.

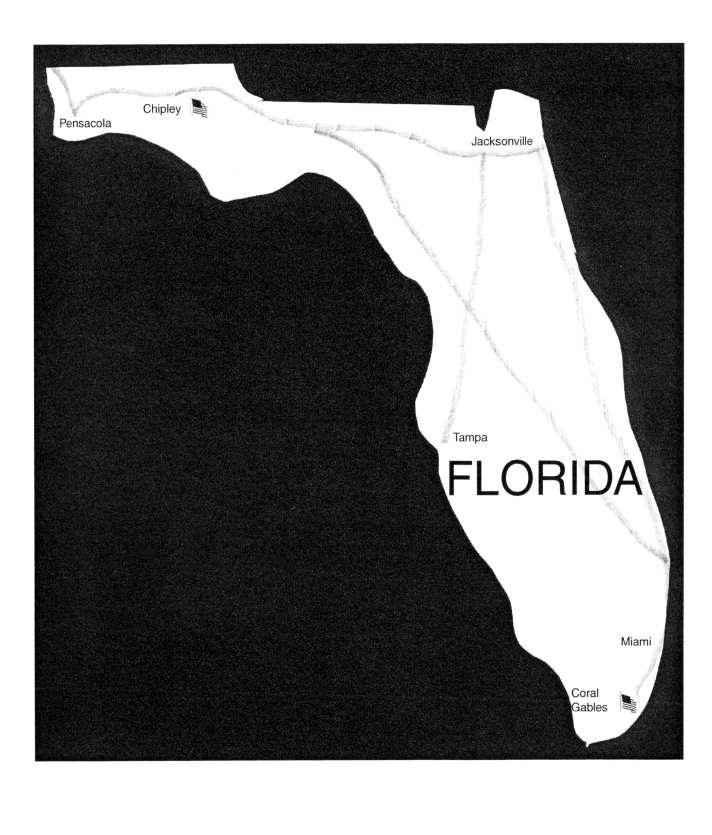

Waterfall Name   Falling Waters Falls

State   Florida

Type   Plunge

Variant Name

Height in feet   100

County   Washington

Topo Map   Wausau

Geo Coord   304327N0853547W

Map Ref Code   30085-F5

Elevation ft   220

Water Source   Falling Waters Creek

Seasonal Flow   Year

Section of State   NW

Directions   Near Chipley at the intersection of Routes 77 and 90, take Rt. 77 S. In 0.6 mile, turn left onto Falling Waters Road (C77A) and go 2.5 miles to State Park Road. Turn left and go 0.6 mile to Falling Waters State Recreation Area. From the parking lot, take the short, easy hike to the falls along the boardwalk trail. Entry fee.

Waterfall Name   Venetian Pools

State   Florida

Type   Tiered/Cascade

Variant Name   Coral Gable Falls/Man-Made

Height in feet   6

County   Dade

Topo Map   South Miami

Geo Coord   254452N0801610W

Map Ref Code   25080-F3

Elevation ft   20

Water Source   Venetian Pools

Seasonal Flow   Year

Section of State   SE

Directions   Five miles south of Maimi in the town of Coral Gables, follow the signs to the Venetian Pools. These are man-made pools. Entry fee.

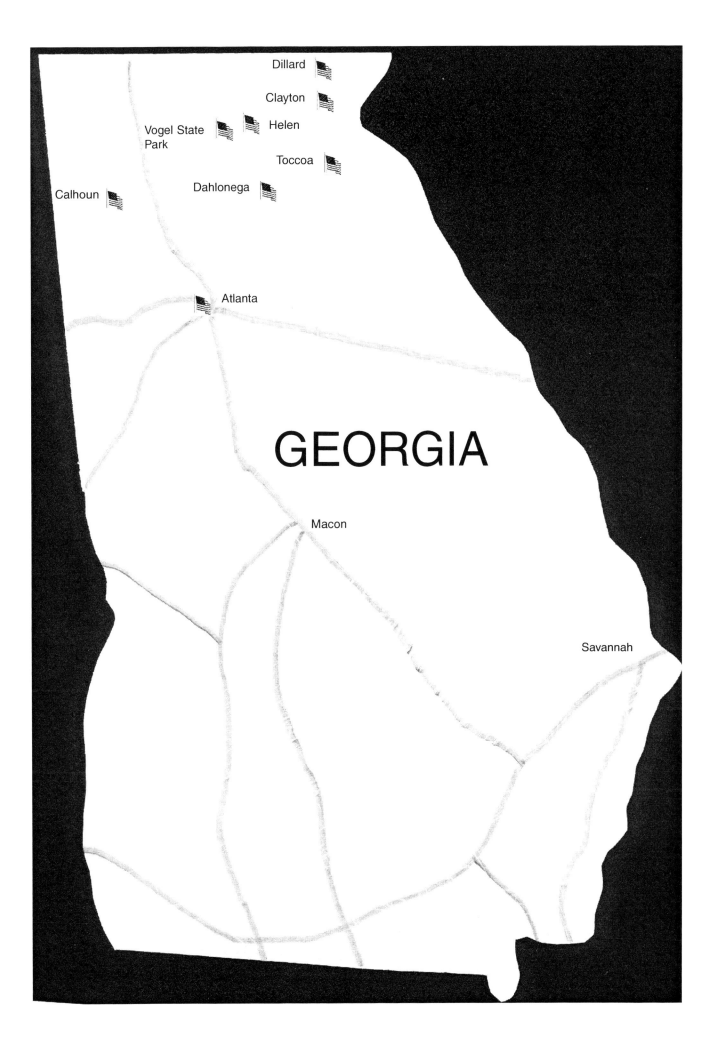

Dillard

Clayton

Vogel State
Park

Helen

Toccoa

Calhoun

Dahlonega

Atlanta

GEORGIA

Macon

Savannah

Waterfall Name	Amicalola Falls
State	Georgia
Type	Cascade
Variant Name	Armacolola Falls
Height in feet	730
County	Dawson
Topo Map	Nimblewill
Geo Coord	343350N0841423W
Map Ref Code	34084-E2
Elevation ft	2400
Water Source	Amicalola Creek
Seasonal Flow	W,Sp,Sm
Section of State	NE

Directions   From Dahlonega, take Hwy. 52 W. 18 miles to Amicalola Falls State Park. From the entrance, proceed to the parking area and trailhead. The trail goes to the base of the falls in 0.3 mile (paved). Entry fee.

Waterfall Name	Ammons Falls
State	Georgia
Type	Cascade
Variant Name	
Height in feet	40
County	Rabun
Topo Map	Rabun Bald
Geo Coord	345904N0831554W
Map Ref Code	34083-H3
Elevation ft	2600
Water Source	Ammons Creek
Seasonal Flow	Year
Section of State	NE

Directions   See directions for Holcomb Creek Falls. The trail continues 0.2 mile further to the viewpoint at Ammons Creek Falls.

Waterfall Name	Blue Hole Falls
State	Georgia
Type	Segmented/Horsetail
Variant Name	
Height in feet	25
County	Towns
Topo Map	Tray Mountain
Geo Coord	344857N0834302W
Map Ref Code	34083-G6
Elevation ft	2560
Water Source	High Shoals Creek
Seasonal Flow	Year
Section of State	NE

Directions   From Helen, take Hwy. 75 N. for 11.4 miles. Make a very sharp right turn onto FR 283 (this turn is just past Unicoi Gap Summit and Mile Mark 2). There will be a sign for High Shoals on the right. Go 1.5 miles to the parking area and trailhead on left. A well-marked trail is 1 mile to Blue Hole Falls.

Waterfall Name	Duke's Creek Falls East
State	Georgia
Type	Tiered/Cascade
Variant Name	Duke's Creek Falls
Height in feet	200
County	White
Topo Map	Cowrock
Geo Coord	344207N0834729W
Map Ref Code	34083-F7
Elevation ft	1800
Water Source	Duke's Creek
Seasonal Flow	Year
Section of State	NE

Directions   From Helen, go north on Hwy. 17/75 for 1.5 miles to Hwy. 356. Turn left and go 2.3 miles. Turn right onto Hwy. 348 (Richard Russell Scenic Byway). Go 1.2 miles to Duke's Creek Recreation Area on left. Hike 1.1 miles down the well-developed trail to the East Falls base passing the main 200-foot falls on the way.

Waterfall Name	Helton Creek Falls
State	Georgia
Type	Fan
Variant Name	
Height in feet	70
County	Union
Topo Map	Coosa Bald
Geo Coord	344509N0835345W
Map Ref Code	34083-G8
Elevation ft	2200
Water Source	Helton Creek
Seasonal Flow	Year
Section of State	NE

Directions   From the junction of Routes 180 W. and 19 near Vogel State Park in the Chattahoochee National Forest, take 19 S. for 1.5 miles. Turn left onto Helton Creek Road (sign reads Helton Creek Cottages). Go 2.3 miles (paved then dirt) to Helton Creek Falls sign on right. Just beyond the sign is a pullout parking area. Walk 0.1 mile to the falls.

Waterfall Name	High Falls
State	Georgia
Type	Cascade
Variant Name	
Height in feet	50
County	Monroe
Topo Map	High Falls
Geo Coord	331020N0840032W
Map Ref Code	33084-B1
Elevation ft	580
Water Source	Towaliga River
Seasonal Flow	Year
Section of State	SW

Directions   From Atlanta, take Interstate 75 S. for approx. 45 miles to Exit 66. Follow the signs to High Falls State Park. Pass by Park entrance on left, cross over the bridge, and park in the State Park parking lot on the left. Cross over the roadway and follow the short trail to the falls. Entry fee.

Waterfall Name	High Shoals Falls
State	Georgia
Type	Fan
Variant Name	
Height in feet	100
County	Towns
Topo Map	Jacks Gap
Geo Coord	344840N0834257W
Map Ref Code	34083-G7
Elevation ft	2600
Water Source	High Shoals Creek
Seasonal Flow	Year
Section of State	NE

Directions	See directions for Blue Hole Falls. High Shoals Falls is 0.2 mile further along the trail, some steep sections.

Waterfall Name	Holcomb Creek Falls
State	Georgia
Type	Tiered/Fan
Variant Name	
Height in feet	120
County	Rabun
Topo Map	Rabun Bald
Geo Coord	345855N0831540W
Map Ref Code	34083-H3
Elevation ft	2600
Water Source	Holcomb Creek
Seasonal Flow	Year
Section of State	NE

Directions	From Dillard, go a short distance north on Rt. 441/23 to Dillard Road (Rt. 246). Turn right (east) for 4.2 miles to Bald Mountain Road. Turn right again and go 4.2 miles to Hale Ridge Road (FR 7, gravel). Turn right and go about 3.7 miles to the junction of FR 86 and FR 7. Park here. The Holcomb Creek Trailhead is marked on the north side of the intersection. A steep 0.3-mile switchback trail leads down to the falls.

Waterfall Name	Keown Falls
State	Georgia
Type	Plunge/Cascade
Variant Name	
Height in feet	40
County	Walker
Topo Map	Sugar Valley
Geo Coord	343648N0850540W
Map Ref Code	34085-E1
Elevation ft	1400
Water Source	Keown Creek
Seasonal Flow	Sp
Section of State	NW

Directions   From Calhoun, take Interstate 75 north to Hwy. 136. Go 7 miles west, then 7 miles north on Rt. 136 to Pocket Road (before the town of Villanow). Turn left (see sign for Keown Falls Recreation Area) and go about 5 miles to FR 702. Turn right (sign for Keown Falls Recreation Area) and follow gravel road for about 3/4 mile to the picnic/parking area. Follow 1-mile trail to the falls, steep and rocky at end. In Chattahoochee National Forest.

Waterfall Name	Minnehaha Falls
State	Georgia
Type	Cascade/Fan
Variant Name	
Height in feet	80
County	Rabun
Topo Map	Tallulah Falls
Geo Coord	344451N0832902W
Map Ref Code	34083-F4
Elevation ft	1900
Water Source	Falls Branch
Seasonal Flow	Year
Section of State	NE

Directions   From Clayton, take Old Highway 441 S. Veer right (west) onto Lake Rabun Rd. Go about 1 mile past Lake Rabun Beach Recreation Area on the left at the west end of the lake. Turn left and cross the bridge below Seed Lake Dam. Continue to stop sign. Go straight on Bear Gap Road (dirt) for about 1.6 miles, cross over creek and park in the pullout on the left. The trailhead is on the right (Minnehaha Trail). Hike 0.3 mile to the falls.

Waterfall Name	Mud Creek Falls
State	Georgia
Type	Fan/Cascade
Variant Name	
Height in feet	70
County	Rabun
Topo Map	Rabun Bald
Geo Coord	345856N0832003W
Map Ref Code	34083-H3
Elevation ft	2500
Water Source	Mud Creek
Seasonal Flow	Year
Section of State	NE

Directions From Dillard, go north a short distance on Hwy. 441/23 to Dillard Road (Rt. 246). Turn right (east) and go 4.2 miles to Bald Mountain Road. Turn right and go about 1 mile to Sky Valley Resort. Turn right and proceed through the gate. Veer left down the main road to the third street (Tahoe Road). Turn right and go 1/2 mile until the pavement ends. Walk or drive the 1/4-mile dirt road to the falls.

Waterfall Name	Raven Cliffs Falls
State	Georgia
Type	Segmented/Tiered/Plunge
Variant Name	
Height in feet	50
County	White
Topo Map	Cowrock
Geo Coord	344304N0834930W
Map Ref Code	34083-F7
Elevation ft	2600
Water Source	Dodd Creek
Seasonal Flow	Year
Section of State	NE

Directions From Helen, go north on Rt. 17/75 for 1.5 miles. Turn left on Hwy. 356 and go 2.3 miles. Turn right on Hwy. 348 (Richard Russell Scenic Byway). Go 3 miles to the parking area on the left (look for Mile Mark 3 and Raven Cliffs Wilderness Area signs). Hike the up/down trail for 2.5 miles to the falls.

Waterfall Name	Toccoa Falls
State	Georgia
Type	Segmented/Plunge
Variant Name	
Height in feet	185
County	Stephens
Topo Map	Toccoa
Geo Coord	343546N0832136W
Map Ref Code	34083-E3
Elevation ft	950
Water Source	Toccoa Creek
Seasonal Flow	Year
Section of State	NE

Directions From downtown Toccoa, go a short distance north on Hwy. 17 to Toccoa Falls College. Turn left into the campus and follow the signs to the falls and the gate cottage. From here, take the short, level walk to the falls. Entry fee.

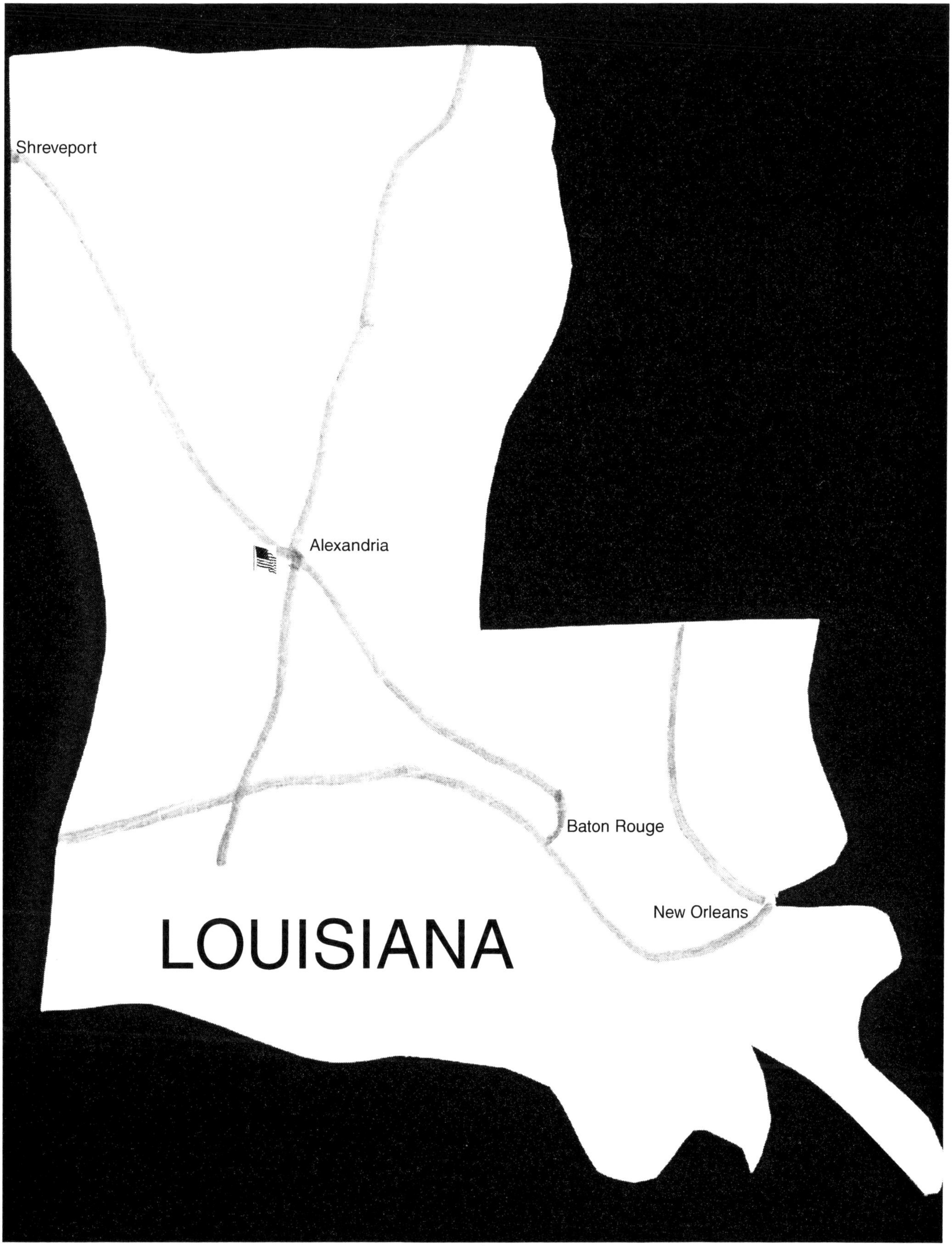

Shreveport

Alexandria

Baton Rouge

New Orleans

LOUISIANA

Waterfall Name	Little Bayou Pierre Cascade
State	Louisiana
Type	Cascade
Variant Name	
Height in feet	5
County	Natchitoches
Topo Map	Gorumor
Geo Coord	312510N0925704W
Map Ref Code	31092-D8
Elevation ft	150
Water Source	Little Bayou Pierre
Seasonal Flow	Year
Section of State	SW

Directions   From Alexandria, take 1 W. to Interstate 49. Take Interstate 49 N. Go about 15 miles to Rt. 8 W. Follow Rt. 8 W. for 16 miles to Mora Road (118) and turn right (west). From the Mora Post Office (on the right), go 8.5 miles to the concrete bridge. The cascade is on the left side of the bridge. In Kisatchie National Forest.

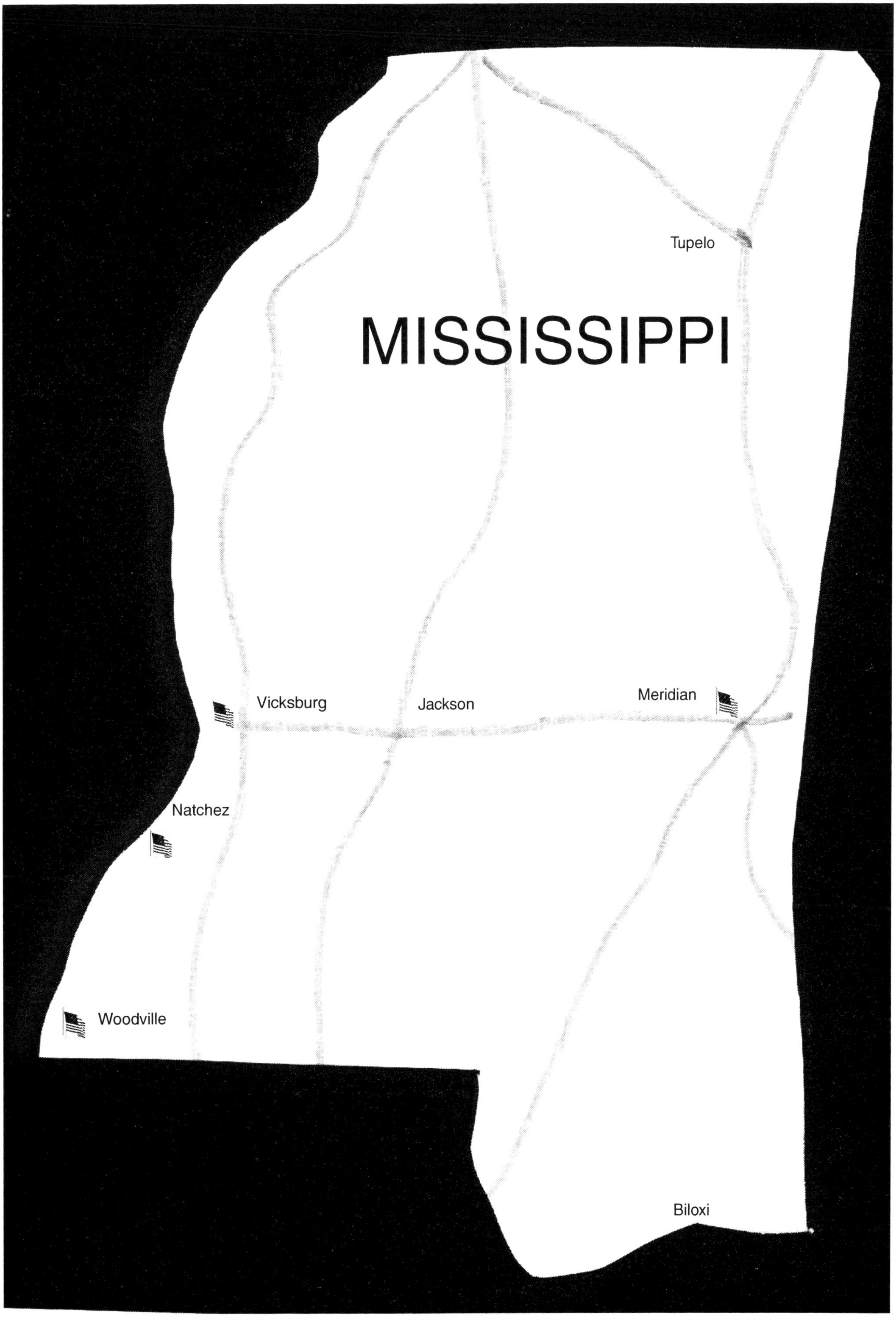

MISSISSIPPI

Tupelo

Vicksburg　　Jackson　　Meridian

Natchez

Woodville

Biloxi

Waterfall Name   Clark Creek Falls #1

State   Mississippi

Type   Segmented/Plunge

Variant Name   First Falls at Clark Creek

Height in feet   40

County   Wilkinson

Topo Map   Fort Adams

Geo Coord   310403N0913050W

Map Ref Code   31091-A5

Elevation ft   300

Water Source   Clark Creek

Seasonal Flow   Year

Section of State   SW

Directions   From Woodville, take Rt. 24 W. Near the city limits, turn left onto the road to Clark Creek Natural Area (follow sign). Go 13 miles to the pond and store (continue to follow signs to Clark Creek Natural Area). A map of the falls trail can be picked up at the store. Drive past the store about 300 yards and park in the dirt lot on the left. The trailhead is at the right end of the parking lot. The trail is steep and rugged in parts. The falls is about a 1/2 hour walk.

Waterfall Name   Clark Creek Falls #3

State   Mississippi

Type   Plunge

Variant Name   Third Falls at Clark Creek

Height in feet   30

County   Wilkinson

Topo Map   Fort Adams

Geo Coord   310410N0913105W

Map Ref Code   31091-A5

Elevation ft   250

Water Source   Clark Creek Branch

Seasonal Flow   Year

Section of State   SW

Directions   See directions for Clark Creek Falls #1. Continue past the 1st falls, stay up on the ridge trail on the right side of the creek and pass 2nd falls. Then follow the stairs that go down to the creek bed. Follow the creek bed downstream to where another creek comes in from the left (about 1/8 mile from 2nd falls). Take this left stream (upstream) about 1/8 mile to the 3rd falls.

Waterfall Name	Dunn's Falls
State	Mississippi
Type	Tiered/Cascade
Variant Name	Dunn's Mill Falls
Height in feet	65
County	Lauderdale
Topo Map	Stonewall
Geo Coord	321343N0884917W
Map Ref Code	32088-B7
Elevation ft	300
Water Source	Dunn's Spring
Seasonal Flow	Year
Section of State	SE

Directions   From Meridian, take Interstate 59 S. about 6 miles to Savoy Exit 142. Turn right (west) at the stop sign. Then make a quick left (south); follow sign to Dunn's Falls. Continue for 0.3 mile and turn left at Dunn's Falls Road. Go 2 miles and park in the lot on the right. The falls, grist mill and picnic area are a short walk down some stairs from the parking area. Entry fee.

Waterfall Name	Mint Spring Bayou Falls
State	Mississippi
Type	Block
Variant Name	Mint Spring Falls
Height in feet	40
County	Warren
Topo Map	Vicksburg East
Geo Coord	322014N0904956W
Map Ref Code	32090-C7
Elevation ft	240
Water Source	Mint Spring Bayou
Seasonal Flow	Year
Section of State	SW

Directions   From downtown Vicksburg, take Business Rt. 61 (Washington St.) N. a short distance to the southern portion of the National Cemetery. The landmarks are 4 large black cannons on the east (right) side of the street, just before the grassy area in front of the concrete arch and gate that mark the cemetery entrance. Park on the left (west) side of the street, near the concrete arch and then walk to it. Facing the arch, make a 90 degree right turn (east) and walk across the grass to a faint trail that leads into the trees and bushes. Continue about 100 yards into the woods to the falls. The hike from the cemetery gate to the falls is about 1/4 mile.

Waterfall Name	Owens Creek Falls
State	Mississippi
Type	Segmented/Tiered/Block
Variant Name	
Height in feet	10
County	Claiborne
Topo Map	Utica West
Geo Coord	320510N0904404W
Map Ref Code	32090-A6
Elevation ft	200
Water Source	Owens Creek
Seasonal Flow	Year
Section of State	SW

Directions   From Natchez, take Rt. 61 N. for about 7 miles to the Natchez Trace Parkway. Go north on the Natchez Trace Parkway to Mile Mark 59 and turn left (towards Utica). At Duke Road (stop sign), turn right towards Utica. Go about 2 miles to Hunt Road and turn right. Proceed 2 more miles on Hunt Road to a large concrete bridge. The falls is on the left side of the bridge.

Waterfall Name	Owens Creek Natchez Trace Falls
State	Mississippi
Type	Block
Variant Name	
Height in feet	15
County	Claiborne
Topo Map	Carlisle
Geo Coord	320340N0905032W
Map Ref Code	32090-A7
Elevation ft	400
Water Source	Owens Creek
Seasonal Flow	Year
Section of State	SW

Directions   From Natchez, take Rt. 61 N. about 7 miles to the Natchez Trace Parkway. Go north on the Natchez Trace Parkway to the picnic area on the left (west), 0.4 mile past Mile Mark 52. Take the short walk to the falls.

Waterfall Name	Rawson Gully Falls
State	Mississippi
Type	Horsetail
Variant Name	Falls at Rawson Gully
Height in feet	40
County	Lauderdale
Topo Map	Toomsuba
Geo Coord	322238N0883230W
Map Ref Code	32088-D5
Elevation ft	400
Water Source	Rawson Creek
Seasonal Flow	Sp
Section of State	SE

Directions   From Meridian, take Interstate 20 E. to the Russell exit. Turn right (south) onto Russell Mountain-Gilead Road and go about 2.5 miles to Betts-Radcliff Road. Continue straight past Betts-Radcliff Rd. about 100 yards to the dirt pullout on the left and park. The gully and falls are about 20 yards in, following the faint trail (CAUTION-steep ravine).

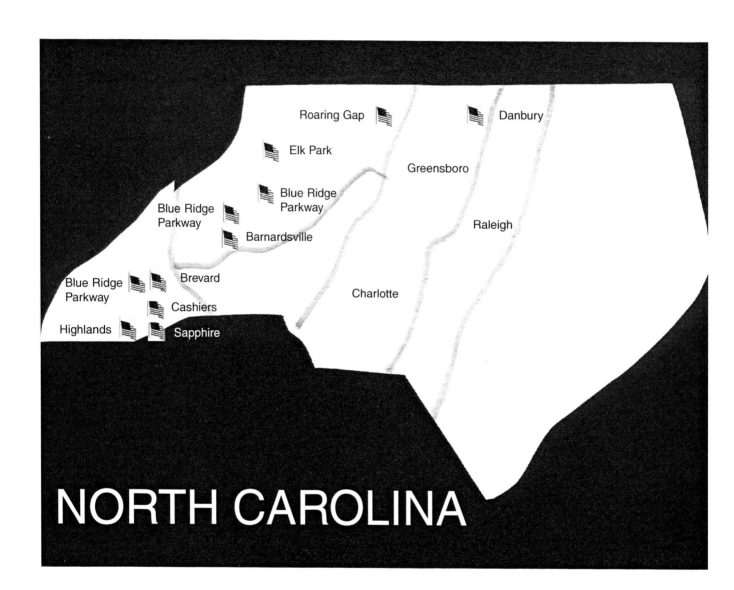

Roaring Gap

Danbury

Elk Park

Greensboro

Blue Ridge
Parkway

Blue Ridge
Parkway

Raleigh

Barnardsville

Brevard

Blue Ridge
Parkway

Charlotte

Cashiers

Highlands

Sapphire

NORTH CAROLINA

Waterfall Name	Cathey's Creek Falls
State	North Carolina
Type	Cascade
Variant Name	
Height in feet	60
County	Transylvania
Topo Map	Roman
Geo Coord	351335N0824813W
Map Ref Code	35082-B7
Elevation ft	3000
Water Source	Cathey's Creek
Seasonal Flow	Year
Section of State	SW

Directions   From downtown Brevard, take Rt. 64 W. about 4 miles and turn right onto Cathey's Creek Road (1401). There is a sign here for Kuykendall National Forest. Make a quick left turn onto Selleca Road (1338). In 0.2 mile, the road will change to gravel. Go an additional 3 miles up the mountain (pass the gauging station and three large bridges that cross Cathey's Creek). At the 3-mile point, park in the turnout on the right (do not go past the 4th bridge). Take the faint trail in the upstream direction traversing the steep hillside to the base of the falls.

Waterfall Name	Connestee Falls
State	North Carolina
Type	Twin/Fan/Tiered/Cascade
Variant Name	
Height in feet	100
County	Transylvania
Topo Map	Brevard
Geo Coord	350949N0824454W
Map Ref Code	35082-B6
Elevation ft	2600
Water Source	Carson Creek and Batson Creek
Seasonal Flow	Year
Section of State	SW

Directions   From Brevard at the junction of Routes 276 and 64, take Rt. 276 S. Go about 6 miles to the large paved parking area on the right and park (sign reads Falls Realty). From the far right corner of the parking area, walk across the bridge to the twin falls overlook.

Waterfall Name	Cullasaja Falls
State	North Carolina
Type	Segmented/Tiered/Cascade
Variant Name	
Height in feet	100
County	Macon
Topo Map	Scaly Mountain
Geo Coord	350700N0831613W
Map Ref Code	35083-A3
Elevation ft	2800
Water Source	Cullasaja River
Seasonal Flow	Year
Section of State	SW

Directions   From Highlands at the junction of Routes 106 and 64, take Rt. 64 W. Go about 9 miles to the small pullout on the left. The falls can be seen from here. Steep cliffs in this area (use CAUTION). In Nantahala National Forest.

Waterfall Name	Douglas Falls
State	North Carolina
Type	Plunge
Variant Name	
Height in feet	60
County	Buncombe
Topo Map	Mount Mitchell
Geo Coord	355234N0822019W
Map Ref Code	35082-G3
Elevation ft	3600
Water Source	Waterfall Creek
Seasonal Flow	Sp
Section of State	NW

Directions   See directions for Walker Falls. Douglas Falls is a short hike from the parking area at the end of FR 74. A total of 8.5 miles from the Corner Rock Picnic Area.

Waterfall Name	Drift Falls
State	North Carolina
Type	Cascade/Slide
Variant Name	
Height in feet	20
County	Transylvania
Topo Map	Reid
Geo Coord	350518N0825740W
Map Ref Code	35082-A8
Elevation ft	3000
Water Source	Horsepasture River
Seasonal Flow	Year
Section of State	SW

Directions   See directions for Rainbow Falls. Drift Falls is on the same trail about 0.2 mile from the parking area.

Waterfall Name	Dry Falls
State	North Carolina
Type	Block/Plunge
Variant Name	
Height in feet	80
County	Macon
Topo Map	Highlands
Geo Coord	350405N0831420W
Map Ref Code	35083-A2
Elevation ft	3500
Water Source	Cullasaja River
Seasonal Flow	Year
Section of State	SW

Directions   From Highlands at the junction of Routes 106 and 64, take Rt. 64 W. Go 3.3 miles to Dry Falls parking area on the left (look for sign). A well-developed asphalt trail goes 200 yards to the falls. In Nantahala National Forest.

Waterfall Name	Elk Falls
State	North Carolina
Type	Horsetail
Variant Name	Big Falls
Height in feet	30
County	Avery
Topo Map	Elk Park
Geo Coord	361156N0815809W
Map Ref Code	36081-B8
Elevation ft	3000
Water Source	Elk River
Seasonal Flow	Year
Section of State	NW

Directions   From Elk Park at the junction of Routes 194 and 19E, take Rt. 19E north. In a very short distance, turn right onto Road 1303 (sign here reads Elk River Falls). Go 0.4 mile and turn left onto Elk River Road (1305). Proceed 2.3 miles and the road changes to gravel; continue another 1.8 miles to the end of the road. Park in the picnic/parking area. A well-marked trail leads about 100 yards to the falls. In Pisgah National Forest.

Waterfall Name	Flat Laurel Creek Falls
State	North Carolina
Type	Horsetail
Variant Name	
Height in feet	100
County	Haywood
Topo Map	Sam Knob
Geo Coord	351910N0825312W
Map Ref Code	35082-C8
Elevation ft	5500
Water Source	Flat Laurel Creek
Seasonal Flow	Sp
Section of State	SW

Directions   From the junction of the Blue Ridge Parkway and Rt. 215, take Rt. 215 N. Go 0.8 mile to the roadside camping area on the right and park (marked with a small triangular camping symbol). Hike down dirt road to Sam Knob Trailhead marker. Follow the trail down to the stream, cross the stream and follow the old dirt roadbed to the falls. From the parking area to the falls is about 0.7 mile. The falls flows under a concrete bridge.

Waterfall Name	Glen Middle Falls
State	North Carolina
Type	Fan/Cascade
Variant Name	Middle Glen Falls
Height in feet	60
County	Macon
Topo Map	Highlands
Geo Coord	350150N0831420W
Map Ref Code	35083-A2
Elevation ft	3700
Water Source	East Fork of Overflow Creek
Seasonal Flow	Year
Section of State	SW

Directions   See directions for Glen Upper Falls.

Waterfall Name	Glen Upper Falls
State	North Carolina
Type	Segmented/Plunge
Variant Name	Upper Glen Falls
Height in feet	60
County	Macon
Topo Map	Highlands
Geo Coord	350151N0831419W
Map Ref Code	35083-A2
Elevation ft	4000
Water Source	East Fork of Overflow Creek
Seasonal Flow	Year
Section of State	SW

Directions   From Highlands, take Rt. 106 S. for 2 miles. Turn left onto the unnamed gravel road at the sign for Glen Falls Scenic Area. Go 1 mile to the parking area at the end of the road. Follow the well-marked trail about 1 mile to see the three main falls. The trail descends about 700 feet in 1 mile.

Waterfall Name	Linville Falls
State	North Carolina
Type	Tiered/Plunge
Variant Name	
Height in feet	55
County	Burke
Topo Map	Linville Falls
Geo Coord	355658N0815537W
Map Ref Code	35081-H8
Elevation ft	4000
Water Source	Linville River
Seasonal Flow	Year
Section of State	NW

Directions   From the Blue Ridge Parkway at Mile Mark 317.4, take Rt. 221 S. and then Rt. 183 S. for a total of 3 miles (follow signs to Linville Falls). Park in the gravel parking lot on the left. There are several viewpoints along the well-marked trail, varying in distance from 1/2 to 1 mile.

Waterfall Name	Looking Glass Falls
State	North Carolina
Type	Block
Variant Name	
Height in feet	50
County	Transylvania
Topo Map	Shining Rock
Geo Coord	351747N0824605W
Map Ref Code	35082-C7
Elevation ft	2400
Water Source	Looking Glass Creek
Seasonal Flow	Year
Section of State	SW

Directions   From Brevard at the junction of Routes 276 and 64, take Rt. 276 N. Go about 5 miles into Pisgah National Forest to the well-marked falls turnout on the right. The falls can be seen from here.

Waterfall Name	Rainbow Falls
State	North Carolina
Type	Fan/Cascade
Variant Name	
Height in feet	150
County	Transylvania
Topo Map	Reid
Geo Coord	350526N0825758W
Map Ref Code	35082-A8
Elevation ft	2800
Water Source	Horsepasture River
Seasonal Flow	Year
Section of State	SW

Directions   From Cashiers at the junction of Routes 107 and 64, take Rt. 64 E. Go about 10 miles to Sapphire and turn right (south) onto Rt. 281. Go 1.8 miles to the pullout on the left and park. Hike north along the guardrail to one of the steep pathways down to the main trail. Take the main trail downstream for about 1/2 mile to the falls. Drift Falls and Turtleback Falls are along the way.

Waterfall Name	Stone Mountain Falls
State	North Carolina
Type	Slide
Variant Name	
Height in feet	200
County	Wilkes
Topo Map	Glade Valley
Geo Coord	362235N0810225W
Map Ref Code	36081-D1
Elevation ft	2000
Water Source	Big Sandy Creek
Seasonal Flow	Year
Section of State	NW

Directions   From Roaring Gap, take Rt. 21 S. Go 7 miles and turn right onto Traphill Road (1002). Follow the signs to Stone Mountain State Park. Go 4.5 miles and turn right onto John Frank Parkway. Proceed another 2.5 miles to the Park entrance. Obtain a Park map. Follow the main Park road to the trailhead parking area. The trail for Stone Mountain Falls is on the left side of the paved parking area at the end of the gravel road.

Waterfall Name   Turtleback Falls

State   North Carolina

Type   Block

Variant Name

Height in feet   20

County   Transylvania

Topo Map   Reid

Geo Coord   350518N0825742W

Map Ref Code   35082-A8

Elevation ft   2900

Water Source   Horsepasture River

Seasonal Flow   Year

Section of State   SW

Directions   See directions for Rainbow Falls.

Waterfall Name   Upper Crabtree Falls

State   North Carolina

Type   Fan

Variant Name   Upper Falls

Height in feet   70

County   Yancey

Topo Map   Celo

Geo Coord   354908N0820904W

Map Ref Code   35082-G2

Elevation ft   3400

Water Source   Crabtree Creek

Seasonal Flow   Year

Section of State   NW

Directions   At Mile Mark 339.5 on the Blue Ridge Parkway, turn into Crabtree Meadows Picnic Area and park. The trailhead is at the lower right-hand corner of the parking lot. Hike about 0.9 mile to the falls.

Waterfall Name	Upper Whitewater Falls
State	North Carolina
Type	Tiered/Plunge
Variant Name	Whitewater Upper Falls
Height in feet	400
County	Transylvania
Topo Map	Cashiers
Geo Coord	350220N0830102W
Map Ref Code	35083-A1
Elevation ft	2680
Water Source	Whitewater River
Seasonal Flow	Year
Section of State	SW

Directions   From Sapphire at the intersection of Routes 281 and 64, take Rt. 281 S. Go about 9 miles to Whitewater Falls Scenic Area (follow signs). Follow the entrance road for about 0.2 mile and park in the parking lot. Hike the easy 0.2 mile to the first overlook. Stairs and steeper terrain go to several other viewpoints.

Waterfall Name	Walker Falls
State	North Carolina
Type	Cascade
Variant Name	
Height in feet	50
County	Buncombe
Topo Map	Mount Mitchell
Geo Coord	354520N0822116W
Map Ref Code	35082-G3
Elevation ft	3400
Water Source	Walker Creek
Seasonal Flow	Sp,Sm
Section of State	NW

Directions   From Barnardsville, take Rt. 197 E. Turn right onto Dillingham Road (2173). Go 5.1 miles, veering left at the Y. Continue straight onto FR 74 (gravel). In 0.4 mile, continue straight past Corner Rock Picnic Area. In another 3.9 miles, Walker Falls can be seen from the road on the left. In Pisgah National Forest.

Waterfall Name	Window Falls
State	North Carolina
Type	Plunge
Variant Name	
Height in feet	20
County	Stokes
Topo Map	Hanging Rock
Geo Coord	362403N0801535W
Map Ref Code	36080-D3
Elevation ft	1400
Water Source	Indian Creek
Seasonal Flow	Sp
Section of State	NW

Directions   From Danbury, take Rt. 89 N. and turn west onto Moore's Spring Road (SR 1001). Go 4 miles to Hanging Rock State Park entrance (follow signs). Obtain a Park map. Follow map to the trailhead for Window Falls. Hike 0.6 mile to the falls.

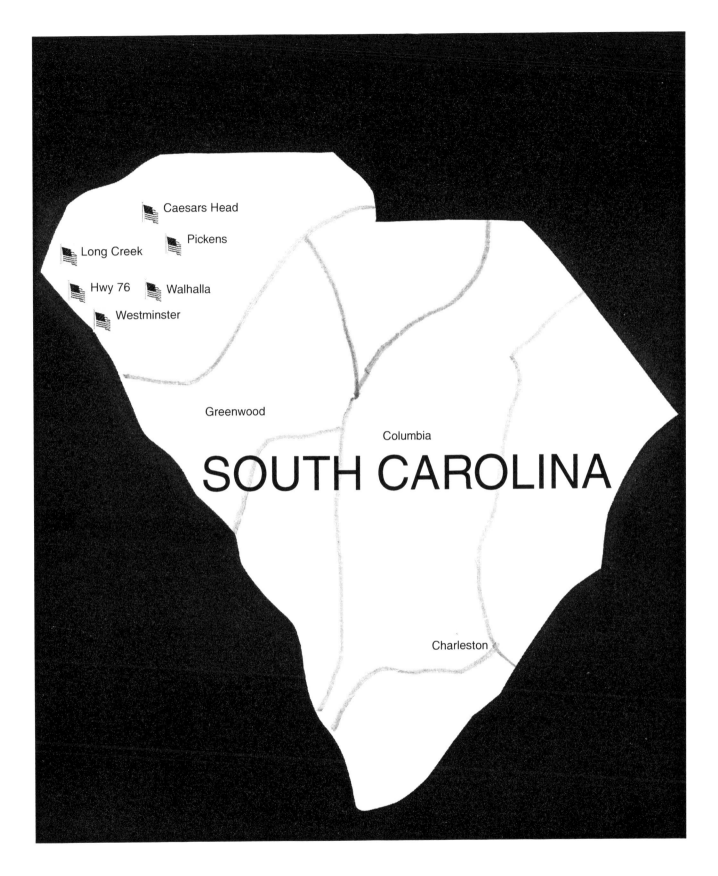

Waterfall Name	Chauga Narrows
State	South Carolina
Type	Cascade
Variant Name	
Height in feet	50
County	Oconee
Topo Map	Whetstone
Geo Coord	344950N0831018W
Map Ref Code	34083-G2
Elevation ft	1400
Water Source	Chauga River
Seasonal Flow	Year
Section of State	NW

Directions   From the bridge over the Chattooga River on Hwy. 76 (at the border of South Carolina and Georgia), take Hwy. 76 E. Go 2.1 miles and turn left onto Chattooga Ridge Road. Go 6 miles and turn right onto Rt. 193 (Whetstone Road) at the 4-way stop sign. Go 1 mile and park near the Chauga Bridge. From the SW corner of the bridge, walk about 1/4 mile down the old roadbed (look for the ruins of the old cabin). At the end of the road, follow the narrow trail another 1/4 mile to the roaring cascade.

Waterfall Name	Fall Creek Falls
State	South Carolina
Type	Fan
Variant Name	
Height in feet	35
County	Oconee
Topo Map	Whetstone
Geo Coord	344904N0831450W
Map Ref Code	34083-G2
Elevation ft	1600
Water Source	Fall Creek
Seasonal Flow	Sp
Section of State	NW

Directions   From the Long Creek Community Fire Station in Sumter National Forest, take Hwy 76 W. (Long Creek Hwy.). Go 2.5 miles and turn right onto Rt. 196 (Chattooga Ridge Rd.). Go 2 miles and turn left onto gravel FR 722 (Fall Creek Rd.). Go 1/2 mile and veer left at the Y; proceed another 1/2 mile and park on right just past where the road crosses over the creek. Walk across the road and follow the faint trail on the NW side of the creek. Follow the steep trail downstream for about 100 yards to the falls (some bushwhacking required).

Waterfall Name	Isaqueena Falls
State	South Carolina
Type	Tiered/Fan
Variant Name	
Height in feet	200
County	Oconee
Topo Map	Walhalla
Geo Coord	344822N0830716W
Map Ref Code	34083-G1
Elevation ft	1400
Water Source	Cane Creek
Seasonal Flow	Year
Section of State	NW

Directions   From Walhalla, take Hwy. 28 N. Go 5.5 miles and turn right into Stumphouse Tunnel Park (follow sign). Follow the signs to the parking area for the falls. The falls viewpoint is a short walk from the parking area.

Waterfall Name	Kings Creek Falls
State	South Carolina
Type	Cascade
Variant Name	
Height in feet	70
County	Oconee
Topo Map	Tamassee
Geo Coord	345750N0830719W
Map Ref Code	34083-H1
Elevation ft	2200
Water Source	Kings Creek
Seasonal Flow	Year
Section of State	NW

Directions   From Walhalla, take Rt. 28 N. Go about 7 miles and turn right (north) onto Rt. 107. Go 10 miles and turn left (west) onto FR 708 (New Burrells Ford Road). Go 2.4 miles and park in the Burrells Ford Campground parking area on the left. The trail starts behind the information board. Hike 0.6 mile to the falls. Most of the trail is easy with the last few hundred yards becoming steep. After crossing Kings Creek, follow the trail upstream to the falls.

Waterfall Name	Long Creek Falls
State	South Carolina
Type	Segmented/Tiered/Cascade
Variant Name	
Height in feet	40
County	Oconee
Topo Map	Rainy Mountain
Geo Coord	344520N0831633W
Map Ref Code	34083-G3
Elevation ft	1800
Water Source	Long Creek
Seasonal Flow	Year
Section of State	NW

Directions   From Westminster, take Hwy. 76 W. Go about 13 miles and turn left onto Damascus Church Road (96). Go 0.8 mile and turn right onto Battle Creek Rd. (102). Go 1.9 miles and turn right onto gravel Turkey Ridge Rd. (755). Proceed to the large parking area. From here, the road is not maintained, so 4WD vehicles only are recommended. Go 1 more mile to the trailhead at the end of the road. From here, hike 1 mile to the falls along the old roadbed. The first 1/2 mile is in a westerly direction. The next 1/2 mile is in a northerly direction. At this point, the main path is blocked by tree limbs and foliage. Take the steep downhill trail to the left about 50 yards through lots of rhododendrons and laurel. Upon reaching the confluence of the Chattooga River and Long Creek, look upstream on Long Creek to see the falls in full view. In Sumter National Forest.

Waterfall Name	Oconee Station Falls
State	South Carolina
Type	Fan/Cascade
Variant Name	
Height in feet	60
County	Oconee
Topo Map	Walhalla
Geo Coord	344508N0830310W
Map Ref Code	34083-G1
Elevation ft	1000
Water Source	Oconee Station Creek
Seasonal Flow	Year
Section of State	NW

Directions   From Walhalla, take Hwy. 183 N. Go 3 miles and turn north onto Hwy. 11. Go 2 miles and turn left onto Oconee Station Road. In 2.2 miles, continue straight past the Oconee Station Park entrance. In another 0.2 mile, park in the pullout on the left. Hike from here on the well-marked trail for about 0.7 mile to the falls.

Waterfall Name	Rainbow Falls
State	South Carolina
Type	Plunge
Variant Name	
Height in feet	100
County	Greenville
Topo Map	Standingstone Mountain
Geo Coord	350804N0823518W
Map Ref Code	35082-B5
Elevation ft	2500
Water Source	Cox Camp Creek
Seasonal Flow	Year
Section of State	NW

Directions   From Caesars Head, take US 276 N. Pass Caesars Head State Park. Turn right onto Camp Greenville Road. Go 4.3 miles to the end of the road at the YMCA Camp Office. The falls is located on the Camp's property. Obtain permission at the office as well as directions. The one hour, round-trip hike to the falls is strenuous and requires the use of some ropes (provided) to help traverse some of the steeper sections.

Waterfall Name	Raven Cliff Falls
State	South Carolina
Type	Tiered/Plunge
Variant Name	
Height in feet	400
County	Greenville
Topo Map	Table Rock
Geo Coord	350620N0823940W
Map Ref Code	35082-A6
Elevation ft	2600
Water Source	Matthews Creek
Seasonal Flow	Year
Section of State	NW

Directions   From the junction of Routes 11 and 276 near Caesars Head, take Rt. 276 N. Go a short distance past Caesars Head State Park Headquarters and park in the parking area on the right (sign here for the falls). A 2.2-mile, well-maintained trail leads to the falls overlook with some steep sections.

Waterfall Name   Spoonauger Falls

State   South Carolina

Type   Fan/Cascade

Variant Name

Height in feet   100

County   Oconee

Topo Map   Tamassee

Geo Coord   345804N0830712W

Map Ref Code   34083-H1

Elevation ft   2300

Water Source   Spoonauger Creek

Seasonal Flow   W,Sp

Section of State   NW

Directions   See directions for King Creek Falls. However, continue straight past Burrells Ford Campground parking area another 0.3 mile. Park along the shoulder of the road before reaching the bridge over the Chattooga River. Take the trail on the east side of the river and go upstream. In about 0.3 mile, cross over Spoonauger Creek. Turn right and follow the sign and trail upstream for another 200 yards to the falls.

Waterfall Name   Twin Falls

State   South Carolina

Type   Segmented/Plunge

Variant Name

Height in feet   70

County   Pickens

Topo Map   Sunset

Geo Coord   345705N0824505W

Map Ref Code   34082-H7

Elevation ft   1100

Water Source   Reedy Cove Creek

Seasonal Flow   Year

Section of State   NW

Directions   At the junction of Routes 11 and 178 near Pickens, take Rt. 178 N. Go 3.2 miles and turn left at Bob's Place onto Cleo Chapman Road. Go 2 miles and turn right at the T intersection onto Eastatoe Community Road. Go 0.9 mile and turn right onto Waterfalls Road. Proceed over the bridge and continue straight as the road changes to gravel. Follow the road as it veers left towards the woods. In about 0.3 mile, turn right onto Major Drive (gravel). Go about 0.2 mile and park in the Nature Preserve parking area. The trail begins behind the steel gate and follows the creek upstream for about 1/4 mile to the falls.

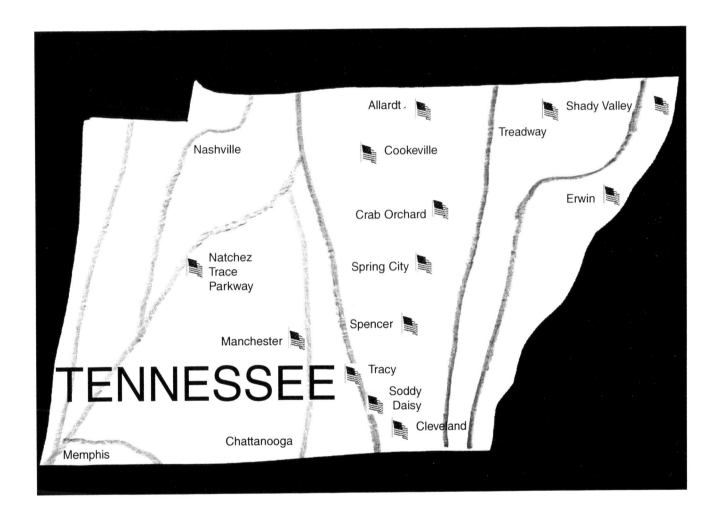

Waterfall Name	Backbone Falls
State	Tennessee
Type	Horsetail
Variant Name	
Height in feet	50
County	Johnson
Topo Map	Laurel Bloomery
Geo Coord	363540N0814950W
Map Ref Code	36081-E7
Elevation ft	2600
Water Source	Backbone Creek
Seasonal Flow	Sp
Section of State	NE

Directions   From Shady Valley at the junction of Routes 421/133/91, take Rt. 133 N. Go 9.7 miles to parking area on right just before the river and Backbone Rock. Take the Backbone Falls Trail for 0.4 mile to the falls. Use CAUTION; the trail is steep and can be slippery. In Cherokee National Forest.

Waterfall Name	Benton Falls
State	Tennessee
Type	Cascade
Variant Name	
Height in feet	70
County	Polk
Topo Map	Oswald Dome
Geo Coord	350827N0843545W
Map Ref Code	35984-B5
Elevation ft	1700
Water Source	Rock Creek
Seasonal Flow	Sp
Section of State	SE

Directions   From Cleveland, take Rt. 64 E. Upon reaching the intersection with Rt. 411, continue straight on Rt. 64 another 7.4 miles and turn left onto FR 77 (sign here reads National Forest Campground-Chilhowee). Go 7 miles up the hill and turn right into the day-use parking area of Chilhowee Camp and Recreation Area. There is a large map of the trail and surrounding area at the trailhead near the parking area. Hike the blue-blazed trail for about 1.5 miles to the falls, last 1/4 mile steepish. In Cherokee National Forest. Entry fee.

Waterfall Name   Burgess Falls

State   Tennessee

Type   Horseshoe/Block

Variant Name

Height in feet   130

County   Putnam

Topo Map   Burgess Falls

Geo Coord   360238N0853554W

Map Ref Code   36085-A5

Elevation ft   950

Water Source   Falling Water River

Seasonal Flow   Year

Section of State   NE

Directions   At the intersection of Interstate 40 and Rt. 135 near Cookeville, take Rt. 135 S. (Burgess Falls Road). Go about 8 miles and park in the lot at Burgess Falls State Natural Area (follow signs). The hike to the falls is about 3/4 mile on a well-marked, well-maintained trail, some stairs along the way. Middle Falls can be seen off to the right on the way to Burgess Falls.

Waterfall Name   Burgess Middle Falls

State   Tennessee

Type   Block

Variant Name   Middle Burgess Falls

Height in feet   40

County   Putnam

Topo Map   Burgess Falls

Geo Coord   360235N0853550W

Map Ref Code   36085-A5

Elevation ft   1000

Water Source   Falling Water River

Seasonal Flow   Year

Section of State   NE

Directions   See directions to Burgess Falls.

Waterfall Name	Chickamauga Pocket Falls
State	Tennessee
Type	Segmented/Horsetail
Variant Name	Chickamauga Falls
Height in feet	40
County	Hamilton
Topo Map	Soddy
Geo Coord	351506N0851454W
Map Ref Code	35085-C2
Elevation ft	1200
Water Source	Chickamauga Gulch Springs
Seasonal Flow	Sp
Section of State	SE

Directions   From Soddy Daisy at the intersection of Sequoyah Road and Dayton Pike, take Dayton Pike south. Go 3.1 miles and turn onto Montlake Road (sign here reads Montlake Golf & Country Club). Go 1.1 miles and turn left into the Bowater North Chickamauga Pocket Wilderness. Park here. Hike or 4WD to the last concrete picnic table (in the upstream direction) on the rough road. Follow the white-blaze trail up the hill (do not follow the main trail which goes along the creek). The falls is about 1 mile total from the parking area. A small cascade must be crossed (continue to follow the white blaze) on the way to the second creek and falls.

Waterfall Name	Elrod Falls
State	Tennessee
Type	Horsetail
Variant Name	
Height in feet	70
County	Hancock
Topo Map	Lee Valley
Geo Coord	362608N0831458W
Map Ref Code	36083-D2
Elevation ft	1400
Water Source	Flat Creek
Seasonal Flow	Sp
Section of State	NE

Directions   From Treadway at the junction of Routes 131 and 31, take Rt. 31 N. Go 2 miles and turn left onto the unnamed gravel road (brown and orange sign here reads "Elrod Falls"). Go 0.7 mile and turn left onto another unnamed gravel road (blue and brown sign here reads "Falls"). Go 1/2 mile and park in the parking area. Follow the well-developed trail a few hundred yards to the falls.

Waterfall Name	Fall Creek Falls
State	Tennessee
Type	Segmented/Plunge
Variant Name	Falls Creek Falls
Height in feet	255
County	Van Buren
Topo Map	Sampson
Geo Coord	353957N0852121W
Map Ref Code	35085-F3
Elevation ft	1600
Water Source	Fall Creek
Seasonal Flow	Year
Section of State	SE

Directions   From Spencer, take Rt. 111 S. Go 8 miles and turn left towards Fall Creek Falls State Park onto Rt. 284. Go 8 miles to the Park entrance. Follow the signs to the Information Center. Obtain a map and directions to the falls. From the Falls Creek Falls Overlook parking area, take the short walk to see the falls. There is also a steep 0.4-mile hike to the bottom of the falls from the overlook.

Waterfall Name	Foster Falls
State	Tennessee
Type	Plunge
Variant Name	
Height in feet	60
County	Marion
Topo Map	White City
Geo Coord	351054N0854033W
Map Ref Code	35085-B6
Elevation ft	1600
Water Source	Little Gizzard Creek
Seasonal Flow	Year
Section of State	SE

Directions   From Tracy at the junction of Routes 56 and 41, take Rt. 41 S. Go 8 miles (follow signs for Foster Falls) and turn towards the parking area. From the parking area, the falls overlook is closeby.

Waterfall Name	Jackson Falls
State	Tennessee
Type	Tiered/Fan
Variant Name	
Height in feet	30
County	Hickman
Topo Map	Greenfield Bend
Geo Coord	354148N0872801W
Map Ref Code	35087-F3
Elevation ft	600
Water Source	Jackson Branch
Seasonal Flow	Sp
Section of State	SW

Directions   Park in the parking area at Mile Mark 404.7 of the Natchez Trace Parkway. Follow the well-developed trail for 100 yards to the falls.

Waterfall Name	Northup Falls
State	Tennessee
Type	Plunge
Variant Name	
Height in feet	65
County	Fentress
Topo Map	Burrville
Geo Coord	362129N0845219W
Map Ref Code	36084-C7
Elevation ft	1700
Water Source	Big Branch
Seasonal Flow	Sp
Section of State	NE

Directions   From Allardt at the junction of Routes 52 and 296 W., take Rt. 52 E. Go 1.2 miles and turn right onto Northup Falls Road (signs here read Colditz Cove State Natural Area/Crooked Creek Lodge). Go 1 mile and park in the parking area for Colditz Cove Natural Area. Hike on the well-maintained trail (past the blue gate) for about 1/4 mile to the bridge over the creek and the brink of the falls. To get to the base of the falls, continue on the trail across the bridge another 1/4 mile as it descends into the gorge.

Waterfall Name	Ozone Falls
State	Tennessee
Type	Plunge
Variant Name	
Height in feet	110
County	Cumberland
Topo Map	Ozone
Geo Coord	355248N0844840W
Map Ref Code	35084-H7
Elevation ft	700
Water Source	Fall Creek
Seasonal Flow	Sp,Sm
Section of State	SE

Directions   From Interstate 40, take Exit 329 to Crab Orchard and Rt. 70. Take Rt. 70 E. for 4.5 miles and park in the small pullout on the right at Ozone Falls State Natural Area (follow sign). Follow the well-marked, steep, rocky trail for about 1/8 mile to the falls.

Waterfall Name	Piney Falls
State	Tennessee
Type	Plunge
Variant Name	
Height in feet	50
County	Van Buren
Topo Map	Spencer
Geo Coord	354023N0852303W
Map Ref Code	35085-F4
Elevation ft	1700
Water Source	Piney Creek
Seasonal Flow	Year
Section of State	SE

Directions   See directions to Fall Creek Falls. Piney Falls is located in the same Park. Obtain directions from the Information Center. The hike to the falls is about 1/2 mile.

Waterfall Name	Rutledge Falls
State	Tennessee
Type	Tiered/Block
Variant Name	
Height in feet	40
County	Coffee
Topo Map	Normandy Lake
Geo Coord	352519N0860816W
Map Ref Code	35086-D2
Elevation ft	900
Water Source	Crumpton Creek
Seasonal Flow	Year
Section of State	SE

Directions   From Manchester at the junction of Routes 41 and 55, take Rt. 55 S. Go about 3.5 miles to the John Deere Co. building on left. Continue straight another 1.2 miles and turn left onto Rutledge Falls Road. Go 1.5 miles and turn right at Rutledge Falls Church (still on Rutledge Falls Road). Go 0.1 mile and park in the gravel pullout on the right. There is a sign posted here with instructions on how to view the falls. They are on private land, but public access is allowed. A short, easy walk.

Waterfall Name	Spivey Falls
State	Tennessee
Type	Block/Plunge
Variant Name	
Height in feet	30
County	Unicoi
Topo Map	Chestoa
Geo Coord	360228N0822828W
Map Ref Code	36082-A4
Elevation ft	2600
Water Source	Spivey Creek
Seasonal Flow	Year
Section of State	NE

Directions   From Erwin at the junction of Routes 81/107 and 23/19W, take Rt. 23/19W south. Go 6.3 miles to Exit 12 (to 19W south and 352 West). Continue south on Rt. 19W. Go 5.2 miles up the mountain and park in the pullout on the right. Walk up the road a few hundred feet to the private driveway and Spivey Falls sign on the right. The owners of the property have graciously allowed public access to the falls via the 250 stairs down the cliffside.

Waterfall Name	Upper Piney Falls
State	Tennessee
Type	Plunge
Variant Name	
Height in feet	80
County	Rhea
Topo Map	Spring City
Geo Coord	354352N0845149W
Map Ref Code	35084-F7
Elevation ft	1300
Water Source	Little Piney Creek
Seasonal Flow	Year
Section of State	SE

Directions   At the junction of Routes 27 and 68 near Spring City, take Rt. 68 N. (Wassom Memorial Hwy). Go 4.9 miles up the mountain and turn sharply left onto Firetower Rd. Follow the sign to Piney Falls State Natural Area. Go 1.5 miles and park in the small pullout on the right. There is a 4WD road leading down the hillside at the pullout. The pullout is before the firetower and before the high power lines (no sign). Hike down the dirt 4WD road about 3/4 mile to the rustic camping area. At this point, follow the path to the left and down the cliffside. Veer right at the Y and continue another 1/4 mile to the base of the falls. By veering left at the Y, the trail leads to Lower Piney Falls.

Waterfall Name	Apple Orchard Falls
State	Virginia
Type	Fan
Variant Name	
Height in feet	200
County	Botetourt
Topo Map	Arnold Valley
Geo Coord	373056N0793157W
Map Ref Code	37079-E5
Elevation ft	2400
Water Source	North Creek
Seasonal Flow	Sp
Section of State	NW

Directions   From the Blue Ridge Parkway at the Sunset Fields Overlook parking area (between Mile Marks 78 and 79), take FS 812 (gravel) down the mountain. FS 812 is on the north side of the parking area. Go 2.9 miles (veering left at the first Y) and turn left onto FS 3034. Go 2 miles and park in the parking area at the end of the road. Follow the signs to the falls for about 1/2 mile up the rocky, strenuous trail.

Waterfall Name	Cascade Falls
State	Virginia
Type	Plunge/Cascade
Variant Name	Cascades Falls
Height in feet	65
County	Giles
Topo Map	Eggleston
Geo Coord	372218N0803452W
Map Ref Code	37080-C5
Elevation ft	3000
Water Source	Stoney Creek
Seasonal Flow	Year
Section of State	SW

Directions   From Pembroke at the intersection of Main St. (Rt. 460) and Cascade Rd. (Rt. 623), take Cascade Rd. north. Go 4 miles to Jefferson National Forest Recreation Site/Cascades (follow sign). Take the well-marked trail 2 miles to the falls (gradual uphill). Entry fee.

Waterfall Name	Crabtree Falls
State	Virginia
Type	Tiered/Horsetail
Variant Name	
Height in feet	400
County	Nelson
Topo Map	Massies Mill
Geo Coord	375035N0790429W
Map Ref Code	37079-G1
Elevation ft	2600
Water Source	Crabtree Creek
Seasonal Flow	Year
Section of State	NW

Directions   From the Blue Ridge Parkway near Montebello, take Rt. 56 E. Go 7 miles and park in the George Washington National Forest Recreation Site/Crabtree Falls parking area on right (follow signs). Hike the uphill trail 1.4 miles viewing the 1200 feet of cascades along the way.

Waterfall Name	Cypress Falls
State	Virginia
Type	Segmented/Cascade
Variant Name	Twin Falls
Height in feet	35
County	Rockbridge
Topo Map	Cornwall
Geo Coord	374740N0792005W
Map Ref Code	37079-G3
Elevation ft	1000
Water Source	Sheep Creek
Seasonal Flow	Sp
Section of State	NW

No
Photo
Available

Directions   From Buena Vista at the junction of Rt. 60 and Catalpa Rd., take Catalpa Road north. Go 0.7 mile and turn right onto Longhollow Rd. (631). Go 1.3 miles and veer left onto Old Buena Vista Road (631). Continue another 1.7 miles and turn right onto South River Road (608). Go 1.8 miles and park in the pullout on the left. The falls can be viewed across the river from here.

Waterfall Name	Dismal Falls
State	Virginia
Type	Segmented/Block
Variant Name	Falls of Dismal
Height in feet	15
County	Giles
Topo Map	Mechanicsburg
Geo Coord	371118N0805402W
Map Ref Code	37080-B8
Elevation ft	2300
Water Source	Dismal Creek
Seasonal Flow	Year
Section of State	SW

Directions   From Bland at the junction of Routes 42 E. and 52, take Rt. 42 E. Go 13.4 miles and turn left (north) onto Road 606. Go about 1 mile and turn right onto Road 201 (just past the bridge). Go 0.4 mile and the road changes to gravel (border of Jefferson National Forest). Continue straight another 1/2 mile and park in the turnout on the right (sign here for Dismal Falls). Follow the trail about 400 feet to the falls.

Waterfall Name	Falling Spring Falls
State	Virginia
Type	Segmented/Plunge
Variant Name	
Height in feet	70
County	Alleghany
Topo Map	Covington
Geo Coord	375222N0795722W
Map Ref Code	37079-G8
Elevation ft	2300
Water Source	Falling Spring
Seasonal Flow	Year
Section of State	NW

Directions   From Interstate 64 and Rt. 220 (Exit 16 in Covington), go north on Rt. 220. Go 9.7 miles and park in the large parking area on the left (west) side of the road. A sign for Falling Spring Viewpoint is located about 1000 feet before the parking area.

Waterfall Name	Garrett Creek Falls
State	Virginia
Type	Segmented/Block
Variant Name	
Height in feet	25
County	Washington
Topo Map	Brumley
Geo Coord	364510N0850501W
Map Ref Code	36085-G1
Elevation ft	1700
Water Source	Garrett Creek
Seasonal Flow	Year
Section of State	SW

Directions From Lebanon at the junction of Rt. 19, Business 19, and Rt. 660, take Rt. 19 S. Go 11.7 miles and turn right (west) onto Road 611 (just past the Holston River Bridge). Go 2.1 miles (road changes to gravel) and the falls can be viewed off to the right. There is a small pullout on the right for parking just past the falls. On private property.

Waterfall Name	Great Falls
State	Virginia
Type	Cascade
Variant Name	Great Falls of the Potomac
Height in feet	70
County	Fairfax
Topo Map	Vienna
Geo Coord	385955N0771517W
Map Ref Code	38077-H3
Elevation ft	550
Water Source	Potomac River
Seasonal Flow	Year
Section of State	NE

Directions At the intersection of Interstate 495 and Rt. 193 (Exit 13, Georgetown Pike) near Washington D.C., take Rt. 193 NW. Go 9 miles and turn right onto Old Dominion Dr. Go 1 mile and park at Great Falls Park (follow signs). The falls viewpoints are a short walk from the parking area. Entry fee.

Waterfall Name	Little Stoney Creek Lower Falls
State	Virginia
Type	Block/Cascade
Variant Name	Lower Little Stoney Creek Falls
Height in feet	15
County	Scott
Topo Map	Dungannon
Geo Coord	365150N0822720W
Map Ref Code	36082-G4
Elevation ft	2200
Water Source	Little Stoney Creek
Seasonal Flow	Year
Section of State	SW

Directions From Dungannon, take Rt. 72 N. Go 8.6 miles and turn left onto Road 664 (Corder Town Road). Go 1.1 miles and turn left onto the unnamed gravel road (sign reads Jefferson National Forest/Falls of Little Stoney). Go about 2 miles and turn left onto gravel Road 701 (sign for Falls National Recreation Trail). Go 1 mile and park in the large parking area on the left. The trail starts at the far end of the parking area. Hike 0.2 mile to Upper Falls and 0.2 mile further to Lower Falls.

Waterfall Name	Little Stoney Creek Upper Falls
State	Virginia
Type	Plunge
Variant Name	Upper Little Stoney Creek Falls
Height in feet	25
County	Scott
Topo Map	Dungannon
Geo Coord	365155N0822718W
Map Ref Code	36082-G4
Elevation ft	2250
Water Source	Little Stoney Creek
Seasonal Flow	Year
Section of State	SW

Directions See directions for Little Stoney Creek Lower Falls.

Waterfall Name	Panther Falls
State	Virginia
Type	Block
Variant Name	
Height in feet	15
County	Amherst
Topo Map	Buena Vista
Geo Coord	374235N0791728W
Map Ref Code	37079-F3
Elevation ft	1300
Water Source	Pedlar River
Seasonal Flow	Year
Section of State	NW

Directions   From the Blue Ridge Parkway between Mile Marks 40 and 50, take Rt. 60 E. Go about 0.1 mile and turn right onto the first gravel road (Panther Falls Road/FS 315). Go 3.6 miles and turn left onto gravel FS 315A. Go 1/2 mile and park in the parking area on the left. Hike down the dirt road past the locked gate. At the bottom of the hill, take the trail to the left (upstream). The falls will come into view in a short distance. Total hike from the parking area to falls is about 1/2 mile.

Waterfall Name	Roaring Run Lower Falls
State	Virginia
Type	Slide
Variant Name	Lower Roaring Run Falls
Height in feet	20
County	Botetourt
Topo Map	Strom
Geo Coord	374230N0795430W
Map Ref Code	37079-F8
Elevation ft	1300
Water Source	Roaring Run
Seasonal Flow	Year
Section of State	NW

Directions   From Interstate 64 and Rt. 696 (Exit 21 to Low Moor), take Rt. 696 S. Go 0.4 mile and turn right onto Rt. 616 (Rich Patch Road). Go 5.5 miles and turn left onto Rt. 621 (Roaring Run Road). Go 3.3 miles and turn right towards Jefferson National Forest Historic Site/Roaring Run Furnace. Go 0.3 mile to parking area. Follow the trail about 0.6 mile, taking in several falls and cascades along the way. The largest falls is past the third wooden bridge.

Waterfall Name	Roaring Run Upper Falls
State	Virginia
Type	Slide
Variant Name	Upper Roaring Run Falls
Height in feet	40
County	Botetourt
Topo Map	Strom
Geo Coord	374229N0795426W
Map Ref Code	37079-F8
Elevation ft	1400
Water Source	Roaring Run
Seasonal Flow	Year
Section of State	NW

Directions   See directions for Roaring Run Lower Falls.

Waterfall Name	White Branch Falls
State	Virginia
Type	Horsetail/Plunge
Variant Name	
Height in feet	40
County	Lee
Topo Map	Rose Hill
Geo Coord	364204N0832226W
Map Ref Code	36083-F3
Elevation ft	1900
Water Source	White Branch
Seasonal Flow	Year
Section of State	SW

Directions   From Rose Hill at the junction of Routes 58 and 673 (near the Post Office), take Rt. 673 N. Go 0.7 mile and turn left onto Road 797 (4WD recommended). Park in pullout on right. Walk up Road 797 for about 0.3 mile to where road turns sharply right. At this point, continue straight up the mountainside on the overgrown logging road. The creek will be to the left. A little bushwhacking is required. Cross the creek (creek now on the right) and follow the faint trail steeply up the mountainside to the falls. Total distance from the pullout to the falls is about 1/2 mile.

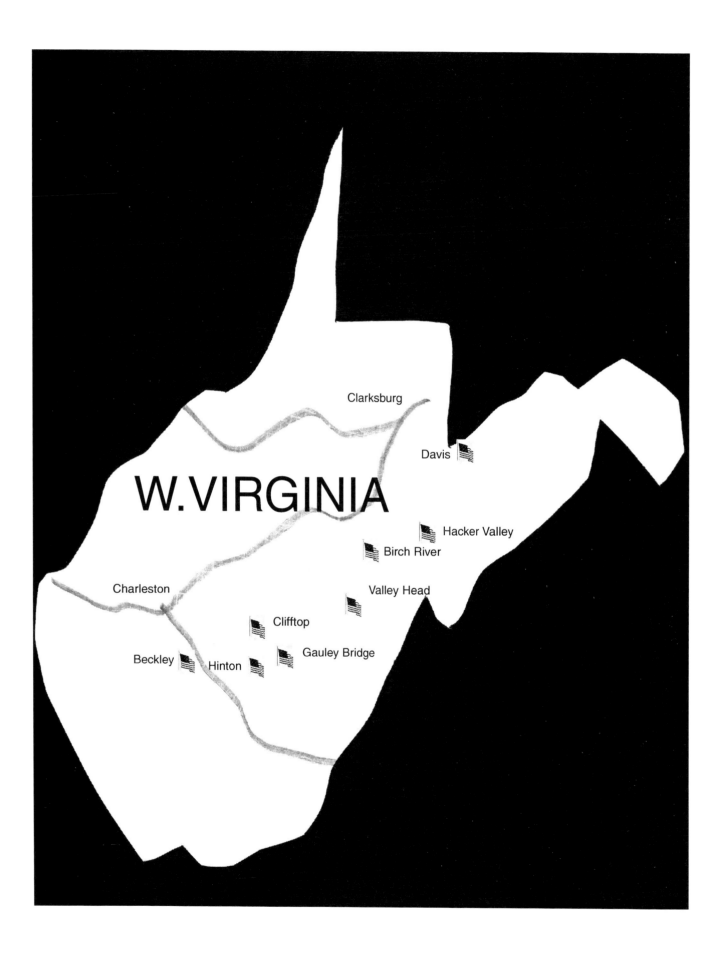

Waterfall Name	Blackwater Falls
State	West Virginia
Type	Horseshoe/Block
Variant Name	
Height in feet	65
County	Tucker
Topo Map	Blackwater Falls
Geo Coord	390649N0792900W
Map Ref Code	39079-A4
Elevation ft	3100
Water Source	Blackwater River
Seasonal Flow	Year
Section of State	NE

Directions   From Davis at the junction of Route 32 and Blackwater Falls Road 29, take Blackwater Falls Road to the SW. Go about 1.5 miles to Blackwater Falls State Park entrance (follow sign). Follow the signs to the parking area for the falls. From the parking area, take 214 stairs down to the falls viewpoints.

Waterfall Name	Cathedral Falls
State	West Virginia
Type	Horsetail
Variant Name	Falls at Gauley Bridge
Height in feet	80
County	Fayette
Topo Map	Gauley Bridge
Geo Coord	380912N0811007W
Map Ref Code	38081-B2
Elevation ft	700
Water Source	Cane Branch
Seasonal Flow	Sp
Section of State	SW

Directions   From Gauley Bridge at the junction of Routes 16/39/60, take Rt. 60 E. Go 1.8 miles and park in the parking area on the left (just past the RR crossing). Take the very short walk to the falls from here.

Waterfall Name	Falls of Elakala-Lower
State	West Virginia
Type	Cascade
Variant Name	Lower Falls of Elakala
Height in feet	30
County	Tucker
Topo Map	Mozark Mountain
Geo Coord	390608N0793010W
Map Ref Code	39079-A5
Elevation ft	3200
Water Source	Elakala Creek
Seasonal Flow	Year
Section of State	NE
Directions	Same directions as Falls of Elakala-Upper.

Waterfall Name	Falls of Elakala-Upper
State	West Virginia
Type	Segmented/Block
Variant Name	Upper Falls of Elakala
Height in feet	20
County	Tucker
Topo Map	Mozark Mountain
Geo Coord	390612N0793002W
Map Ref Code	39079-A5
Elevation ft	3250
Water Source	Elakala Creek
Seasonal Flow	Year
Section of State	NE
Directions	See directions for Blackwater Falls. Once in the Park, follow the signs to Blackwater Lodge. Follow the trail at the south end of Blackwater Lodge parking lot. Walk about 1/8 mile to the falls and cascades.

Waterfall Name	Glade Creek Falls
State	West Virginia
Type	Segmented/Cascade
Variant Name	Grist Mill Falls
Height in feet	12
County	Fayette
Topo Map	Danese
Geo Coord	375812N0805710W
Map Ref Code	37080-H8
Elevation ft	2280
Water Source	Glade Creek
Seasonal Flow	Year
Section of State	SW

Directions   From Clifftop, take Rt. 41 S. Go 4 miles and turn into Babcock State Park. Follow signs to Grist Mill and Park Office. The falls are a few stairsteps away from the office.

Waterfall Name	McCoy Falls
State	West Virginia
Type	Segmented/Plunge
Variant Name	
Height in feet	15
County	Webster
Topo Map	Tioga
Geo Coord	382904N0803935W
Map Ref Code	38080-D6
Elevation ft	1400
Water Source	Birch River
Seasonal Flow	Sp,Sm
Section of State	SE

Directions   From Birch River at the junction of Routes 19 and 82 E., take Rt. 82 E. Go 7.6 miles and park in the gravel turnout on the left (east) side of the road. The falls are directly across the road. Follow the narrow, steep trail down to the falls.

Waterfall Name	Sandstone Falls
State	West Virginia
Type	Block
Variant Name	
Height in feet	20
County	Raleigh
Topo Map	Meadow Creek
Geo Coord	374530N0805420W
Map Ref Code	37080-G8
Elevation ft	1300
Water Source	New River
Seasonal Flow	Year
Section of State	SE

Directions   In Hinton at the junction of Rt. 20 and River Rd. at the west end of the bridge over the New River, take River Road north. Go 9 miles on this one-lane road and park in the parking area on the right. Follow the wooden boardwalk for several hundred yards to the numerous view-points. The falls are over 1500 feet wide.

Waterfall Name	Shupe's Chute
State	West Virginia
Type	Horsetail
Variant Name	
Height in feet	15
County	Webster
Topo Map	Goshen
Geo Coord	383738N0801808W
Map Ref Code	38080-F3
Elevation ft	1800
Water Source	Fall Run
Seasonal Flow	W,Sp,Sm
Section of State	SE

Directions   From Hacker Valley at the Post Office, take Rt. 20 N. Go 0.9 mile and turn right onto Left Fork Holly River Road. Go 4.2 miles (changes to gravel) and park in the parking area for Upper Falls/Potatoe Knob/Shupe's Chute on the right. Hike down the old dirt road for 1/8 mile to the falls. In Holly River State Park.

Waterfall Name	Upper Twin Falls
State	West Virginia
Type	Plunge
Variant Name	
Height in feet	20
County	Wyoming
Topo Map	Mullens
Geo Coord	373720N0812510W
Map Ref Code	37081-E4
Elevation ft	1800
Water Source	Bearpen Branch/Horsepen Branch
Seasonal Flow	Sp
Section of State	SW

Directions   From Beckley at the junction of West Virginia Turnpike 77 and Rt. 16 (Exit 42), take Rt. 16 S. Go 4.2 miles and turn south onto Rt. 54 S. (Sign here to Twin Falls State Park.) Go 14 miles and turn right onto Rt. 97. Go 5.5 miles and turn left at the stop sign onto Bear Hole Road. From here, follow the signs to the falls. Follow the rocky trail to the Lower Falls off to the right. Continue on the main trail (veering left at the Y) to the end and the Upper Falls (about 0.3 mile total).

Waterfall Name	Whitaker Falls
State	West Virginia
Type	Tiered/Cascade
Variant Name	
Height in feet	10
County	Randolph
Topo Map	Samp
Geo Coord	383130N0801103W
Map Ref Code	38080-E2
Elevation ft	2300
Water Source	Elk River
Seasonal Flow	Year
Section of State	SE

Directions   From Valley Head at the junction of Routes 219 and 15 W., take Rt. 15 W. Go 4.5 miles and turn left just past the quarry onto Rt. 49. Go 6.5 miles (road changes to gravel) to view the falls from the road on the left. In Monongahela National Forest.

CHAPTER 6

The North Eastern States

Connecticut
Maine
Maryland
Massachusetts
New Hampshire
New Jersey
New York
Pennsylvania
Rhode Island
Vermont

Taughannock Falls
NEW YORK

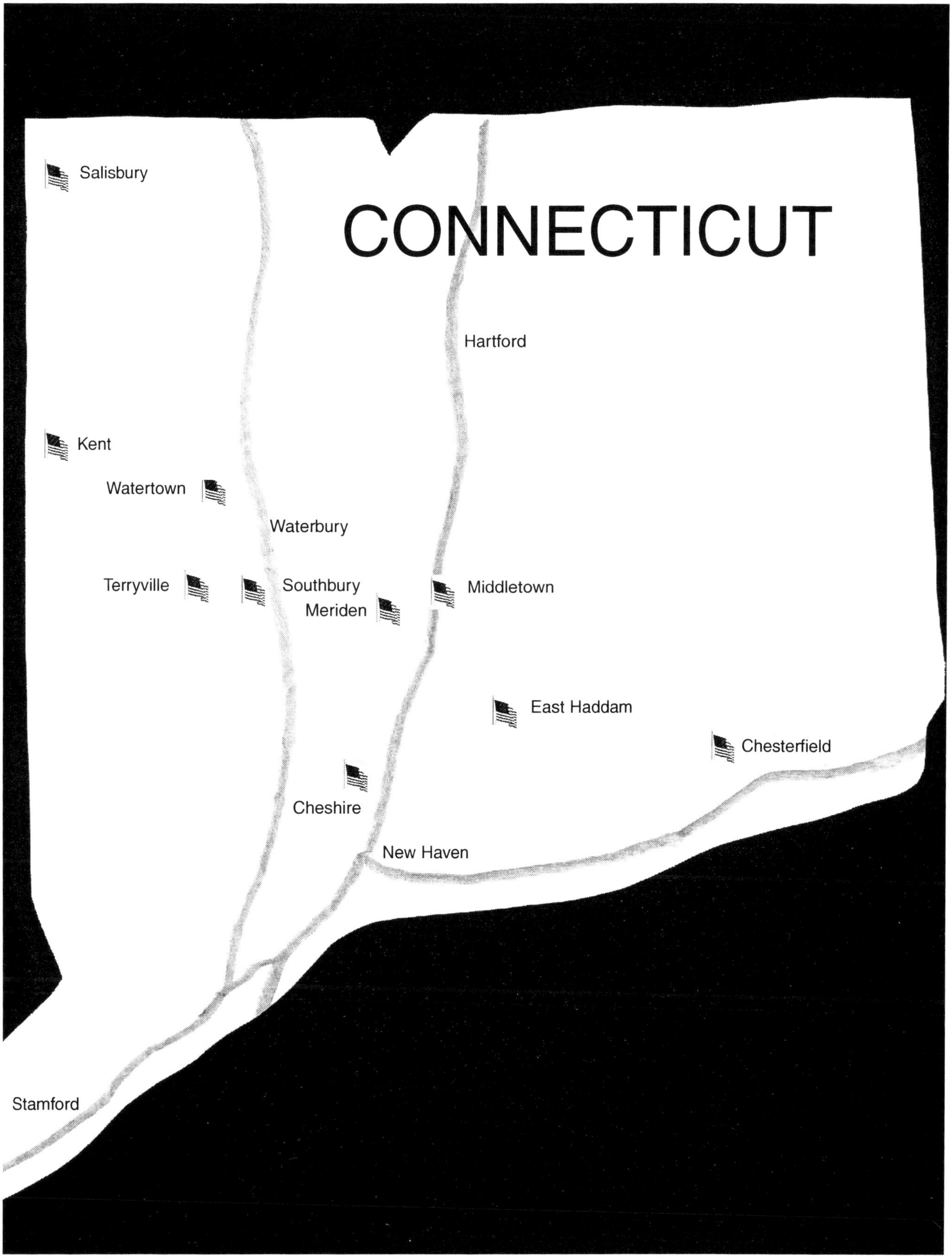

CONNECTICUT

Salisbury

Hartford

Kent

Watertown

Waterbury

Terryville   Southbury   Middletown
               Meriden

East Haddam

Chesterfield

Cheshire

New Haven

Stamford

Waterfall Name	Buttermilk Falls
State	Connecticut
Type	Segmented/Horsetail
Variant Name	
Height in feet	40
County	Litchfield
Topo Map	Thomaston
Geo Coord	413838N0730019W
Map Ref Code	41073-F1
Elevation ft	700
Water Source	Indian Heaven Creek
Seasonal Flow	W,Sp,Sm
Section of State	NW

Directions   In Terryville at the junction of Rt. 6 and S. Main St., go south on S. Main St. for 0.3 mile. Veer right at the Y staying on S. Main St. for another windy 1.2 miles. Coming to an intersection, turn right to stay on S. Main St. for another 1.2 miles to Lane Hill Rd. Turn left and go uphill for 0.2 mile to a small turnout on the right and park. Sign for Nature Sanctuary here. Follow the blue-blazed trail for 100 feet to the falls.

Waterfall Name	Chapman Falls
State	Connecticut
Type	Tiered/Segmented/Cascade
Variant Name	
Height in feet	60
County	Middlesex
Topo Map	Hamburg
Geo Coord	412900N0722028W
Map Ref Code	41072-D3
Elevation ft	260
Water Source	Eight Mile River
Seasonal Flow	Year
Section of State	SE

Directions   Near East Haddam at the junction of Routes 82 and 156 (Devil's Hopyard Rd.), take Rt.156 N. about 3 miles to Devil's Hopyard State Park. Turn into the park and follow the signs to the falls. The falls is a short distance from the parking area.

Waterfall Name   Kent Lower Falls

State   Connecticut

Type   Tiered/Cascade

Variant Name   Lower Kent Falls

Height in feet   80

County   Litchfield

Topo Map   Ellsworth

Geo Coord   414602N0732410W

Map Ref Code   41073-G4

Elevation ft   550

Water Source   Kent Falls Brook

Seasonal Flow   Year

Section of State   NW

Directions   In Kent from the junction of Routes 7 and 341, go north on Rt. 7 for 5.1 miles to Kent Falls State Park. The Lower Falls can be seen from the parking area; the Upper Falls requires a steep 1/4-mile hike, but is well worth the effort.

Waterfall Name   Kent Upper Falls

State   Connecticut

Type   Segmented/Plunge

Variant Name   Upper Kent Falls

Height in feet   60

County   Litchfield

Topo Map   Ellsworth

Geo Coord   414550N0732405W

Map Ref Code   41073-G4

Elevation ft   750

Water Source   Kent Falls Brook

Seasonal Flow   Year

Section of State   NW

Directions   See directions to Kent Lower Falls.

Waterfall Name	Nonnewaug Falls
State	Connecticut
Type	Horsetail/Plunge
Variant Name	
Height in feet	30
County	Litchfield
Topo Map	Woodbury
Geo Coord	413658N0730958W
Map Ref Code	41073-E2
Elevation ft	600
Water Source	Watertown Branch
Seasonal Flow	Sp
Section of State	SW

Directions   Just south of Watertown from the junction of Routes 6 W. and 61 N., take Rt. 61 N. for 0.8 mile. Veer right onto Nonnewaug Rd. Go 0.6 mile and continue straight at the Y (Hickory Lane goes left). In 0.1 mile, continue straight onto Falls Road (dirt). Go another 0.2 mile and park in the pullout on the right. The sign here will read "No motorized vehicles beyond this point". Walk up the rock roadway to the right and veer right at the Y. Continue up the rock roadway another 1/4 mile to a meadow. Walk 100 yards across the meadow and through the trees to the ravine and the falls.

Waterfall Name	Roaring Brook Falls
State	Connecticut
Type	Horsetail
Variant Name	
Height in feet	40
County	Hartford
Topo Map	Mount Carmel
Geo Coord	412850N0725630W
Map Ref Code	41072-D8
Elevation ft	600
Water Source	Roaring Brook
Seasonal Flow	Sp
Section of State	NW

Directions   From the junction of Routes 10 and 42 just south of Cheshire, go west on Rt. 42 (North Brooksvale Rd.) for 1.4 miles to Mountain Road. Turn right and go 0.4 mile to Roaring Brook Rd. Turn left and go 0.2 mile to the end of the road and park. The trailhead sign is at the gate on the dirt road. Follow the orange-blaze steep trail about 1/2 mile to the falls.

Waterfall Name	Silver Falls
State	Connecticut
Type	Cascade
Variant Name	
Height in feet	15
County	New London
Topo Map	Montville
Geo Coord	412443N0721309W
Map Ref Code	41072-D2
Elevation ft	160
Water Source	Latimer Brook
Seasonal Flow	Sp
Section of State	SE

Directions   In Chesterfield at the junction of Routes 85 and 161, take Rt. 161 S. for 0.9 mile to the second road on the left (unmarked). Turn left and go 0.3 mile. After crossing the bridge, there will be a large lawn area on the left (look for concrete picnic table). Park here. The falls is down the small stairway.

Waterfall Name	Southford Falls
State	Connecticut
Type	Tiered/Cascade
Variant Name	
Height in feet	60
County	New Haven
Topo Map	Southbury
Geo Coord	412720N0731001W
Map Ref Code	41073-D2
Elevation ft	600
Water Source	Papermill Creek
Seasonal Flow	Year
Section of State	SW

Directions   From the junction of Interstate 84 and Rt. 67 (Exit 15 just south of Southbury), take Rt. 67 S. for 3 miles to Rt. 188. Turn right (south) and go approx. 0.4 mile to Southford Falls State Park. The parking area is on the left. The falls and covered bridge are a short hike from the parking area south of the small lake.

Waterfall Name	The Cascades
State	Connecticut
Type	Cascade
Variant Name	Cascades
Height in feet	40
County	Litchfield
Topo Map	Bash Bish Falls (MA)
Geo Coord	420201N0732720W
Map Ref Code	42073-A4
Elevation ft	1700
Water Source	Wachoeastinook Creek
Seasonal Flow	Year
Section of State	NW

Directions   In Salisbury at the junction of Main St. (Rt. 41) and Factory/Washinee Rd. (on the south side of Town Hall), go west on Factory/Washinee Rd. In 0.2 mile, veer right at the Y staying on F/W Road. Go another 1/2 mile to Mt. Riga Rd. (sign says Mt. Riga). Turn left and go 0.1 mile to the Y and veer right to stay on Mt. Riga Rd. Go 2.2 more miles (road turns to gravel) and park in the pullout on the right (sign for "The Cascades"). Hike about 100 feet to the falls, steepish. In Mt. Riga Forest Preserve.

Waterfall Name	Wadsworth Falls
State	Connecticut
Type	Block/Cascade
Variant Name	
Height in feet	30
County	Middlesex
Topo Map	Middletown
Geo Coord	413132N0724149W
Map Ref Code	41072-E6
Elevation ft	200
Water Source	Coginchaug River
Seasonal Flow	Year
Section of State	SE

Directions   From Middletown, take Rt. 66 W. to Rt. 157. Take Rt. 157 S. for about 2.7 miles (follow signs for Wadsworth Falls State Park). At Cherry Hill Rd., turn left and go 0.2 mile to the parking area on the left. The falls is a short, easy walk from the parking area.

Waterfall Name	Westfield Falls
State	Connecticut
Type	Horsetail
Variant Name	
Height in feet	20
County	Middlesex
Topo Map	Middletown
Geo Coord	413449N0724255W
Map Ref Code	41072-E6
Elevation ft	140
Water Source	Fall Brook
Seasonal Flow	Sp
Section of State	SE

Directions   Heading north on Interstate 91 just north of Meriden, take Exit 20 (Country Club Road). Go east (right). Make an immediate left onto Miner St. Go 0.9 mile to a small pullout on the left and park. Large concrete blocks frame the pullout. Take the short, rocky 50-yard hike down to the falls from the parking area.

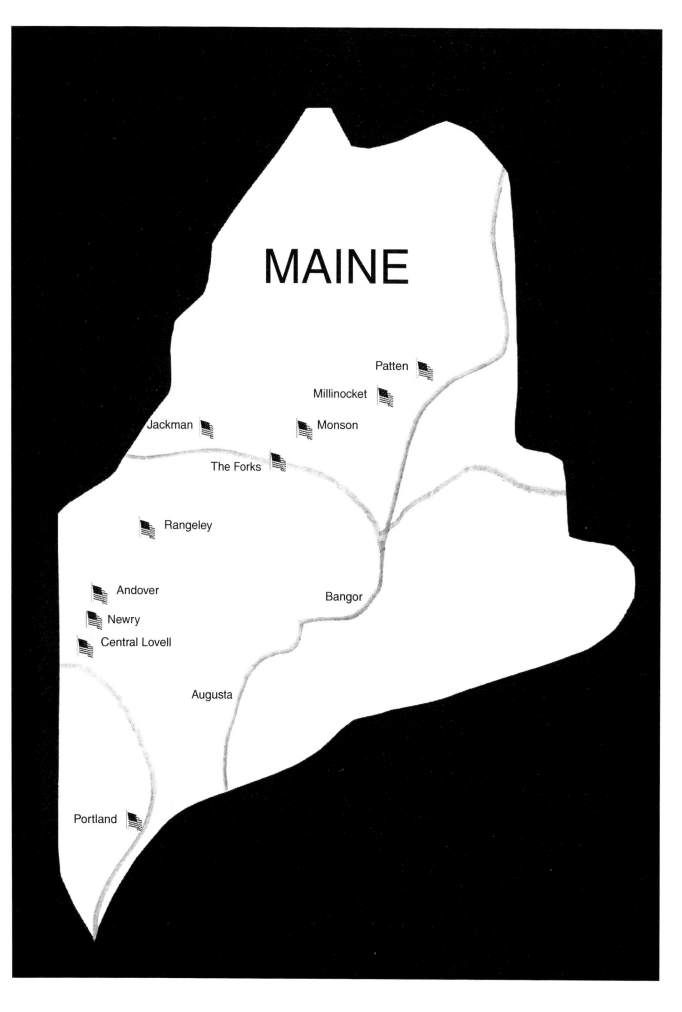

MAINE

Patten

Millinocket

Jackman   Monson

The Forks

Rangeley

Andover

Newry   Bangor

Central Lovell

Augusta

Portland

Waterfall Name	Big Niagara Falls
State	Maine
Type	Tiered/Block/Cascade
Variant Name	
Height in feet	25
County	Piscataquis
Topo Map	Rainbow Lake East
Geo Coord	455213N0690216W
Map Ref Code	45069-G1
Elevation ft	880
Water Source	Nesowadnehunk Stream
Seasonal Flow	Year
Section of State	NE

Directions   From Millinocket, take Rt. 157 N. about 18 miles to Baxter State Park (follow signs). At the Togue Pond Gatehouse (entrance to park), obtain a map and directions to Daicey Pond parking area. The hike from Daicey Pond parking area to Big Niagara is 1.2 miles, traveling south on the Appalachian Trail. Entry fee. No motorcycles. No vehicles over 9' tall, 7' wide, and 22' long.

Waterfall Name	Dunn Falls
State	Maine
Type	Horsetail
Variant Name	
Height in feet	75
County	Oxford
Topo Map	B Pond
Geo Coord	443949N0705302W
Map Ref Code	44070-F8
Elevation ft	1400
Water Source	West Branch Ellis River
Seasonal Flow	Year
Section of State	SW

Directions   In Andover at the junction of Newton St. and Main St., go west (towards Upton) on Newton St. (becomes East Bee Hill Rd). In about 8.3 miles, park in the pullout on the left (white trail blazes on the trees mark the access to the Appalachian Trail). Follow the Appalachian Trail to the left (downhill) to the sign reading "Cascade Trail 0.6 mile to Ellis River and 0.7 mile to Junction Side Trail to Falls". Follow the Cascade Trail downstream, cross 3 streams, following the blue blazes all the way to the sign for "Base of Falls 740 feet". From the pullout to the falls is approx. 0.9 mile, with some rocky and steep sections. In Mahoosucs Public Reserved Land area.

Waterfall Name	Haskell Pitch Falls
State	Maine
Type	Tiered/Block/Cascade
Variant Name	Haskell Rock Pitch Falls
Height in feet	30
County	Penobscot
Topo Map	The Traveler
Geo Coord	460430N0684525W
Map Ref Code	46068-A7
Elevation ft	620
Water Source	E Branch Penobscot River
Seasonal Flow	Year
Section of State	NE

Directions   From Patten, take Rt. 159 W. about 24 miles to the bridge over the East Branch Penobscot River (just past the Matagamon Wilderness Campground). From here, go another 0.2 mile on Rt. 159 W. to the second gravel road on the left after bridge (unnamed) and turn left. Go 1.9 miles to Crossover Road (also called GNP Road) and turn left. Go 0.4 mile to River Road and continue straight. In 2.6 miles, look for Mile Mark 5 (up in tree on left) and continue straight another 1.2 miles. Park in the small pullout on the left (before the hill). Walk up the hill and in about 0.1 mile, veer left at the fork onto the old rocky 4WD road. Pass Pond Pitch sign (on the left), pass the green 7-mile sign, and then veer left where the road forks. The road becomes a small trail at this point. At the next fork, veer left and follow the sound of falling water to the falls. From the pullout to the falls is about 1 mile total. The trail parallels the river going downstream.

Waterfall Name	Jewell Falls
State	Maine
Type	Tiered/Horsetail
Variant Name	
Height in feet	30
County	Cumberland
Topo Map	Portland West
Geo Coord	434017N0701956W
Map Ref Code	43070-F3
Elevation ft	60
Water Source	Fore River
Seasonal Flow	Sp,Sm
Section of State	SE

Directions   In Portland at the junction of Interstate 295 and Congress St. (Rt. 22), go 1.2 miles west on Congress St. Turn right onto Frost St. and make a quick left into the parking lot (address here is 1601 Congress St. and is also marked by "Parking for Fore River Trail/Sanctuary"). Walk west on Congress St. to the trailhead on the right (well-marked, about 100 feet). Hike the easy trail about 1 mile following the blue blazes and signs to Jewell Falls.

Waterfall Name	Kezar Falls
State	Maine
Type	Horsetail
Variant Name	
Height in feet	30
County	Oxford
Topo Map	North Waterford
Geo Coord	441153N0704854W
Map Ref Code	44070-B7
Elevation ft	600
Water Source	Kezar River
Seasonal Flow	Year
Section of State	SW

Directions   From Central Lovell at the junction of Rt. 5 and Eastman Hill Rd., go east on Eastman Hill Road 1.8 miles to the T intersection. Turn left onto the unsigned paved road and go 0.8 mile (road turns to dirt). In another 1/2 mile, veer left at the fork. Go 1.3 miles and veer left again at the fork. Go 1.1 miles and veer left for the third time and park in what appears to be a turn-around. (If you get to the house on the right, you went too far). The unmarked trail goes down a steep ravine about 200 feet to the gorge and falls. Use CAUTION.

Waterfall Name	Little Niagara Falls
State	Maine
Type	Block
Variant Name	
Height in feet	15
County	Piscataquis
Topo Map	Rainbow Lake East
Geo Coord	455226N0690228W
Map Ref Code	45069-G1
Elevation ft	1000
Water Source	Nesowadnehunk Stream
Seasonal Flow	Year
Section of State	NE

Directions   See directions for Big Niagara Falls. Little Niagara is about 1/4 mile upstream from Big Niagara on the same trail.

Waterfall Name   Little Wilson Falls

State   Maine

Type   Tiered/Horsetail

Variant Name

Height in feet   50

County   Piscataquis

Topo Map   Monson East

Geo Coord   452226N0692820W

Map Ref Code   45069-C4

Elevation ft   900

Water Source   Little Wilson Stream

Seasonal Flow   Year

Section of State   NW

Directions   From the north end of the town of Monson at the junction of Routes 6 W.,15 N. and Elliotsville Road, go east on Elliotsville Road. In 7.7 miles, turn left onto the unmarked gravel road (just before bridge over Big Wilson Stream and sign for Borestone Mountain Sanctuary). Go 0.8 mile straight to the end of the road and park at the west end of the campground. Take the trail at the west end of the campground upstream for about 1/2 mile. From here, the main trail veers left away from the stream and goes uphill. Follow this main trail to the white-blazed Appalachian Trail. Turn left and follow the Appalachian Trail to the falls. Total hike to falls is about 1 mile.

Waterfall Name   Moxie Falls

State   Maine

Type   Plunge/Horsetail

Variant Name

Height in feet   90

County   Somerset

Topo Map   The Forks

Geo Coord   452153N0695625W

Map Ref Code   45069-C8

Elevation ft   700

Water Source   Moxie Stream

Seasonal Flow   Year

Section of State   NW

Directions   From The Forks at the junction of Rt. 201 and the road towards Moxie Lake (just south of the bridge over the Kennebuc River), go east on the road to Moxie Lake. In 1.9 miles, park at the parking area for Moxie Falls Scenic Area. Hike 0.6 mile on the well-maintained trail to the falls.

Waterfall Name	Screw Auger Falls
State	Maine
Type	Tiered/Plunge
Variant Name	
Height in feet	40
County	Oxford
Topo Map	Old Speck Mountain
Geo Coord	443419N0705438W
Map Ref Code	44070-E8
Elevation ft	1100
Water Source	Bear River
Seasonal Flow	Year
Section of State	SW

Directions From Newry at the junction of Routes 2/5/26, take Rt. 26 N. for 9.6 miles to the entrance to Screw Auger Falls on the left. (Located in Grafton Notch State Park.) The falls is a very short walk from the parking lot. Entry fee.

Waterfall Name	Shin Falls
State	Maine
Type	Segmented/Horsetail/Cascade
Variant Name	
Height in feet	40
County	Penobscot
Topo Map	Hay Brook Mountain
Geo Coord	460821N0683651W
Map Ref Code	46068-B5
Elevation ft	700
Water Source	Shin Brook
Seasonal Flow	Year
Section of State	NE

Directions From Patten at the junction of Routes 11 N. and 159, take 159 W. for 14.9 miles to a small pull-out on the left. Large boulders block the trail. Park here. Hike on the trail and in 1/2 mile, veer left at the fork (the right fork goes to the upper overlook of the falls but the view is partially blocked). In about 100 yards, take the first small trail to the right and follow it down the hill to the falls brink. The bottom of the falls can be accessed from here, a steep descent.

Waterfall Name   Smalls Falls

State   Maine

Type   Tiered/Horsetail

Variant Name

Height in feet   60

County   Franklin

Topo Map   Jackson Mountain

Geo Coord   445132N0703102W

Map Ref Code   44070-G5

Elevation ft   1140

Water Source   Sandy River

Seasonal Flow   Year

Section of State   NW

Directions   From Rangeley at the junction of Routes 16 E. and 4 S., take Rt. 4 S. for 12.6 miles to Smalls Falls Rest Area on the right. The falls is at the north end of the rest area, a few yards to the bridge viewpoint.

Waterfall Name   Step Falls

State   Maine

Type   Cascade

Variant Name

Height in feet   150

County   Oxford

Topo Map   Old Speck Mountain

Geo Coord   443502N0705142W

Map Ref Code   44070-E8

Elevation ft   1200

Water Source   Wight Brook

Seasonal Flow   Year

Section of State   SW

Directions   From Newry at the junction of Routes 2/5/26, take Rt. 26 N. for 8 miles to Wight Brook Preserve (on the right) and park. Hike uphill about 1/4 mile to a series of cascades and chutes.

Waterfall Name	The Cataracts
State	Maine
Type	Tiered/Horsetail/Plunge
Variant Name	
Height in feet	50
County	Oxford
Topo Map	Andover
Geo Coord	443819N0705139W
Map Ref Code	44070-F7
Elevation ft	1200
Water Source	Frye Brook
Seasonal Flow	Year
Section of State	SW

Directions — From Andover at the junction of Newton St. and Main St., go west (towards Upton) on Newton St. (becomes East Bee Hill Road). In 5.5 miles park in the pullout on the right (just before the concrete bridge). The trailhead is across the road (with a posted map). Hike about 1/2 mile up the yellow-blazed trail. The falls will be on the right where the split rail fence guards the cliff.

Waterfall Name	The Falls
State	Maine
Type	Horsetail
Variant Name	
Height in feet	45
County	Somerset
Topo Map	Jackman
Geo Coord	454358N0701745W
Map Ref Code	45070-F3
Elevation ft	1700
Water Source	Sandy Stream
Seasonal Flow	Year
Section of State	NW

Directions — From the junction of Routes N201/E6 and 6/15 just south of Jackman, go north on N201/E6 for 9.2 miles to The Falls Rest Area on the right. Park here. The Falls is at the north end of the rest area.

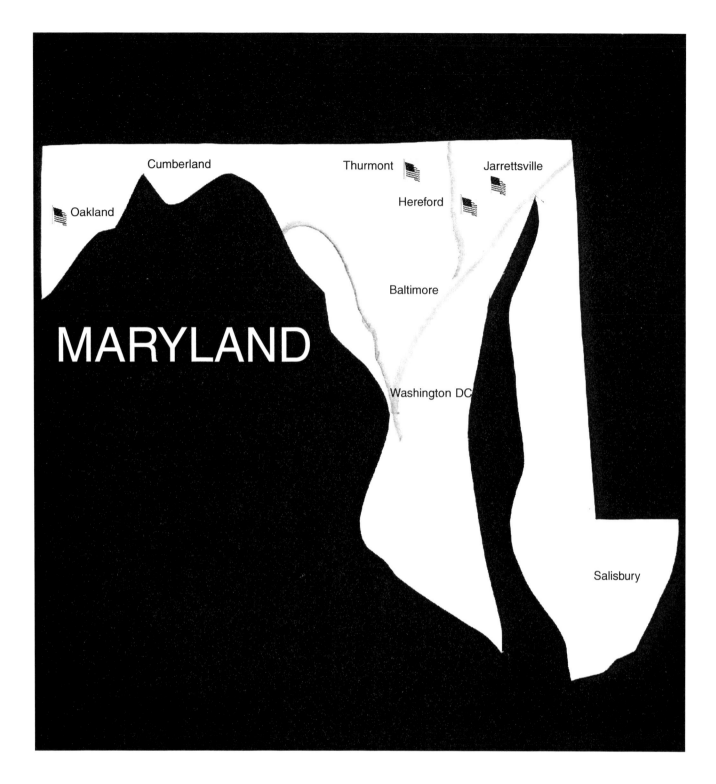

Waterfall Name	Cunningham Falls
State	Maryland
Type	Tiered/Cascade
Variant Name	
Height in feet	80
County	Frederick
Topo Map	Blue Ridge Summit (PA)
Geo Coord	393753N0772818W
Map Ref Code	39077-F4
Elevation ft	1300
Water Source	Big Hunting Creek
Seasonal Flow	Sp
Section of State	NW

Directions   From Thurmont at the junction of Routes 15 and 77, take Rt. 77 west for 2.8 miles to Catoctin Hollow Road and turn left (sign reads Cunningham Falls State Park). Go 1.3 miles to the park entrance and turn right. Proceed 0.4 miles to the booth, obtain a trail map and park. The trail is 3/4 mile to the falls following the red-blaze trail. The trailhead is at the edge of the woods near Hunting Creek Lake beach. The trail goes upstream paralleling Big Hunting Creek. Entry fee.

Waterfall Name	Kilgore Falls
State	Maryland
Type	Block
Variant Name	Falling Branch Falls
Height in feet	20
County	Harford
Topo Map	Fawn Grove
Geo Coord	394048N0762507W
Map Ref Code	39076-F4
Elevation ft	400
Water Source	Falling Branch
Seasonal Flow	Sp,Sm
Section of State	NE

Directions   From Jarrettsville, take Rt. 165 N. for 9 miles to the junction with Rt. 24. Go north on Rt. 24 for 1.4 miles to St. Marys Road and turn left (west). Go 1/2 mile to Falling Branch Road (gravel) and turn right. Go 0.6 mile to gravel entrance of Falling Branch Area (look for sign). Turn right and proceed 0.1 mile to the parking area. Follow the well-marked, easy, 1/4-mile trail through a meadow to Kilgore Falls.

Waterfall Name	Muddy Falls
State	Maryland
Type	Cascade
Variant Name	Muddy Creek Falls
Height in feet	50
County	Garrett
Topo Map	Sang Run
Geo Coord	393001N0792504W
Map Ref Code	39079-E4
Elevation ft	2300
Water Source	Muddy Creek
Seasonal Flow	Year
Section of State	NW

Directions   From Oakland at the junction of Rt. 219 and Green, take Green NW for 7.7 miles to Swallow Falls State Park (sign). Turn left into the park and proceed 0.4 mile to parking area. Note—Green becomes Liberty which becomes Swallow Falls Road en route to the Park (follow signs). Obtain a trail map. The falls is a 1/4-mile hike from the parking area on an easy, well-marked trail. Entry fee.

Waterfall Name	Raven Run Falls
State	Maryland
Type	Horsetail
Variant Name	Gunpowder Falls
Height in feet	50
County	Baltimore
Topo Map	Phoenix
Geo Coord	393650N0763726W
Map Ref Code	39076-E5
Elevation ft	400
Water Source	Raven Run Branch
Seasonal Flow	Sp
Section of State	NE

Directions   From Hereford at the junction of Interstate 83 and Rt. 137 (Mount Carmel Road, Exit 27), take Rt. 137 E. for 0.4 mile to York Road. Turn left (north) and go 1.8 miles to gravel parking area just before the bridge over the Big Gunpowder Falls River. This is part of the Gunpowder Falls State Park/Hereford Area. Trail maps can be obtained at the Ranger Station in Monkton. The trailhead is unmarked. Walk to the NE side of the bridge (use caution, no walkway provided). Continue N along the guardrail. A faint trail begins at guardrail metal post #21 (counting from the NE end of bridge). Climb over the rail and walk down what looks like a small drainage to the blue-blazed, overgrown trail. This is the Gunpowder North Trail. Follow this east downstream 0.9 mile to the falls on the left.

Waterfall Name	Swallow Falls
State	Maryland
Type	Cascade
Variant Name	
Height in feet	20
County	Garrett
Topo Map	Oakland
Geo Coord	392927N0792501W
Map Ref Code	39079-D4
Elevation ft	2300
Water Source	Youghiogheny River
Seasonal Flow	Year
Section of State	NW

Directions   See directions for Muddy Falls. Swallow Falls is a 2/3-mile hike from the parking area on a well-marked trail. Entry fee.

MASSACHUSETTS

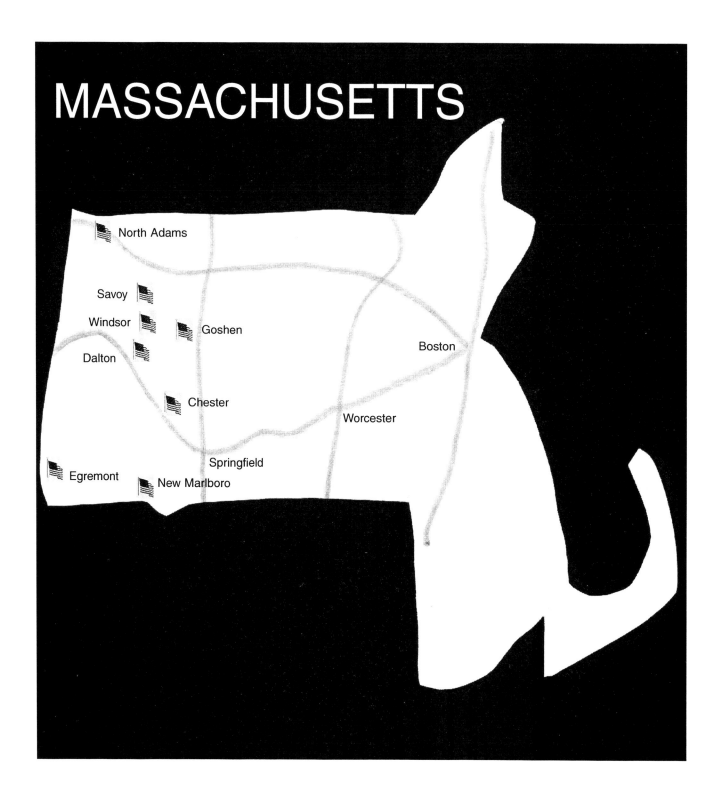

Waterfall Name	Bash Bish Falls
State	Massachusetts
Type	Segmented/Plunge/Horsetail
Variant Name	Bashapish Falls
Height in feet	40
County	Berkshire
Topo Map	Bash Bish Falls
Geo Coord	420653N0732936W
Map Ref Code	42073-A4
Elevation ft	1100
Water Source	Bash Bish Brook
Seasonal Flow	Year
Section of State	SW

Directions   From Egremont at the junction of Routes 41 and 23, take Rt. 41 S. for 0.2 mile to Mt. Washington Rd. (sign reads Mt. Washington State Forest). Turn right and proceed 7.7 miles to Cross Road and turn right (sign reads Bash Bish Falls 4 miles). Go 1.7 miles to Falls Road and turn left (road is unmarked but sign reads Bash Bish Falls 2 miles). Go 1.5 miles to a large parking area on the left and park. Signs point to the trailhead. The trail is rocky and slippery with some stairs, about 1/3 mile to the falls.

Waterfall Name	Campbell Falls
State	Massachusetts
Type	Tiered/Cascade
Variant Name	
Height in feet	60
County	Berkshire
Topo Map	South Sandisfield
Geo Coord	420245N0731400W
Map Ref Code	42073-A2
Elevation ft	1100
Water Source	Ginger Creek
Seasonal Flow	Year
Section of State	SW

Directions   From New Marlboro at the intersection of Rt. 57 and New Marlboro-Southfield Road, go south towards Southfield on New Marlboro-Southfield Rd. In 1.3 miles, veer left at the Y towards Southfield (road is unnamed). Go 0.7 mile (look for sign reading Norfolk, Conn.) and continue straight (road name changes to Norfolk Road). Follow Norfolk Road for 3.8 miles to Campbell Falls Road (gravel). Turn right and go 0.4 mile to the State Park parking area on the left. The trailhead is at the west side of the parking area. Follow the white-blazed trail a steep 100 yards to the falls.

Waterfall Name	Cascade Falls
State	Massachusetts
Type	Cascade
Variant Name	The Cascades
Height in feet	40
County	Berkshire
Topo Map	Williamstown
Geo Coord	424140N0730735W
Map Ref Code	42073-F2
Elevation ft	1100
Water Source	Notch Brook
Seasonal Flow	Sp
Section of State	NW

Directions   From North Adams at the junction of Routes 8 and 2, go west on Rt. 2 about 1 mile to Marion Ave. Turn left and go 0.4 mile to the end of the road and park. Note—this is a residential area, so only park in designated spots. Walk upstream on the trail for about 1/2 mile to the falls. In Cascade Park.

Waterfall Name	Chapel Falls
State	Massachusetts
Type	Horsetail
Variant Name	Chapel Brook Falls
Height in feet	30
County	Franklin
Topo Map	Goshen
Geo Coord	422855N0724537W
Map Ref Code	42072-D7
Elevation ft	1100
Water Source	Chapel Brook
Seasonal Flow	Sp
Section of State	NW

Directions   Several miles north of Goshen at the junction of Routes 9 and 112 N., proceed north on Rt. 112 for 1/2 mile to the DAR State Forest entrance. Obtain a map here. Drive on the main park road (Moore Hill Road) to the locked gate and park. The group camp area is on the left. Hike past the gate on the paved road, stay straight on Ludwig Road, pass West Road, and turn left at the T intersection (Williamsburg Road, unmarked). Follow this road to Chapel Brook Reservation. Turn right and follow the sign and trail downstream to the falls. The total hike from parking spot to the falls is about 1.5 miles. Entry fee.

Waterfall Name	Sanderson Brook Falls
State	Massachusetts
Type	Segmented/Horsetail
Variant Name	Sanderson Falls
Height in feet	80
County	Hampden
Topo Map	Blandford
Geo Coord	421457N0725729W
Map Ref Code	42072-B8
Elevation ft	800
Water Source	Sanderson Brook
Seasonal Flow	Sp
Section of State	SW

Directions   From Chester, take Rt. 20 E. to Mile Mark 35. Go an additional 2.7 miles east on Rt. 20 to Sanderson Brook Road (gravel) and turn right (just before bridge over creek). Go 0.6 mile and park at the big dirt mounds across the road. Hike on the road (uphill) for about 1/4 mile to the first trail on the right. Go right for about 1/8 mile to the falls. In Chester-Blandford State Forest.

Waterfall Name	Tannery Falls
State	Massachusetts
Type	Segmented/Horsetail
Variant Name	
Height in feet	100
County	Berkshire
Topo Map	Windsor
Geo Coord	423728N0730014W
Map Ref Code	42073-E1
Elevation ft	1600
Water Source	Tannery Brook
Seasonal Flow	Sp
Section of State	NW

Directions   From Savoy at the church, go south on Rt. 116 for 1.2 miles to Loop Rd. and turn left. Go 1.4 miles to Chapel Rd. and turn left. Proceed 3.9 miles (stay on main paved road; name changes to Black Brook Road) to Tannery Road (gravel). The sign for Tannery Road is on the left and faces the opposite direction, so it can only be seen after passing it. Turn left onto Tannery Road and go 0.7 mile to the parking area on the right (sign for falls on a tree). Follow the blue-blaze trail for 1/4 mile downstream to the falls. The trail is steep with some stairs. In Savoy Mountain State Forest.

Waterfall Name	Wahconah Falls
State	Massachusetts
Type	Fan
Variant Name	
Height in feet	35
County	Berkshire
Topo Map	Peru
Geo Coord	422918N0730637W
Map Ref Code	42073-D1
Elevation ft	1450
Water Source	Wahconah Falls Brook
Seasonal Flow	Sp
Section of State	NW

Directions   From Dalton, take Rt. 9 E. about 3 miles to North Street and turn right (sign reads Wahconah Falls State Park). Continue on North St. as it changes to gravel and is now named Wahconah Falls Road. Park in the parking area on the right. The falls is 200 feet away via an easy, well-marked trail.

Waterfall Name	Windsor Jambs Falls
State	Massachusetts
Type	Cascade
Variant Name	Windsor Jams
Height in feet	100
County	Berkshire
Topo Map	Plainfield
Geo Coord	423120N0725935W
Map Ref Code	42072-E8
Elevation ft	1400
Water Source	Windsor Jambs Brook
Seasonal Flow	Year
Section of State	NW

Directions   From Windsor at the junction of Routes 9 and 8A North, go east on Rt. 9 for 5.2 miles. Turn left onto the unnamed road at the Windsor Jambs sign. Go 0.1 mile and turn left onto River Road (follow sign for Windsor State Forest). Go 3 miles to the large parking area on the left (Park Headquarters located here). Obtain a trail map. The trailhead is located behind the restrooms in the campground. The 1-mile, blue-blazed trail will go upstream along the cliffside to the falls. Entry fee.

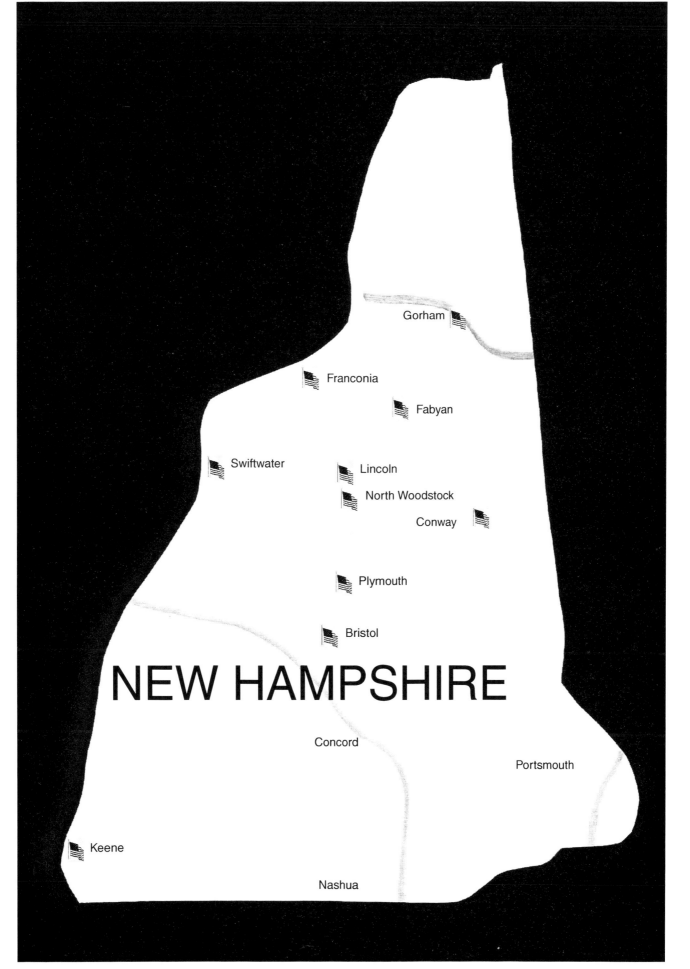

Gorham

Franconia

Fabyan

Swiftwater

Lincoln

North Woodstock

Conway

Plymouth

Bristol

NEW HAMPSHIRE

Concord

Portsmouth

Keene

Nashua

Waterfall Name	Agassiz Basin Lower Falls
State	New Hampshire
Type	Plunge
Variant Name	Lower Agassiz Basin Falls
Height in feet	15
County	Grafton
Topo Map	Lincoln
Geo Coord	440204N0714230W
Map Ref Code	44071-A6
Elevation ft	860
Water Source	Moosilauke Brook
Seasonal Flow	Year
Section of State	NW
Directions	See directions for Agassiz Basin Upper Falls. The Lower Falls are downstream about 50 yards.

Waterfall Name	Agassiz Basin Upper Falls
State	New Hampshire
Type	Segmented/Plunge/Cascade
Variant Name	Upper Agassiz Basin Falls
Height in feet	20
County	Grafton
Topo Map	Lincoln
Geo Coord	440205N0714240W
Map Ref Code	44071-A6
Elevation ft	900
Water Source	Moosilauke Brook
Seasonal Flow	Year
Section of State	NW

Directions   Near the town of N. Woodstock at the junction of Routes 112 and 118, take Rt. 112 E. Go about 1 mile and park on the right next to the restaurant (across from Mountain Side Road). The falls is behind the restaurant. In White Mountain National Forest.

Waterfall Name	Bridal Veil Falls
State	New Hampshire
Type	Horsetail
Variant Name	
Height in feet	80
County	Grafton
Topo Map	Franconia
Geo Coord	440937N0714327W
Map Ref Code	44071-B6
Elevation ft	2200
Water Source	Coppermine Brook
Seasonal Flow	Sp,Sm
Section of State	NW

Directions   From Franconia at the junction of Interstate 93 and Rt. 116, take Rt. 116 S. Go 3.5 miles and turn left onto the unnamed dirt road (sign for Coppermine Village on right). Go 0.1 mile and park in the pullout on the left (just before sign that reads "No Trailhead Parking Past This Point"). Hike on the road about 1/2 mile to the trailhead hiker sign. Follow the main trail into the woods (Coppermine Trail) for 2 miles to the falls. A moderately difficult rocky trail that parallels Coppermine Brook. In White Mountain National Forest.

Waterfall Name	Chesterfield Gorge Falls
State	New Hampshire
Type	Horsetail
Variant Name	Falls at Chesterfield Gorge
Height in feet	25
County	Cheshire
Topo Map	Spofford
Geo Coord	425010N0722905W
Map Ref Code	42072-H4
Elevation ft	1000
Water Source	Wilde Brook
Seasonal Flow	Sp,Sm
Section of State	SW

Directions   At the junction of Routes 10/12/9 near Keene, take Rt. 9 W. for 5.8 miles to Chesterfield Gorge State Wayside on the right. Take the well-marked 0.7-mile hike from the parking area to the falls. Obtain a trail map and information from the Visitors Center located near the parking area.

Waterfall Name	Cloudland Falls
State	New Hampshire
Type	Fan
Variant Name	
Height in feet	60
County	Grafton
Topo Map	Franconia
Geo Coord	440750N0713952W
Map Ref Code	44071-B6
Elevation ft	3000
Water Source	Dry Brook
Seasonal Flow	Year
Section of State	NW

Directions   From Lincoln, take Interstate 93 N. to "Trailhead Parking" on the right (follow sign). The parking area is just past Mile Mark 108 and is opposite Lafayette Campground. Hike the steep, strenuous, rocky Falling Waters Trail for 1.4 miles to the falls. In Franconia Notch State Park.

Waterfall Name	Erebus Falls
State	New Hampshire
Type	Segmented/Horsetail
Variant Name	Triple Falls
Height in feet	25
County	Coos
Topo Map	Carter Dome
Geo Coord	442131N0711445W
Map Ref Code	44071-C2
Elevation ft	1600
Water Source	Town Line Brook
Seasonal Flow	Sp
Section of State	NE

Directions   From Gorham at the junction of Routes 16 N. and 2 W., take Rt. 2 W. Go 4.6 miles and turn left onto Pinkham B Road (sign here reads Horton Center). Go 1.8 miles (road turns to gravel) into the White Mountains National Forest and park in the pullout on the left. Hike on the Town Line Brook Trail (across the road) up the mountainside for 200 yards to the falls.

Waterfall Name	Giant Falls
State	New Hampshire
Type	Fan
Variant Name	
Height in feet	200
County	Coos
Topo Map	Shelburne
Geo Coord	442556N0710629W
Map Ref Code	44071-D1
Elevation ft	1600
Water Source	Peabody Brook
Seasonal Flow	Sp
Section of State	NE

No
Photo
Available

Directions   From Gorham, take Rt. 2 east for 3 miles. Turn left onto North Road. Go about 1 mile. Park in the pullout on the right, just past the cemetery. Follow the Appalachian Trail/Peabody Brook Trail for 1.5 miles to the falls.

Waterfall Name	Glen Ellis Falls
State	New Hampshire
Type	Horsetail
Variant Name	
Height in feet	65
County	Coos/Carroll
Topo Map	Stairs Mountain
Geo Coord	441438N0711507W
Map Ref Code	44071-B3
Elevation ft	2000
Water Source	Ellis River
Seasonal Flow	Year
Section of State	NE

Directions   From Gorham, take Rt. 16 S. to the Pinkham Notch Visitors Center. Continue another 0.7 mile on Rt. 16 S. to the Glen Ellis Falls Scenic Area on the right. The walk from the parking area to the falls is 600 feet and several stairs must be descended to get there. In White Mountain National Forest.

Waterfall Name	Livermore Falls
State	New Hampshire
Type	Cascade
Variant Name	
Height in feet	35
County	Grafton
Topo Map	Plymouth
Geo Coord	434705N0714008W
Map Ref Code	43071-G6
Elevation ft	600
Water Source	Pemigewasset River
Seasonal Flow	Year
Section of State	NW

Directions   From Plymouth, take Interstate 93 N. for a couple miles to Exit 27 (Blair Bridge) and turn right (east) towards Blair Bridge. Go 0.1 mile to Rt. 3 and turn right (south). Proceed 2.1 miles to the 2 dirt pullouts on the left and park. Hike down the hill on the path between the 2 pullouts (in a NE direction) to the falls. Total hike is about 1/4 mile. In Livermore Falls State Forest.

Waterfall Name	Profile Falls
State	New Hampshire
Type	Segmented/Fan
Variant Name	
Height in feet	40
County	Grafton
Topo Map	Bristol
Geo Coord	433403N0714420W
Map Ref Code	43071-E6
Elevation ft	520
Water Source	Smith River
Seasonal Flow	Year
Section of State	SW

Directions   From Bristol at the junction of Routes 3A and 104, take Rt. 3A south. Go 2.1 miles and turn left onto Profile Falls Road (just before the bridge over the Smith River). Go 0.3 mile and make a sharp right turn; continue another 0.1 mile to the parking area on the right. Walk about 400 feet uphill and to the left to the falls.

Waterfall Name	Rocky Gorge Falls
State	New Hampshire
Type	Segmented/Cascade
Variant Name	
Height in feet	15
County	Carroll
Topo Map	Bartlett
Geo Coord	440201N0711710W
Map Ref Code	44071-A3
Elevation ft	1200
Water Source	Swift River
Seasonal Flow	Year
Section of State	NE

Directions   From Conway at the junction of Routes 112 W. and 16, take Rt. 112 W. Go 8.7 miles to the Rocky Gorge Scenic Area on the right. The falls is a short distance from the parking area. In White Mountain National Forest.

Waterfall Name	Swiftwater Falls
State	New Hampshire
Type	Tiered/Cascade
Variant Name	
Height in feet	15
County	Grafton
Topo Map	Lisbon
Geo Coord	440735N0715725W
Map Ref Code	44071-B8
Elevation ft	690
Water Source	Wild Ammonoosuc River
Seasonal Flow	Year
Section of State	NW

Directions   The village of Swiftwater is on Rt. 112, 2.2 miles east of the junction of Routes 302 and 112. Once in town, take a left off of Rt. 112 onto Covered Bridge 29 Road. Drive through the covered bridge and turn left into the first dirt parking area. The falls can be seen from here directly under the bridge.

Waterfall Name	Tama Falls
State	New Hampshire
Type	Segmented/Cascade
Variant Name	
Height in feet	40
County	Coos
Topo Map	Mt. Washington
Geo Coord	442110N0711730W
Map Ref Code	44071-C3
Elevation ft	1500
Water Source	Snyder Brook
Seasonal Flow	Year
Section of State	NE

Directions   From Gorham at the junction of Routes 2 W. and 16 N., take Rt. 2 W. Go 5.5 miles to the large parking area on the left for Snyder Brook Scenic Area. Park at the east end of the parking area. Begin hiking, following the sign to "Fallsway to Valley Way, to the Falls". Go 0.6 mile past the RR tracks to another sign reading "Fallsway Up the West Side of Snyder Brook to Gordon, Sabroc and Tama Falls". The strenuous uphill hike is about 1 mile from the parking area to the falls. In White Mountain National Forest.

Waterfall Name	Upper Ammonoosuc Falls
State	New Hampshire
Type	Tiered/Cascade
Variant Name	
Height in feet	15
County	Coos
Topo Map	Mt. Washington
Geo Coord	441550N0712505W
Map Ref Code	44071-C3
Elevation ft	1770
Water Source	Ammonoosuc River
Seasonal Flow	Year
Section of State	NE

Directions   From the junction of Rt. 3 and 302, take 302 east about 5 miles to the village of Fabyan. Go left (north) on Base Road. A sign on the corner of this intersection reads "Ride the Mt. Washington Cog Railway". Go 2.3 miles to the pullout on the right and park (large boulders here block the entrance to an open grassy area). The falls is a short walk through the trees.

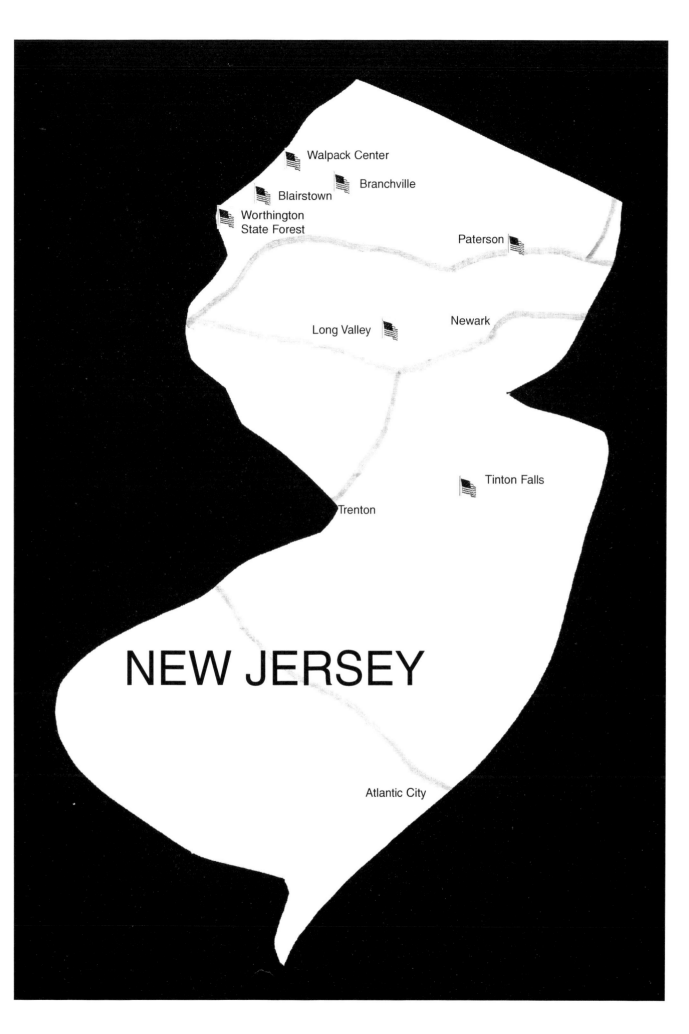

Walpack Center

Branchville

Blairstown

Worthington
State Forest

Paterson

Long Valley

Newark

Tinton Falls

Trenton

NEW JERSEY

Atlantic City

Waterfall Name	Buttermilk Falls
State	New Jersey
Type	Tiered/Horsetail/Plunge
Variant Name	
Height in feet	80
County	Sussex
Topo Map	Lake Maskenozha (PA-NJ)
Geo Coord	410735N0745240W
Map Ref Code	41074-B8
Elevation ft	800
Water Source	Buttermilk Creek
Seasonal Flow	Sp
Section of State	NW

Directions　From Walpack Center (located in the Delaware Water Gap National Recreation Area) at the Walpack Post Office on Rt. 615, go east on the unnamed road. Go past several homes, over the one-lane bridge (about 1/2 mile total) and turn right, just past the cemetery, onto the gravel road (Mountain Rd., unsigned). In 2.1 miles, the falls will be on the left. Park on the right.

Waterfall Name	Great Falls of the Passaic
State	New Jersey
Type	Segmented/Block
Variant Name	Passaic Falls, Totawa Falls
Height in feet	70
County	Passaic
Topo Map	Paterson
Geo Coord	405459N0741057W
Map Ref Code	40074-H2
Elevation ft	176
Water Source	Passaic River
Seasonal Flow	Year
Section of State	NE

Directions　From Paterson, take Rt. 80 west to Exit 57C. At the end of the exit ramp, turn left onto Main St. Go to the 2nd stop light and turn left onto Grand St. Go 4 blocks and turn right onto Spruce St. Go 4 more blocks and turn right onto McBride Ave. Park at the Great Falls Visitors Center on the right. The falls is directly across the street.

Waterfall Name	Hidden Falls
State	New Jersey
Type	Tiered/Horsetail/Plunge
Variant Name	
Height in feet	35
County	Sussex
Topo Map	Lake Maskenozha (PA-NJ)
Geo Coord	410740N0745233W
Map Ref Code	41074-B8
Elevation ft	700
Water Source	Hidden Creek
Seasonal Flow	Sp
Section of State	NW

Directions   See directions for Buttermilk Falls. After turning right onto the gravel road, just past the cemetery, go 1.5 miles to the one-car pullout on the left and park. Two big logs mark the pullout. Take the trail leading into the trees from the pullout and veer left at the Y's. Follow the creek upstream to the falls. Total hike is about 1/4 mile.

Waterfall Name	Laurel Falls
State	New Jersey
Type	Tiered/Cascade
Variant Name	
Height in feet	40
County	Warren
Topo Map	Bushkill (PA-NJ)
Geo Coord	410210N0750450W
Map Ref Code	41075-A1
Elevation ft	1300
Water Source	Sunfish Creek
Seasonal Flow	Sp
Section of State	NW

Directions   From Interstate 80, take Exit 1 (River Rd./Old Mine Rd.). Go NE on River Rd./Old Mine Rd. to Mile Mark 4 and park in the north side of the Douglas parking area. This is very near the Worthington State Forest Campground. Follow the Douglas Trail (directly across the street) up the steep terrain next to the stream. Several falls and cascades are within 1/4 mile. Near Delaware Water Gap National Recreation Area.

Waterfall Name	Tillman Lower Falls
State	New Jersey
Type	Horsetail
Variant Name	Lower Tillman Falls
Height in feet	80˚
County	Sussex
Topo Map	Culvers Gap
Geo Coord	410928N0745132W
Map Ref Code	41074-B7
Elevation ft	800
Water Source	Tillman Brook
Seasonal Flow	Sp
Section of State	NW

Directions   Near Branchville at the junction of Routes 206/521 and 560, take Rt. 206/521 S. Go 0.7 mile and turn right (west) onto Struble Road. Go 4 miles to the second Tillman Ravine parking area on the left. The falls is a few hundred yards down the hillside. In Stokes State Forest.

Waterfall Name	Tinton Falls
State	New Jersey
Type	Cascade
Variant Name	
Height in feet	10
County	Monmouth
Topo Map	Long Branch
Geo Coord	401755N0740705W
Map Ref Code	40074-C8
Elevation ft	200
Water Source	Pine Brook
Seasonal Flow	Sp
Section of State	NE

Directions   The falls is on the north corner of the intersection of Tinton Ave., Sycamore Ave., and Water St. in the town of Tinton Falls. It is downstream from the bridge on Tinton Ave. and behind the Grist Mill Restaurant.

Waterfall Name	Trout Brook Falls
State	New Jersey
Type	Tiered/Cascade
Variant Name	
Height in feet	20
County	Morris
Topo Map	Chester
Geo Coord	404510N0744450W
Map Ref Code	40074-G6
Elevation ft	500
Water Source	Trout Brook
Seasonal Flow	Sp
Section of State	NW

Directions From Long Valley at the junction of Routes 24/513 East and 24/517, take Rt. 24/513 E. Go 3.2 miles and turn right (south) onto State Park Road (sign for Hacklebarney State Park). Go 1.8 miles and take a very sharp right turn, continuing on State Park Road. Go another 0.7 mile to the park entrance (follow signs to Hacklebarney State Park). Follow the main road through the park for another 0.3 mile and park in the parking area. The falls is a short hike (follow signs). Entry fee.

Waterfall Name	Van Campens Glen Falls
State	New Jersey
Type	Tiered/Cascade
Variant Name	Falls at Van Campens Glen
Height in feet	30
County	Warren
Topo Map	Flatbrookville
Geo Coord	410432N0745940W
Map Ref Code	41074-A8
Elevation ft	500
Water Source	Van Campens Brook
Seasonal Flow	Year
Section of State	NW

Directions From Blairstown, take Rt. 602 N. to Millbrook. In the village, go west on Old Mine Rd. for 2.2 miles to Van Campens Glen parking area on the left. From here, hike upstream about 1/2 mile to the falls. In Delaware Water Gap National Recreation Area.

NEW YORK

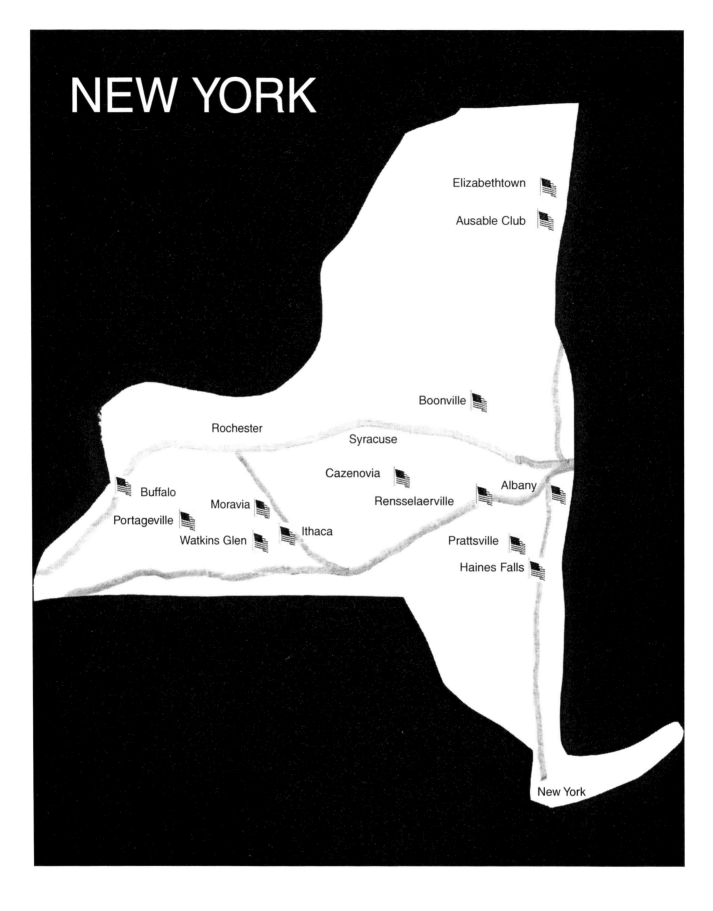

Elizabethtown

Ausable Club

Boonville

Rochester

Syracuse

Cazenovia

Buffalo

Albany

Moravia

Rensselaerville

Portageville

Watkins Glen

Ithaca

Prattsville

Haines Falls

New York

Waterfall Name	Beaver Meadow Falls
State	New York
Type	Fan
Variant Name	
Height in feet	50
County	Essex
Topo Map	Keene Valley
Geo Coord	440745N0734858W
Map Ref Code	44073-B7
Elevation ft	2100
Water Source	Wolfjaw Brook
Seasonal Flow	Year
Section of State	NE

Directions   See directions for Rainbow Falls-Adirondacks. From Lower Ausable Lake, cross over the bridge to the West River Trail. Follow the trail downstream for about 3/4 mile to Beaver Meadow Falls on the left. The West River Trail is marked by round orange ATIS blazes. The trail is rocky with a few up and down sections.

Waterfall Name	Bridal Veil Falls
State	New York
Type	Fan
Variant Name	
Height in feet	120
County	Niagara
Topo Map	Niagara Falls
Geo Coord	430501N0790414W
Map Ref Code	43079-A1
Elevation ft	550
Water Source	Niagara River
Seasonal Flow	Year
Section of State	NW

Directions   From Buffalo, take Interstate 190 N. to Niagara Falls (follow signs). Bridal Veil Falls is one of the three separate falls that make up the waterfalls in the town of Niagara Falls. Bridal Veil Falls is the middle falls of the three.

Waterfall Name	Chittenango Falls
State	New York
Type	Tiered/Cascade
Variant Name	
Height in feet	165
County	Madison
Topo Map	Cazenovia
Geo Coord	425843N0755031W
Map Ref Code	42075-H7
Elevation ft	800
Water Source	Chittenango Creek
Seasonal Flow	Year
Section of State	NE

Directions From Cazenovia, take Rt. 13 N. for 4 miles to Chittenango Falls State Park. Follow the signs to the falls parking area. The trail to the overlook of the falls is a short walk from the parking area, steep with stairs. Entry Fee.

Waterfall Name	Hector Falls
State	New York
Type	Cascade
Variant Name	
Height in feet	70
County	Schuyler
Topo Map	Burdett
Geo Coord	422504N0765156W
Map Ref Code	42076-D7
Elevation ft	600
Water Source	Hector Falls Creek
Seasonal Flow	Sp,Sm
Section of State	NW

Directions From Watkins Glen, take Rt. 414 N. From the intersection with Rt. 79 E., continue on Rt. 414 N. for 1.7 more miles to the falls on the right. Park on the shoulder near the bridge over Hector Falls Creek.

Waterfall Name	Hogback Falls
State	New York
Type	Cascade
Variant Name	
Height in feet	80
County	Cayuga
Topo Map	Moravia
Geo Coord	424105N0762307W
Map Ref Code	42076-F4
Elevation ft	1400
Water Source	Dry Creek
Seasonal Flow	Sp
Section of State	NW

Directions From Moravia, take Rt. 38 S. for 1 mile to Fillmore Glen State Park. Obtain a park map at the entry booth. Follow the signs to the parking area for the Gorge Trail. Take the Gorge Trail for about 1.5 miles to the falls on the right. The trail goes gradually uphill with some stairs. Entry fee.

Waterfall Name	Horseshoe Falls
State	New York
Type	Horseshoe/Plunge
Variant Name	Niagara Falls
Height in feet	120
County	Niagara
Topo Map	Niagara Falls
Geo Coord	430438N0790430W
Map Ref Code	43079-A1
Elevation ft	550
Water Source	Niagara River
Seasonal Flow	Year
Section of State	NW

Directions See directions for Bridal Veil Falls. Horseshoe Falls is the largest of the three falls in Niagara Falls. It is one of the few falls that truly is a horseshoe shape. For a view up close, travel to the Canada side of the river.

Waterfall Name	Ithaca Falls
State	New York
Type	Block/Cascade
Variant Name	
Height in feet	150
County	Tompkins
Topo Map	Ithaca East
Geo Coord	422710N0762931W
Map Ref Code	42076-D4
Elevation ft	750
Water Source	Fall Creek
Seasonal Flow	Year
Section of State	NW

Directions   From Ithaca at the intersection of Meadow St. (Rt. 13/34) and Hancock St. at the north end of town, take Meadow St. north. Go 1.4 miles to the Stewart Park/Auburn exit. At the exit stop sign, turn right onto unmarked East Shore Dr. (also named Lake St.). Go 0.8 mile and park in the parking area on the left, where Lake St. intersects with Falls St. The falls can be seen to the left from the bridge, just before the parking area. The base of the falls is a short walk.

Waterfall Name	Kaaterskill Falls
State	New York
Type	Tiered/Plunge
Variant Name	Caterskill Falls
Height in feet	260
County	Greene
Topo Map	Kaaterskill
Geo Coord	421136N0744413W
Map Ref Code	42074-B1
Elevation ft	2000
Water Source	Lake Creek
Seasonal Flow	Year
Section of State	NE

Directions   From Haines Falls village at the junction of Rt. 23A and North Lake Rd., take Rt. 23A east. The sign at this intersection reads "North/South Lake Campground". Go 1.3 miles down the mountain and park in the large parking area on the right. Hike CAUTIOUSLY to the east on 23A for 0.2 more mile and cross the bridge over Bastion Falls. The trailhead for Kaaterskill Falls starts on the left at the far side of the bridge. Follow the yellow blazes for 1/2 mile on this rocky, strenuous trail to the falls. In Catskill Forest Preserve.

Waterfall Name	Letchworth Lower Falls
State	New York
Type	Block
Variant Name	Lower Falls at Letchworth
Height in feet	50
County	Wyoming
Topo Map	Portageville
Geo Coord	423507N0780115W
Map Ref Code	42078-E1
Elevation ft	1000
Water Source	Genesee River
Seasonal Flow	Year
Section of State	NW

Directions	See directions for Letchworth Middle Falls.

Waterfall Name	Letchworth Middle Falls
State	New York
Type	Segmented/Block
Variant Name	Middle Falls at Letchworth
Height in feet	100
County	Wyoming
Topo Map	Portageville
Geo Coord	425438N0780234W
Map Ref Code	42078-E1
Elevation ft	1100
Water Source	Genesee River
Seasonal Flow	Year
Section of State	NW

Directions	From Portageville, take Rt. 19A north to Letchworth State Park. Obtain a park map and directions at the entrance. The trailheads and trail are well-marked and maintained for all 3 falls located here (Lower, Middle, and Upper). Entry fee.

Waterfall Name   Mossy Cascade

State   New York

Type   Horsetail

Variant Name

Height in feet   40

County   Essex

Topo Map   Keene Valley

Geo Coord   441002N0734550W

Map Ref Code   44073-B7

Elevation ft   1200

Water Source   Mossy Cascade Brook

Seasonal Flow   Sp

Section of State   NE

Directions   From Albany, take Interstate 87 N. to Exit 30. Go 2.2 miles north on Rt. 9 and turn west (left) onto Rt. 73. Go 6.6 miles and park in the small pullout on the right (small wooden sign here for Hopkins/Mossy Cascade). The pullout is after the sign for St. Huberts and before the Ausable River sign. Hike about 3/4 mile to the falls following the orange ATIS trail blazes and the signs. In Adirondack Mountains Forest Preserve.

Waterfall Name   Niagara Falls

State   New York

Type   Block/Horseshoe

Variant Name   American/Bridal Veil/Horseshoe Falls

Height in feet   120

County   Niagara

Topo Map   Niagara Falls

Geo Coord   430500N0790415W

Map Ref Code   43079-A1

Elevation ft   550

Water Source   Niagara River

Seasonal Flow   Year

Section of State   NW

Directions   See directions to Bridal Veil Falls. Niagara Falls is the name commonly given to the three falls (Bridal Veil, American, and Horseshoe) that make up the falls at the city of Niagara Falls.

Waterfall Name	Pixley Falls
State	New York
Type	Segmented/Block
Variant Name	
Height in feet	50
County	Oneida
Topo Map	Boonville
Geo Coord	432408N0752040W
Map Ref Code	43075-D3
Elevation ft	900
Water Source	Mohawk River
Seasonal Flow	Year
Section of State	NE

Directions   From Boonville, take Rt. 46 S. about 6 miles to Pixley Falls State Park. Obtain a map at the entrance. Park in the far right parking area. From here, take the gradual downhill walk about 50 yards to the falls. Entry fee.

Waterfall Name	Rainbow Falls
State	New York
Type	Twin/Plunge/Cascade
Variant Name	Watkins Glen Gorge Falls
Height in feet	80
County	Schuyler
Topo Map	Burdett
Geo Coord	422231N0765229W
Map Ref Code	42076-D7
Elevation ft	460
Water Source	Glen Creek
Seasonal Flow	Year
Section of State	NW

Directions   From Watkins Glen, take Franklin St. (14) to the entrance of Watkins Glen State Park (follow signs). Obtain a trail map at the entrance. From the main entrance take the Gorge Trail for 3/4 mile to the falls. Several sections of stairs and some slippery surfaces will be encountered along the way, use CAUTION. Entry fee.

Waterfall Name	Rainbow Falls
State	New York
Type	Plunge/Fan
Variant Name	Rainbow Falls-Adirondacks
Height in feet	100
County	Essex
Topo Map	Dix Mountain
Geo Coord	440707N0734930W
Map Ref Code	44073-A7
Elevation ft	2300
Water Source	Cascade Brook
Seasonal Flow	Year
Section of State	NE

Directions   At Exit 30 off of Interstate 87 (near Elizabethtown), take Rt. 9 N. for 2.2 miles to Rt. 73 W. Go 5.5 miles on 73 W. and turn left onto the unnamed dirt road (sign reads Trail Parking). Go 0.1 mile to the parking area. This is private property owned by the Ausable Club Lodge but is open to the public for hiking. Hike up the dirt road towards the lodge and through the golf course (about 1/2 mile). Turn left between the 2 tennis courts to the Trailhead Registration Booth. Obtain a trail map. The easiest hike to Rainbow Falls is to follow the main dirt road to Lower Ausable Lake (3 miles gradual incline), then follow the signs for another 0.3 mile to the falls.

Waterfall Name	Red Falls
State	New York
Type	Segmented/Cascade
Variant Name	
Height in feet	25
County	Greene
Topo Map	Prattsville
Geo Coord	421730N0742307W
Map Ref Code	42074-C4
Elevation ft	1200
Water Source	Batavia Kill River
Seasonal Flow	Year
Section of State	NE

Directions   From the junction of Routes 23 and 23A near Prattsville, take Rt. 23 E. Go 1.7 miles to the pullout on the right and park (just before the sign for Red Falls Lodge). The falls can be viewed from here. There is also a short, easy trail to the base of the falls from the pullout.

Waterfall Name	Rensselaerville Falls
State	New York
Type	Tiered/Cascade
Variant Name	
Height in feet	100
County	Albany
Topo Map	Rensselaerville
Geo Coord	423053N0740838W
Map Ref Code	42074-E2
Elevation ft	1400
Water Source	Ten Mile Creek
Seasonal Flow	Sp,Sm
Section of State	NE

Directions   In the town of Rensselaerville at the junction of Routes 85 and 353 W., take Rt. 353 W. Go 0.1 mile to Edmund Niles Huyck Nature Preserve (the sign for the Preserve is on the right, next to the white building, before the bridge over the creek). Turn right into the parking lot and park at the end of the gravel. The trail (see posted maps and information) starts here and is about a 1/8-mile level walk to the bridge overlooking the falls.

Waterfall Name	Roaring Brook Falls
State	New York
Type	Horsetail
Variant Name	
Height in feet	200
County	Essex
Topo Map	Keene Valley
Geo Coord	440920N0734518W
Map Ref Code	44073-B7
Elevation ft	1800
Water Source	Roaring Brook
Seasonal Flow	Sp
Section of State	NE

Directions   At Exit 30 off of Interstate 87 (near Elizabethtown), take Rt. 9 N. Go 2.2 miles and turn west onto Rt. 73. Go 5.1 miles to the pullout on the right. The falls can be seen from here. To see the base of the falls close up, continue another 0.4 mile on Rt. 73 to the large parking area on the right. From here, hike the easy 0.3-mile to the falls base. In Adirondack Mountains Forest Preserve.

Waterfall Name	Taughannock Falls
State	New York
Type	Plunge
Variant Name	Taghanic Falls
Height in feet	210
County	Tompkins
Topo Map	Ludlowville
Geo Coord	423208N0763640W
Map Ref Code	42076-E5
Elevation ft	800
Water Source	Taughannock Creek
Seasonal Flow	Year
Section of State	NW

Directions   From Ithaca, take Rt. 89 approx. 8 miles to Taughannock State Park. Park in the parking lot opposite the Park Office. Parking fee required. Take the Gorge Trail about 3/4 mile to the falls.

Waterfall Name	Watkins Glen Cascade
State	New York
Type	Cascade
Variant Name	The Cascade
Height in feet	20
County	Schuyler
Topo Map	Burdett
Geo Coord	422233N0765229W
Map Ref Code	42076-D7
Elevation ft	400
Water Source	Glen Creek
Seasonal Flow	Year
Section of State	NW

Directions   See directions for Rainbow Falls at Watkins Glen. The Cascade is about halfway up the gorge on the same trail.

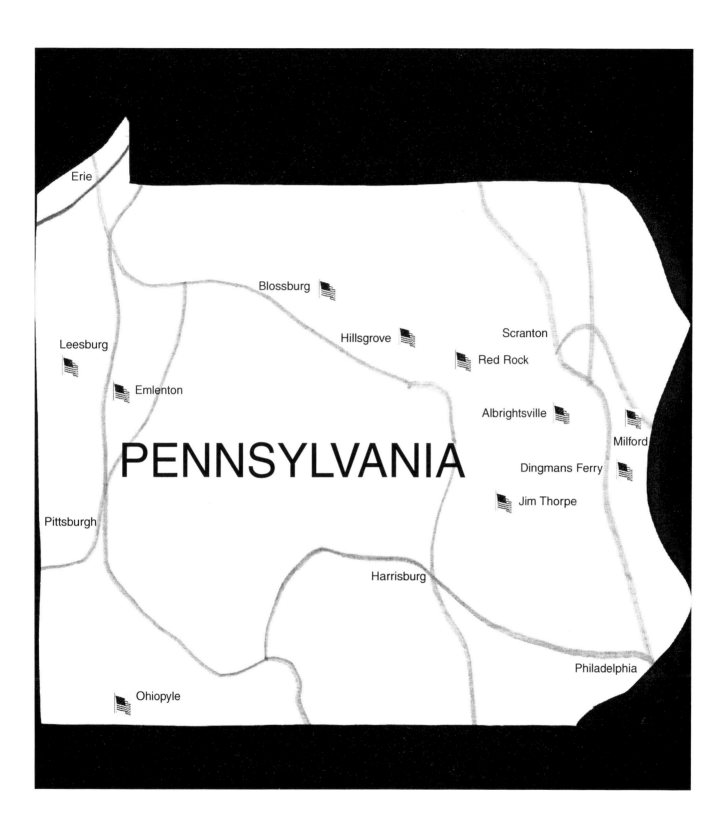

Waterfall Name	Adams Falls
State	Pennsylvania
Type	Horsetail
Variant Name	
Height in feet	25
County	Luzerne
Topo Map	Red Rock
Geo Coord	411754N0761624W
Map Ref Code	41076-C3
Elevation ft	1250
Water Source	Kitchen Creek
Seasonal Flow	Sp,Sm
Section of State	NE

Directions   From Red Rock at the junction of Routes 118 and 487, take Rt. 118 E. Go 1.6 miles and park in the parking area on the right (follow sign for Adams Falls). The falls is a short walk down a few stairs from the parking area. In Ricketts Glen State Park.

Waterfall Name	Cucumber Falls
State	Pennsylvania
Type	Plunge
Variant Name	
Height in feet	50
County	Fayette
Topo Map	Fort Necessity
Geo Coord	395146N0793012W
Map Ref Code	39079-G5
Elevation ft	1320
Water Source	Cucumber Run
Seasonal Flow	Sp
Section of State	SW

Directions   From Ohiopyle at the junction of Rt. 381 and Sheridan St., take Rt. 381 S. Go 1/2 mile and turn right onto unnamed road (first road after the bridge). There is a sign for Cucumber Falls on the corner. Go 0.4 mile and park along the right side of the road in the pulloffs (sign). From here, take the short walk down some stairs to the falls (follow sign).

Waterfall Name	Deer Leap Falls
State	Pennsylvania
Type	Tiered/Plunge
Variant Name	
Height in feet	30
County	Pike
Topo Map	Lake Maskenozha
Geo Coord	411406N0745456W
Map Ref Code	41074-B8
Elevation ft	900
Water Source	Dingmans Creek
Seasonal Flow	Year
Section of State	NE

Directions   Near Dingmans Ferry at the intersection of Routes 209 and 739 (just north of Mile Mark 13 on Rt. 209), take Rt. 739 N. Go 1.2 miles and turn left (west) onto Silver Lake Rd. Go 1.7 miles and park in the George Childs Park parking area on the left. Follow the trail from the parking area for about 1 mile to Deer Leap Falls. Deer Leap Falls is the third of the three falls seen from this trail. In Delaware Water Gap National Recreation Area.

Waterfall Name	Dry Run Falls
State	Pennsylvania
Type	Cascade
Variant Name	
Height in feet	20
County	Sullivan
Topo Map	Hillsgrove
Geo Coord	412548N0764015W
Map Ref Code	41076-D6
Elevation ft	1200
Water Source	Dry Run
Seasonal Flow	Sp
Section of State	NE

Directions   From Hillsgrove, take Rt. 87 S. From the bridge over Loyalsock Creek, proceed another 0.4 mile and turn left onto Dry Run Rd. (sign reads Wyoming State Forest, Hillsgrove Ranger Station). Go up the mountain (the road will change to gravel) for 2.1 miles to the falls view on the right. Falls can be seen from the road.

Waterfall Name	East Branch Falls
State	Pennsylvania
Type	Tiered/Horsetail
Variant Name	
Height in feet	60
County	Sullivan
Topo Map	Barbours
Geo Coord	412955N0764505W
Map Ref Code	41076-D7
Elevation ft	1700
Water Source	East Branch
Seasonal Flow	Sp,Sm
Section of State	NE

Directions   From Hillsgrove, take Rt. 87 N. Turn left (west) onto Mill Creek Road (gravel) and go 4 miles. Turn right onto Camels Road. Go 0.1 mile and turn left onto Walker Rd. Go 0.9 mile and park in the turnout on the left. Do not pass the sign for Middle Trail. Hike down the steep hillside on the faint trail to the falls. In Wyoming State Forest.

Waterfall Name	Fall Brook Falls
State	Pennsylvania
Type	Tiered/Cascade
Variant Name	
Height in feet	20
County	Tioga
Topo Map	Gleason
Geo Coord	414039N0765918W
Map Ref Code	41076-F8
Elevation ft	1800
Water Source	Fall Brook
Seasonal Flow	Sp
Section of State	NE

Directions   From Blossburg at the junction of Routes 15 and 2017 (Main St.), take 2017 E. Go 2 miles and turn left onto Rt. 2014 (sign here reads Morris Run and Fall Brook). Go 3.9 miles (pass through Morris Run, follow main road, changes to gravel) and park in the pullout on the right. The pull-out is just before the bridge over Fall Brook. Walk past the gate and down the old roadbed. In about 30 yards, veer left at the Y onto a smaller trail. Stay left upon reaching the creek. The falls are about 100 yards from the parking area. In Tioga State Forest.

Waterfall Name	Ganoga Falls
State	Pennsylvania
Type	Cascade
Variant Name	
Height in feet	95
County	Luzerne
Topo Map	Red Rock
Geo Coord	411930N0761708W
Map Ref Code	41076-C3
Elevation ft	2000
Water Source	Kitchen Creek
Seasonal Flow	Sp,Sm
Section of State	NE

Directions From Red Rock at the junction of Routes 118 and 487, take Rt. 487 N. Go about 4 miles to the entrance to Ricketts Glen State Park/Lake Jean Area on the right. Obtain a map at the Park Office. Follow the signs to the falls trailhead. Ganoga Falls is the 4th falls seen from the Ganoga Glen Trail. This trail is a steep, rocky, sometimes slippery 3-mile loop trail that allows viewing of 22 falls.

Waterfall Name	Glen Onoko Falls
State	Pennsylvania
Type	Tiered/Cascade
Variant Name	
Height in feet	30
County	Carbon
Topo Map	Weatherly
Geo Coord	405235N0754533W
Map Ref Code	40075-H7
Elevation ft	1000
Water Source	Glen Onoko Run
Seasonal Flow	Sp,Sm
Section of State	NE

Directions Near Jim Thorpe at the junction of Routes 209 and 903 N., take Rt. 903 N. Cross the bridge and veer left onto Front St. (still called Rt. 903). Continue straight at the stop sign (about 0.4 mile from the 209/903 junction) through the intersection and pass the Whitewater Rafting sign. Go 0.4 mile and turn left towards Lehigh Gorge State Park, Glen Onoko Access (follow sign). Go 1.7 miles and park in the parking area just past the bridge over the Lehigh River. Follow the trail from the north side of the parking area (near the middle), cross over the RR tracks at signpost 125, and continue up the trail from there. From the parking area to the falls is about 1/2 steep miles.

Waterfall Name	Hawk Falls
State	Pennsylvania
Type	Tiered/Fan
Variant Name	
Height in feet	25
County	Carbon
Topo Map	Hickory Run
Geo Coord	410023N0753803W
Map Ref Code	41075-A6
Elevation ft	1380
Water Source	Hawk Run
Seasonal Flow	Sp,Sm
Section of State	SE

Directions   Near Albrightsville at the junction of Routes 903 and 534, take Rt. 534 W. Go about 2.6 miles (just before the Turnpike overpass) and park in the large lot on the left. The trailhead starts near the west end of the parking area. Look for a small wooden sign pointing to Hawk Falls. Hike about 3/4 mile to the falls. The falls is about 30 feet off the main trail on a small spur trail, so listen for the sound of falling water as a guide. Located in Hickory Run State Park.

Waterfall Name	Huron Falls
State	Pennsylvania
Type	Horsetail/Cascade
Variant Name	
Height in feet	40
County	Luzerne
Topo Map	Red Rock
Geo Coord	411936N0761630W
Map Ref Code	41076-C3
Elevation ft	1900
Water Source	Kitchen Creek
Seasonal Flow	Sp,Sm
Section of State	NE

Directions   See directions for Ganoga Falls. Huron Falls is the 4th falls on the Glen Leigh Trail. This trail starts at the same location as Ganoga Glen Trail. Both trails intersect at the bottom of the canyon. Taking both trails makes up the 3-mile (22 waterfalls) loop trail.

Waterfall Name	Leesburg Falls
State	Pennsylvania
Type	Block
Variant Name	Springfield Falls
Height in feet	25
County	Mercer
Topo Map	Mercer
Geo Coord	410856N0801250W
Map Ref Code	41080-B2
Elevation ft	1150
Water Source	Leesburg Creek
Seasonal Flow	Year
Section of State	NW
Directions	From Leesburg at the junction of Interstate 79 and Rt. 208, take Rt. 208 W. Go 2.2 miles and turn right onto Old Mercer Road. Go 1/2 mile and turn left onto Falls Road. Go 0.8 mile and park in the small gravel parking lot on the left. The falls is directly across the road down a short, steep trail.

Waterfall Name	Little Scrubgrass Creek Falls
State	Pennsylvania
Type	Cascade
Variant Name	Little Scrubgrass Falls
Height in feet	10
County	Venango
Topo Map	Eau Claire
Geo Coord	411115N0794728W
Map Ref Code	41079-B7
Elevation ft	1200
Water Source	Little Scrubgrass Creek
Seasonal Flow	Sp,Sm
Section of State	NW
Directions	Near Emlenton at the junction of Interstate 80 and Rt. 38, take Rt. 38 N. Go 0.2 mile and turn left (west) onto Rt. 208. Go 2.5 miles and veer left onto the unnamed gravel road (just before the bridge over Little Scrubgrass Creek). Go 0.2 mile to the end of the road and park. Step over the low cable guardrail and follow the faint trail (in a northerly direction) down the hillside to the creek and falls. Total walk is about 100 feet.

Waterfall Name	Ohiopyle Falls
State	Pennsylvania
Type	Tiered/Block
Variant Name	
Height in feet	25
County	Fayette
Topo Map	Ohiopyle
Geo Coord	395204N0792945W
Map Ref Code	39079-G4
Elevation ft	1180
Water Source	Youghiogheny River
Seasonal Flow	Year
Section of State	SW

Directions   From Ohiopyle at the junction of Rt. 381 and Sheridan St., park in the parking lot located on the corner. From the parking lot, follow the signs to the falls. About a 100-yard walk. In Ohiopyle State Park.

Waterfall Name	Raymondskill Falls
State	Pennsylvania
Type	Tiered/Horsetail
Variant Name	
Height in feet	130
County	Pike
Topo Map	Milford
Geo Coord	411719N0745031W
Map Ref Code	41074-C7
Elevation ft	700
Water Source	Raymondskill Creek
Seasonal Flow	Year
Section of State	NE

Directions   From Milford, take Rt. 209 S. At Mile Mark 18.5, turn west onto Rt. 2009 (follow sign to Raymondskill Falls). Go 1/2 mile and park in the parking area on the left. The trail at the left side of the parking area leads to the bottom of the falls (a few stairs on the way). The trail at the right side of the parking area leads to the top of the falls. Both trails are about 100 yards in length. In Delaware Water Gap National Recreation Area.

Waterfall Name	Shohola Falls
State	Pennsylvania
Type	Tiered/Cascade
Variant Name	
Height in feet	40
County	Pike
Topo Map	Shohola
Geo Coord	412328N0745809W
Map Ref Code	41074-D8
Elevation ft	1120
Water Source	Shohola Creek
Seasonal Flow	Year
Section of State	NE

Directions   At the junction of Interstate 84 and Rt. 6 (just north of Milford, Exit 10), take Rt. 6 W. Go 10 miles and turn left onto the unnamed road (sign here reads Shohola Falls Inn). Go 0.3 mile (veering right at the T) and park in the Shohola Recreation Area parking lot (follow sign). Falls can be viewed a short walk from the parking lot.

RHODE ISLAND

Providence

Newport

Exeter

Waterfall Name	Stepstone Falls
State	Rhode Island
Type	Tiered/Block
Variant Name	
Height in feet	5
County	Washington
Topo Map	Voluntown (CT)
Geo Coord	413642N0714539W
Map Ref Code	41071-E7
Elevation ft	300
Water Source	Wood River
Seasonal Flow	Sp
Section of State	SE

Directions   From Exeter, take Rt. 102 W. At the junction with Routes 3 and 165, take Rt. 165 W. Go 5.4 miles and turn right onto Escoheag Hill Road. Go 2.4 miles and turn right onto Falls River Rd. (a sand and gravel road). Go 0.7 mile and park in the small parking area on the right just before the small concrete bridge. The falls is a short walk downstream from the parking area. In Arcadia Management Area.

VERMONT

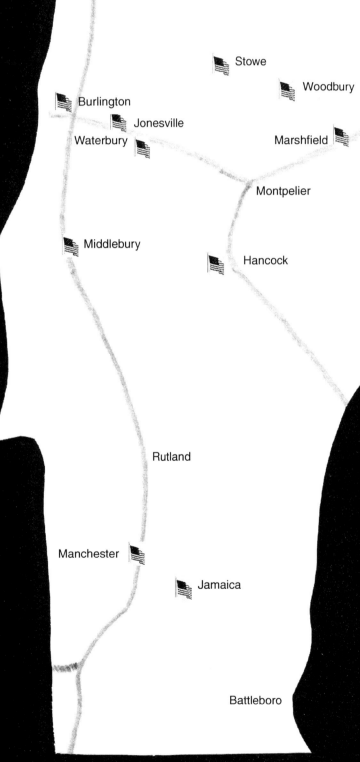

Stowe

Woodbury

Burlington

Jonesville

Waterbury

Marshfield

Montpelier

Middlebury

Hancock

Rutland

Manchester

Jamaica

Battleboro

Waterfall Name	Depot Brook Falls
State	Vermont
Type	Fan
Variant Name	
Height in feet	40
County	Washington
Topo Map	Marshfield
Geo Coord	442042N0722219W
Map Ref Code	44072-C3
Elevation ft	900
Water Source	Depot Brook
Seasonal Flow	Sp
Section of State	NE

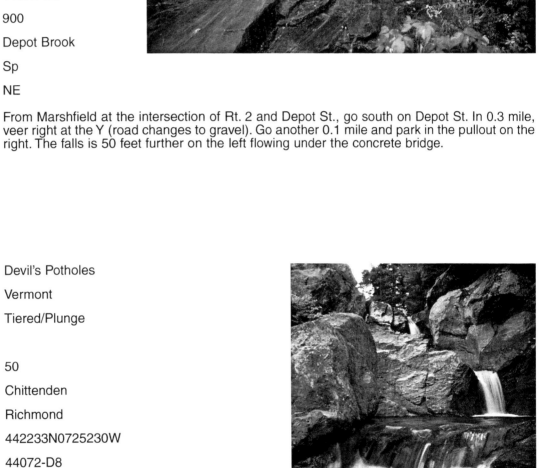

Directions   From Marshfield at the intersection of Rt. 2 and Depot St., go south on Depot St. In 0.3 mile, veer right at the Y (road changes to gravel). Go another 0.1 mile and park in the pullout on the right. The falls is 50 feet further on the left flowing under the concrete bridge.

Waterfall Name	Devil's Potholes
State	Vermont
Type	Tiered/Plunge
Variant Name	
Height in feet	50
County	Chittenden
Topo Map	Richmond
Geo Coord	442233N0725230W
Map Ref Code	44072-D8
Elevation ft	500
Water Source	Joiner Brook
Seasonal Flow	Year
Section of State	NW

Directions   From Waterbury, take Rt. 2 W. Go 7 miles and turn right onto the unnamed road toward Bolton Valley Ski Area. Go 0.2 mile and park in the pullout on the right. Hike over the granite rocks on the right to the stream; go downstream to the falls. The hike is about 200 yards. Use CAUTION—steep and can be slippery.

Waterfall Name	Falls of Lana
State	Vermont
Type	Tiered/Horsetail
Variant Name	Sucker Brook Falls
Height in feet	60
County	Addison
Topo Map	East Middlebury
Geo Coord	435415N0730347W
Map Ref Code	43073-H1
Elevation ft	800
Water Source	Sucker Brook
Seasonal Flow	Year
Section of State	NW

Directions   From Middlebury, take Rt. 7 S. Go 7 miles and turn left (south) onto Rt. 53. Go 4 miles and park in the parking area on the left (sign here reads Silver Lake/Falls of Lana). Follow the signed trail to the falls. The trail goes uphill for about 1/2 mile. In Green Mountain National Forest.

Waterfall Name	Hamilton Falls
State	Vermont
Type	Tiered/Plunge/Segmented/Horsetail
Variant Name	Jamaica Falls
Height in feet	125
County	Windham
Topo Map	Jamaica
Geo Coord	430710N0724502W
Map Ref Code	43072-A7
Elevation ft	960
Water Source	Cobb Brook
Seasonal Flow	Year
Section of State	SE

Directions   From Jamaica at the junction of Rt. 30 and Depot St., take Depot St. to the NE. Go 1/2 mile to Jamaica State Park. Obtain a trail map at the entrance. The trailhead is located at the far end of the beach/picnic parking area. Hike upstream along the West River about 2 miles. Turn right on the trail to the falls. Go another 3/4 mile uphill on this steep, rocky trail. Entry fee.

Waterfall Name	Huntington Gorge Falls
State	Vermont
Type	Horsetail
Variant Name	
Height in feet	30
County	Chittenden
Topo Map	Huntington
Geo Coord	442212N0725750W
Map Ref Code	44072-C8
Elevation ft	600
Water Source	Huntington River
Seasonal Flow	Year
Section of State	NW

Directions   From Jonesville on Rt. 2, turn south on the unnamed road across from the post office. Cross the green metal bridge and in 1/2 mile, turn left onto Dugway Road. Go 1.8 miles (road changes to gravel) and park in the large pullout on the left (just past the sign for Huntington Gorge). Walk back to the sign and follow the trail to the gorge and falls. From the parking area to the falls is about 100 yards.

Waterfall Name	Lower Bingham Falls
State	Vermont
Type	Plunge
Variant Name	
Height in feet	30
County	Lamoille
Topo Map	Mount Mansfield
Geo Coord	443110N0724603W
Map Ref Code	44072-E7
Elevation ft	1300
Water Source	W. Branch Waterbury River
Seasonal Flow	Year
Section of State	NE

Directions   From Stowe at the junction of Routes 100 and 108, take 108 W. Go 6.4 miles and park in the pullout on the right. A wide trail leads 1/4 mile down to the river and the falls. Two more sections of the falls are a bit further downstream, very steep, use CAUTION.

Waterfall Name   Lye Brook Falls

State   Vermont

Type   Fan/Horsetail

Variant Name

Height in feet   100

County   Bennington

Topo Map   Manchester

Geo Coord   430739N0730230W

Map Ref Code   43073-B1

Elevation ft   1600

Water Source   Lye Brook

Seasonal Flow   Sp

Section of State   SW

Directions   From Rt. 7 near Manchester, take Rt. 11/30 W. at Exit 4. Go 1 mile and turn left onto Richville Road at the traffic light. Go 0.4 mile and turn left onto E. Manchester Road. Go 0.6 mile and turn right onto Glen Road. Go 0.2 mile (road changes to gravel) and continue straight at the sign for Lye Brook Wilderness Access. Proceed another 0.4 mile and park in the parking area. Hike the wide trail past the bulletin board through the grassy clearing. Continue past the large rock firepit and then veer left uphill to the registration box. Follow the light blue-blaze trail from here for a moderately strenuous ascent of 2.3 miles to the falls. Follow the signs. In Green Mountain National Forest.

Waterfall Name   Moss Glen Brook Falls

State   Vermont

Type   Tiered/Horsetail/Fan

Variant Name   Moss Glen Falls

Height in feet   100

County   Lamoille

Topo Map   Mount Worcester

Geo Coord   442855N0723728W

Map Ref Code   44072-D5

Elevation ft   1000

Water Source   Moss Glen Brook

Seasonal Flow   Year

Section of State   NE

Directions   From Stowe at the junction of Routes 108 and 100, take Rt. 100 N. Go about 4 miles and turn right onto Randolph Rd. Go 0.4 mile and turn right onto Moss Glen Falls Rd. (dirt). Go 1/2 mile and park in the large parking area on the left (look for the wooden sign on the tree for "Falls"). Follow the trail upstream for about 1/4 mile to the falls.

Waterfall Name	Moss Glen Falls at Deer Hollow
State	Vermont
Type	Fan
Variant Name	Deer Hollow Brook Falls
Height in feet	60
County	Addison
Topo Map	Warren
Geo Coord	440105N0725103W
Map Ref Code	44072-A7
Elevation ft	1300
Water Source	Deer Hollow Brook
Seasonal Flow	Year
Section of State	NW

Directions   In Hancock at the junction of Routes 125 and 100, take Rt.100 N. Go 7 miles and park in the parking area on the left. The falls can be seen from here. In Green Mountain National Forest.

Waterfall Name	Texas Falls
State	Vermont
Type	Tiered/Horsetail
Variant Name	
Height in feet	50
County	Addison
Topo Map	Bread Loaf
Geo Coord	435605N0725403W
Map Ref Code	43072-H8
Elevation ft	1200
Water Source	Hancock Branch
Seasonal Flow	Year
Section of State	NW

Directions   In Hancock at the junction of Routes 125 and 100, take Rt. 125 W. Go 3.2 miles and turn right (north) onto the unnamed road (sign here reads Green Mountain National Forest Recreation Area/Texas Falls). Go 0.4 mile and park in the parking area on the left. The falls can be seen off to the right near the roadway.

Waterfall Name	Winooski Falls
State	Vermont
Type	Block
Variant Name	
Height in feet	10
County	Chittenden
Topo Map	Burlington
Geo Coord	442930N0731115W
Map Ref Code	44073-D2
Elevation ft	100
Water Source	Winooski River
Seasonal Flow	Year
Section of State	NW

Directions   From Burlington, take Interstate 89 N. At Exit 16, take Main St. (Rt. 7) south towards Winooski. Go 1.2 miles to the bridge over the Winooski River. The falls can be seen off to the left upstream.

Waterfall Name	Woodbury Falls
State	Vermont
Type	Horsetail
Variant Name	
Height in feet	40
County	Washington
Topo Map	Woodbury
Geo Coord	442804N0722310W
Map Ref Code	44072-D4
Elevation ft	1200
Water Source	Woodbury Creek
Seasonal Flow	Sp
Section of State	NE

Directions   From Woodbury at the post office, take Rt. 14 N. Go 2.8 miles and park in the small pullout on the left. The falls can be seen from here flowing next to the road.

INDEX

ABOUT THE AUTHORS

Jim, a native of Illinois, has an Engineering degree from Purdue University. He has over 14 years experience in travel, land navigation, direction writing, and photography. Having worked with an adventure travel company 8 years, he has toured across the U.S. at least twice a year and adventured in 40 different countries, guiding people to places of geological beauty, historical significance and cultural diversity. He has captured hundreds of people, places and experiences on photographic film. In his spare time, Jim works as a carpenter and handyman.

Carla is a native Californian with a Music degree from San Jose State University. She has an eclectic background in business, travel and the visual and performing arts, namely, from organizer/budgeter to writer/editor/proofreader, from 'having the eye' and creating nature photo greeting cards to outdoor enthusiast and avid hiker, from voice-over artist to video/film on-camera performer. In her spare time, Carla works as a personal aquafitness trainer and life manager.

Both Jim and Carla believe strongly in the priorities and work of the Sierra Club, Nature Conservancy, Wilderness Society, American Wildlands, National Wildlife Federation, Regional Open Space Districts and all other similar organizations devoted to nature preservation and world sustainability. They wish to encourage local, county, state and federal involvement in the acquisition and conservation of precious waterfall areas that are currently unprotected.

MAIL ORDER FORM

WATERFALLS USA
A HIKING GUIDE AND TRAVEL PLANNER

First Name_____Last Name_____

Address_____City_____

State/Province_____Zip_____Country_____

E-Mail_____Phone (_____)_____

Price per book $ 40.00 x _____   = $_____

Shipping & handling for Book 1 $ 3.95 x ___1___   = $_____3.95_____

Shipping & handling for Book 2 or more $ 3.50 x _____   = $_____

Illinois residents ONLY add 6.75% sales tax x total book price = $_____
  (no tax on shipping & handling)

                                                                Total $_____

Complete this Order Form and
Mail with your Check or Money Order to:

JRG Inc.
46 Castle Rock Lane
Bloomingdale, IL 60108

Expect your *WATERFALLS USA* book(s) in 2-4 weeks

THANK YOU FOR YOUR ORDER!

E-mail contact: info@waterfallsusa.com